THE
MONEY
MAZE

Warning

Stock market investments (including gilts and loan stocks), unit trusts, investment trusts, insurance products, property and alternative investments, can go down as well as up. The income from most securities can also go down as well as up. When you seek advice, also ask about marketability. The shares, gilts, loan stocks, investment trusts and unit trusts referred to in the text of this book are for illustrative purposes only and are not an invitation to deal in them. This book was originally written in October 1997. But market conditions change. Neither the publisher nor the author accept any legal responsibility for the contents of the work, which is not a substitute for detailed professional advice. Readers should conduct their own investment activity through an appropriately authorized person.

THE
MONEY
MAZE

A Do-It-Yourself Guide To Managing Your Money
And Achieving Financial Security

BERNICE COHEN

ORION BUSINESS
BOOKS

To Alan – A partner to treasure

This edition first published in Great Britain
in 1999 by Orion Business
An imprint of The Orion Publishing Group Ltd
Orion House, 5 Upper St Martin's Lane,
London WC2H 9EA

A CIP catalogue record for this book
is available from the British Library.

ISBN 0-75281-333-1

Printed and bound in Great Britain by
Butler & Tanner Ltd, Frome and London

CONTENTS

PREFACE TO PAPERBACK EDITION

A year can be a very long time in the lives of people trying to manage their money in a sensible way. It certainly seems to be a long time in the life of the global economy. When I wrote *The Money Maze* in 1997, economies everywhere were booming; international stock markets responded euphorically by lifting prices to ever higher levels and commentators spoke optimistically about a 'New Age' with unending growth and prosperity. In Britain, the newly elected Labour government was promising an end to the damaging boom and bust cycle that has dogged the nation for decades.

Sadly, during the summer of 1998, most of this optimism evaporated abruptly. Indeed, a gathering pessimism seemed to have sneaked in when very few people were looking. What a change, and how quickly it rushed onto the general scene. Suddenly, we discovered that over 40 per cent of the world's trading nations were mired in recession; Russia, Japan and the tiger economies of South-East Asia were all affected, while prospects in Latin America looked increasingly bleak.

So should we worry about deteriorating economic conditions on the other side of the world? Unfortunately, even though Britain is an island, today we live in a global village. It is difficult to escape the impact of problems in other regions, since we trade with so many different nations that if they move into recession, they will buy less of our exports and services than they did during the boom times. In addition, fewer tourists will arrive to spend their money in our historic towns and busy shopping centres. This reduction in world trade spells retrenchment everywhere; shops and factories close, jobs are lost, there are declining sales on the high street and, before we know it, we are all tightening our belts and becoming more pessimistic about the chances of avoiding an outright recession.

To people buying their own home, saving for a pension, or for a major future event, the sudden possibility of recession seems bad news. However, there is a good side to this gloomy picture if you are taking the trouble to learn the secrets of managing your money more wisely. It is all a matter of having the right long-term perspective. Sir John Templeton, who spent his whole working life looking for sound investment opportunities, and made a fortune by doing so, has words of wisdom for coping at such times; 'Bull markets,' he says, 'are born on pessimism, grow on scepticism, mature on optimism and die on euphoria. The time of maximum pessimism is the best time to buy, and the time of maximum optimism is the best time to sell.'

Whatever the conditions in the economy around us, we can all make a resounding success of our financial affairs if we take the trouble to learn how to do it well.

October 1998

INTRODUCTION

HOPELESS WITH MONEY

'I'm hopeless with money.'

'I could never do what you've done.'

'I simply wouldn't know where to start.'

'I leave all that to my partner.' (or accountant, financial adviser).

'Money is a foreign language to me, but I do like to spend it.'

In the winter of 1996, when I was doing some radio interviews to promote my book *The Armchair Investor*, I was amazed by the relaxed, happy-go-lucky comments on managing money or rather, the declared inability to manage money, freely expressed to me by some of the young women who were steering me through my interviews. I lost count of the number of seemingly well-educated, immaculately dressed 'bright young things' who tossed off casual remarks over their shoulders as they chaperoned me down endless rabbit warren-like passages. I cringed in response to the repeated confessions that sounded suspiciously like boasts: 'I'm hopeless with money.' 'I could never do what you've done.' 'I simply wouldn't know where to start.' And more comments on the same theme.

These carefree, off-the-cuff sentiments, volunteered with such disarming sincerity, gave me the impression, hopefully unintended, that to many people money doesn't matter very much. Or, better still, of course, that somebody else will always be around to sort things out. The unspoken implication seemed to be that there is absolutely no need to sully one's hands with 'filthy lucre'. Just leave that boring side of financial affairs to chaps who know how it all works. As long as there is money in the bank or a friendly credit card to finance what we want to buy, there is little more to worry about.

If Only It Were That Simple

Sadly, however, some of us realise that life is not like that. Although it goes largely unrecognised in our society today, managing money is definitely a skill. As it is not formally taught in schools or at college, for most people, once they get inside the money maze, it can take years to find the right way through, endlessly seeking a financially secure future.

Everyone needs money to buy the absolute essentials at the very least: food, clothing, warmth and somewhere to live. If we are unlucky enough not to earn a regular income for ourselves, then someone else must provide us with these basic essentials or give us money so we can buy them. That someone may be a parent or close friend. But invariably, today it is the state that supplies a minimal income replacement. This welfare provision is only the sparsest of safety nets. Relying on that alone, almost all the little luxuries we so often take for granted would be totally out of reach.

Careful preparation is the key to financial success

The majority of us spend a great deal of our time trying to live within our means, every day, every week and every month. After all, if we had more money at our disposal, I feel sure most of us would happily give up regular work. With access to a golden nest egg, most people would choose to spend their days indulging in exciting leisure interests and hobbies, doing the things they enjoy, rather than being at the beck and call of endlessly demanding bosses. The fact is, most of us are obliged to earn our living.

Few people are lucky enough to afford the luxury of drifting through their lives doing just as they please. But that doesn't mean we must stop dreaming about having our very own golden nest egg. The figures for participation in Britain's Lottery suggest this dream of idle luxury is a national pastime, and some killjoys would rate it as high as a national obsession. Personally, I can see nothing wrong with a bit of luxury dreaming.

As recently as the early part of this century, many people were fortunate enough either to live in homes inherited from deceased relatives, or to enjoy an unearned income handed down from parents or grandparents. The famous crime writer Agatha Christie noted in her autobiography that, as a young woman, prior to the

Introduction

First World War she was able to live quite comfortably on the interest from government bonds inherited from her father. She didn't start working for her living until that war was over, when she found it had become too difficult to manage on the bond interest alone. Indeed, a similar, fortunate situation of living on unearned income was quite commonplace for 'gentle folk' right through from the early nineteenth century, as we can read in Jane Austen's colourful novels of the period and in the details of her own personal life.

Wonderful Welfare

Even during my lifetime the standard of living for the bulk of British people has increased astonishingly. More of us today are enjoying the rising prosperity of the nation than at any previous time in British history. When I was a child of ten, fifty years ago, my family didn't own a motor car, a refrigerator, central heating, a fitted kitchen, a telephone or television.

When you make a balance sheet of your life, you find your assets far outweigh your liabilities

As national prosperity has grown, more of us have come to rely on a middle-class standard of living. Increasingly, many of our most valued or precious material possessions have come to be regarded almost as basic necessities. Nowadays, we tend to take for granted the enjoyments of car ownership, package holidays abroad, having a refrigerator, central heating, a built-in kitchen and bathroom, fitted carpets plus one or more televisions in our homes. And with the increase in prosperity and financial liberation within the economy has grown an increase in our dependence on debt. As a nation, we now have higher levels of debt per household than in any previous era.

During 1997 my intuitive feeling about improved living standards found support in information released on the fiftieth anniversary of the Retail Prices Index (key financial terms are highlighted in bold type and are explained in the glossary of terms on page 230 at the end of the book). In 1947, spending on services accounted for only 8 per cent of consumer spending. While food took over a third (35 per cent) of working class incomes, drink and tobacco, (just beer, whisky, cigarettes and pipe tobacco,) accounted for 22 per cent of household expenses. By 1997 expenditure on food had shrunk to 14 per cent, drink and tobacco were down to 11 per cent and services had risen to 33 per cent.

I believe there are two key reasons for the enormous recent growth in living standards that over 70 per cent of Britons have been lucky enough to start enjoying. First, and undoubtedly the most important reason, is the bliss of over fifty years of peace in western Europe. This has allowed national wealth right across the continent to be ploughed back into the thriving economy: more money than ever before is now spent on building modern homes, schools, hospitals, and factories manufacturing mass consumer goods that everyone wants to own and on developing a wider range of public services. A prolonged period of peace has enabled most of us to acquire many more of those new consumer products that my parents could not afford to buy during my childhood.

Of almost equal importance over the last fifty years, has been the rise of the welfare state. Although increasingly we recognise that, in many respects, it is certainly not a perfect panacea for all our wants, we know it has brought free health, education, law and order and vital community services to almost all of us. There is not one family in the land who has not derived some benefit from this provision of free public services.

The welfare state was devised initially to be a very modest safety net just to help people in times of serious trouble. But it has expanded and developed into a much more all-embracing service. Today, it is there as a minimum lifeline for millions of people, to which we gratefully turn whenever disaster strikes, confident it will help to see us through short bouts of accidents, sickness and unemployment. And this splendid welfare state provides a basic, albeit extremely frugal, pension for the growing army of pensioners who have begun to enjoy a longer, fitter lifespan than was thought possible as recently as fifty years ago. Because health and welfare services have improved so vastly, many more of us can now look forward to the possibility of living to a ripe old age, well into our eighties and beyond, a possibility that was quite unheard of in any previous period.

« *What people don't understand they fear, and what they fear they reject.* »

Pauline Green, MEP for North London, 1995

Living On And On

Over the past forty years, reliance on the welfare state has grown as the system itself has expanded to deal with ever more of our needs. Prior to 1976, the level of unemployment was below a million people, but it is now over twenty years since that level was last seen. Today, in excess of a million people live on long-term unemployment benefit. In addition, there are far more old age pensioners today, over 10 million, than there were in 1945 when the welfare state was first introduced. Among these, over 8,000 are centenarians, having reached the astonishing age of one hundred years or older. And forecasts for centenarians are equally amazing. Their numbers are set to grow to around 30,000 over the next thirty years.

In August 1997, statistics came to light that revealed the reality of the extended longevity now occurring. During that month, an English couple celebrated their seventy-fifth wedding anniversary; the husband was ninety-nine years old and his wife ninety-seven. They had fifteen living descendants: children, grandchildren, great-grandchildren and great-great-grandchildren. In the same month, the oldest man in Britain died at the heroic age of one hundred and nine. But he was a mere stripling compared to the oldest woman in France, who died in the same week at the incredible age of one hundred and twenty-two. The Bible tells us that Moses lived to be one hundred and twenty, so perhaps we are returning to the best biblical lifespans as so many more people are now living well beyond a hundred years. This may be more realistic than we think. David Riddington of Norwich Union, the insurance company, has commented that a man of sixty-five retiring in 1997 had a life expectation of 18.3 years, whereas in 1987 it was 17.5 years. But fifty-five-year-olds in 1997, retiring in 2007, will on average live another 19.1 years, while forty-five-year-olds can expect to live another 19.6 years on retirement in 2017. Similar increases apply to women. Every decade that passes, therefore, brings the possibility of longer lifespans.

Don't spend what you haven't got

David Riddington provided another proven actuarial statistic to encourage us to save more for retirement: the bigger your pension fund when you retire, the longer you will live. This startling fact is well substantiated by statistical evidence. A man with a low fund of around £80,000 will have a 10 per cent shorter life than Mr Average on £100,000, but a man who can accumulate £500,000 will expect to live 10 per cent longer than the average. Obscurely, this life expectancy link does not work for women. But however long you live, who wants to face a poverty-stricken old age?

Increasingly, we realise that the rising prosperity we are enjoying here in the West is partly responsible for the longer lives we can now look forward to. By contrast, in most of eastern Europe and Russia, where the experiment of communism proved to be such an impediment to national prosperity, the average lifespan is still down in the sixties for most of the people who live in those countries.

After the Second World War, at the time when the welfare state was first introduced, the numbers of retired people in Britain were very much lower and the average life expectancy, as in present-day eastern Europe, was little more than seventy years. These statistics give a clear indication of why the promise of welfare provision from the cradle to the grave may now be running into mathematical difficulties. Facing the prospect of twenty to thirty years on a state pension does not inspire much optimism for retirement to be one long, happy holiday, as state provision in Britain is so minimal. It only amounted to around 16.2 per cent of the average wage of about £385 per week in 1997 terms, as revealed by *Social Trends*, a government publication.

The Future May Not Be Like The Past

For young people in Britain, brought up during the last thirty years, with this utopian background of peace in Europe and a benevolent welfare state, it hardly seems surprising that their attitudes to money are so relaxed. But this in-bred optimism may now be misplaced. The welfare state is a twentieth-century vision that is visibly creaking at the seams as we head towards the next millennium. The mathematics of equality for all in essential social services is already revealing itself to be an idyll which cannot cope with the growing expectations of those who live in western industrial democracies. It patently appears to be faltering when it has to tackle the realities of a rising army of elderly citizens and a limited public purse to finance everyone's wants in health, education, law enforcement, income support, pensions and numerous other vital local public services.

When it comes to relying completely on the state, the future may not be as rosy as the past and this will apply to us all, whatever our age or financial situation.

The haphazard attitudes to handling money that I encountered while publicising my book *The Armchair Investor*, merely reinforced similar comments by several people I had already met in the winter of 1996 during many months of filming for an experimental Channel 4 television series on personal finance – the first series of *Mrs Cohen's Money*.

During that filming, I had been absolutely stunned by the genuine lack of understanding and awareness on most financial issues among camera crews, photographers and members of the production team. It seemed that virtually everyone involved in creating this series wanted more information on how to manage their personal finances. After the initial flippant talk about being clueless on coping with money, everyone seemed acutely aware of the need to become more expert in this crucial area of modern life. One of the team ruefully confessed to me that, at the outset, she had not even known what a 'share' was.

But it was not until February 1997 that I was finally struck by the idea of writing this book, *The Money Maze*. It was then that I met someone who told me he thought *The Armchair Investor* was too advanced for pure novices. I was momentarily speechless when he asked me to explain what I meant by 'a belt and braces' approach to picking promising company shares with great growth prospects. It had never crossed my mind that the term 'belt and braces' as a cautionary way of picking stock market winners (because it embraces a wide range of key factors) might be misconstrued as financial jargon that needed to be explained in even simpler terms.

In At The Deep End

As I mulled over these thoughts, my conviction about the extent of the problem was reinforced by knowing that in modern Britain most people are sadly ill-equipped to manage their own finances. This ignorance leaves the majority fearful of taking important financial decisions. Money remains an unfathomable mystery. Grappling with its complexities is best avoided. Many of us are completely unprepared for this most essential and basic requirement in a modern democracy because personal finance is a topic that has fallen through a series of holes in the established norms of preparation for adult life.

« If you think education is expensive, try ignorance. »
Yongyuth Yuthavong,
Director of National Science and Technology Agency, Thailand

In general, these crucial money matters are not taught in primary or secondary school, nor do they feature in the curriculum for college education, or even as part of a training schedule for young new entrants to the jobs market. Understanding about money, budgeting to manage it wisely, the need for saving or handling tax issues, all these vitally important skills lie in an empty no-man's-land, because no one has accepted the responsibility for teaching this essential expertise to the next generation of adults. So if you don't learn basic money principles at home, then, tough. You will have to learn by bitter experience in the grown up world or through a time-consuming trial and error process as you go along.

Indeed, school children are taught the facts of life and know more about sex than they know about money. Young people educated at college will emerge with a degree or other qualification to fit them for a lifetime of work, during which a sum of money perhaps exceeding three quarters of a million, or even a million pounds, depending on luck and the levels of skills they acquire, may pass through their hands. This is serious money by anyone's standards, but it may be no exaggeration to guess that over 80 per cent of these youngsters will have to pick up what they know about money in the most piecemeal and disorganised way.

« Does that mean that because Americans won't listen to sense, you intend to talk nonsense to them? »
John Maynard Keynes, remark to a Treasury official on the way to an International Monetary Conference in 1944 or 1945

When young graduates or school leavers set out to find their first jobs in society, they will be helped to prepare a curriculum vitae of their skills and work experience, shown how to dress correctly for each all-important job interview, told in some detail how to handle the possible questions they may be asked and how to conduct themselves properly so they can win the job. But, unfortunately, learning how to budget with the money that job may bring, or save to repay a student loan or deal with a tax problem are crucial issues which will probably be entirely overlooked in the hectic scramble to enter the jobs market. Learning about how money works or the intricacies of borrowing, saving and investment are essentially extracurricular activities that will have to be bolted on later, rather than sooner.

So it is hardly surprising that for most people, money remains one of those complicated topics that is shrouded in mystery and unfamiliar jargon. It becomes a directionless maze for the thirty-somethings who have been left to fend entirely for themselves to discover what it all means. And most of them are likely to remain hopelessly uninitiated until well into adulthood. They will have to grope their way cautiously towards a reasonable level of understanding through their own determination to acquire a better knowledge of what proper financial planning entails. And for many, sadly, the mystery and the jargon remain insurmountable barriers to ever grasping the crucial fundamentals of coping well with money. The lack of attention to personal finance is, however, not confined to the young alone.

Money Is The Pivot

Inadequate knowledge about personal finances is widespread across all sections of society. Beginning with school leavers and college graduates, it covers people at all stages of their working lives and even those approaching retirement. This lack of awareness is a severe handicap for almost the whole adult population. Money and the way to manage it properly remain remote, unfamiliar subjects so that most of us never come to realise clearly the central role money plays. We know that we have to work to earn our keep and when we cannot do that for ourselves, the state will step in and offer a frugal hand. But beyond accepting that elementary reality, it seems, for far too many of us, there is a 'live for the day' approach, hoping the state will be there, as in the past, to provide for the future if that need arises.

Money is only important when you haven't got enough

This attitude of dependency has prevented most of us from realising how crucial a role money, or the lack of it, will play throughout our lives. We rarely recognise that knowledge about finance can be a valuable key to unlock doors to the exciting realms of true financial freedom. Acquiring some money brings with it peace of mind, financial security, boundless opportunities for travel or for buying those luxuries that make life easier or more fulfilling. Money cannot buy happiness, but it can help to ease your path through life. It can even allow you to become a more generous and giving person, not just to those you love, but to help worthy causes and your favourite charities.

But widespread ignorance about handling money means very few people will appreciate how these financial benefits can be achieved. Money can be easily frittered away in an endless stream of nothings so that luxuries will then have to be bought through borrowing rather than through saving first. Many people become mired in debt simply because they have never been taught the crucial fundamentals about budgeting or coping with money.

How Much Is Enough?

Lack of money all too often becomes a constant nightmare. How will you pay the bills – gas, electricity, rent? Can you afford to buy new shoes for the children or Christmas presents? The struggle to make ends meet becomes a cruel, all-consuming effort for those with inadequate resources.

So how can you judge how much money is enough for a reasonable lifestyle? Everyone will have their own, unique money needs, but I have found a useful way of judging how much money I think is 'enough'. When you feel comfortable with the amount of money you have, then money will cease to be a problem. This may sound rather naive, but this comfort level will differ from person to person. For one person, a few thousand pounds in the bank will bring a sense of contentment, while another might still feel insecure, even with a cushion of hundreds of thousands of pounds available. I think in general, money is only an important factor to those people who do not think they have enough of it. As soon as you feel financially secure, money will stop being a worry to you and then you will realise that you have enough not only for your essential needs but to enjoy a comfortable, relaxed lifestyle.

Don't rely on winning the National Lottery; there are more certain ways to build up your wealth

We all indulge in dreams of exotic places we would like to visit or exciting events we want to attend, halfway around the world. Most of us dream about having an easy life, free of debts, with sufficient money to buy the big luxury items we crave without constantly having to worry whether we can afford them.

And this is not the only blessing that comes from a sense of financial well-being. If your finances are in good shape you can recover far more quickly from a major setback. This happened to me in 1994, when we were faced with a huge repair bill for our house. But in 1995, along came a remarkably strong stock market rise, and I was able within a matter of months to replace all the heavy outlay we had been forced to spend on building repairs, because I had money invested in the rising stock market. What a comfort that turned out to be.

Financial security is not a fixed, unalterable lump of money in the bank. It is a state of mind and will mean a different amount of cash for each individual. I like to think of money as a Goldilocks commodity. If you have too much of it, your life may get hijacked by the demands that others will make on you. If you have too little, you may become obsessed by cravings for all the good things you cannot afford to own or beset by problems over debts. The best solution is to have just that amount which is enough for you to enjoy a full and happy life, doing all the things you want to do without worrying unduly about where the money will come from to pay for them. This solution sounds idyllic, but it can be achieved if you are willing to plan for your financial future so that you can make it secure, rather than having a hit-and-miss attitude which may or may not come right in time. One of my father's favourite sayings was:

« *You make your own luck* »

And when it comes to financial peace of mind, those lucky enough to find it have usually done some preparation and planning to ensure it comes their way.

What A Bore

I know from conversations with people I have met, that many of them find talking or learning about money is a huge bore. These are often people who quickly flick over the money pages in newspapers to read the sporting news. But maybe they have failed to realise that having money creates enormous freedom. If you have the money, you can take trips to watch these sporting events instead of just reading about them in your newspaper. Money offers undreamed of choices. Would you like to go to Mexico to watch a World Cup in person? Do you want a ringside seat at Caesar's Palace in Las Vegas for the heavyweight boxing championship? Why not buy a new television with satellite TV channels so you can view exciting international sports events at the switch of a button every day of the week? Will you have to borrow to buy these tempting goodies, or can you pay for them outright?

Turn the problem into a solution

Perhaps we need a better perspective of what we mean when we say, 'Money is boring.' The lack of money can be a nasty straight-jacket that turns your life into a repetitive and narrow daily routine. That can be boring, with no excitement to relieve the monotony. But knowing how to escape from this tiresome trap is the very opposite of boring as it opens up new possibilities of unimagined excitement, so you can fulfill some of your life's most cherished dreams and desires much sooner than you had ever imagined. Learning how to manage money is the passport to embarking upon this happy adventure.

Fortunately, it is not an impossible task to learn the core essentials of coping well with money and, once the essentials are mastered, you will be pleasantly surprised at how quickly you can acquire the basic skills.

Become Moneywise

The information presented in this book is planned specifically to equip you properly with the essential facts you need to set you on the road to securing a better financial future. We will go through the various stages of planning to help you become more organised and confident enough to proceed.

There are many books on how to invest to make your money grow, but personal finance is a far broader, much more basic skill than this. Currently, it is regularly covered in the money sections of the broadsheet newspapers and in the special supplements they produce periodically, on certain topics of interest. But while they aim to give you up-to-the-minute guidance on various aspects of financial affairs, they rarely present a complete picture of the basic elements of what, in fact, constitutes sound financial planning.

The Money Maze hopes to fill this gap. It is designed to be an easy, step-by-step guide to personal finance. It cannot tell you all the answers to everything you will ever need to know, because the current financial situation is always changing. The markets on which most financial products are based are constantly moving, and governments continue to alter many conditions on products which are already in the market place. But once you have grasped the basics, you will be able to follow the shifting details more easily in newspaper articles. What I hope this book will do is give you the essential blueprint. Armed with that, you will then know how to set about finding and sifting through the huge clutter of available information. You want to capture only the really vital facts that you must have in order to make a sound financial decision. Like many other skills in life, once you have understood the main fundamentals, improving your expertise is simply a matter of time. Moreover, there is such a vast amount of information available, what you really need to know is how to keep the process as simple as possible, so you can distill out the pure essentials alone.

Through The Money Maze

The Money Maze is arranged in two sections. In the first five chapters we shall prepare the ground by covering the broad principles. We shall explore the key points about how money works and the essential facts you need to have at your fingertips so you can look after your own personal financial affairs. In chapters 6, 7 and 8 we shall cover all the key issues in far greater detail. These three chapters are designed to take you through the necessary stages of becoming your own personal financial adviser. A step-by-step guide will make you more proficient on achieving the all-important money skills. In the final chapter, 9, we will set out an easy-to-follow plan to get you started and show you how to put your personal investment plan into action. In addition you will need to know how to stay on track, so you can make a big positive impact on your financial affairs. Chapter 9 also includes a clear summary of all the main topics covered throughout the book, to draw all the threads together.

Throughout the book we shall aim to decode the mysterious jargon which surrounds money like an impenetrable fog. When you are caught up in this, you can feel trapped within the money maze, with no clear route through. A lot of nonsense is often talked about how complicated finance is. Here, we will decode the cryptic codes and make sense of the nonsense, to build an expertise that can confidently take you through all the money stages of your life. *The Money Maze* will provide you with all the essential know-how to guide you successfully through the tangled passages. It will show you how to find the reassuring exit; the one marked 'financial security'.

So let us begin right away by describing in the first chapter the investment staircase we are all climbing, even if you had never before realised that you were, indeed, climbing it.

« *Buy good securities, put them away, and forget them.* »
Timothy Bancroft, American financier

CHAPTER 1

The INVESTMENT
staircase

'I've just reached forty and suddenly I'm realising how quickly the years are slipping away. I haven't started a pension. I haven't saved any money yet. Before I know it I'll be fifty and will I still be where I am today on the money front? Suddenly, it looks a bit scary!'

This is a direct quote from one of the young directors I was working with on the first television series of *Mrs Cohen's Money*. Her plaintive cry for help during idle dinner chatter saddened me greatly. It highlights the shortcomings of an education system that leaves young adults ill-equipped for life in a money-dominated world. They are pitched into the world of work without the necessary skills to prepare themselves properly for an uncertain future. So they stay locked within the money maze, lacking the know-how to see them safely through. Clearly, this young director recognised her dilemma but had no idea how to start putting it right. She obviously knew she was adrift in a financial fog, and she realised she was climbing the investment staircase from forty to fifty, but was at a total loss to know how she should be planning for her financial security.

Sadly, she is not alone; millions of adults, of all ages, know they face similar monetary dilemmas. Longing for an improvement to achieve a better result of course, is not enough. You have to know how to make it happen and that can only come by applying yourself actively to the problem and searching for the right solutions which, in due course, should bring the financial success you crave.

Money, unfortunately, governs our lives in a variety of ways. But it is a most curious commodity that behaves in strange, often mysterious ways. However, once you understand the principles on which it operates, you can tackle the issues of how to manage it properly. This will put you firmly in the driving seat so you can rely more constructively on yourself to achieve financial security.

Invest And Grow Rich

Central to our discussions is the investment staircase that we are all climbing, whether we have realised it or not. Right through life we all pass through a series of many changing circumstances. These affect different age groups in a similar way to that described by Shakespeare in his play *As You Like It*. He used the idea of the seven ages of man: from the reluctant schoolboy, and on, through parenthood to the very old man who had reached his dotage.

On the investment staircase, unhappily, too many of us are like my young director friend, climbing blind and ill-prepared. Most people never fully grasp the magic of money; how it works and how they can exploit this valuable knowledge. But the key concepts are easily stated. And once they are explained, you can plan to increase your funds consistently as you mount the staircase. The idea of a staircase is just a guide. I have split it into six even steps, from the ten-plus age group to the sixty-plus group. The divisions could as easily have been taken as fifteen-plus to sixty-five-plus. Each of the separate stairs, from whatever age you begin, is meant to cover one facet of life viewed from the perspective of your financial needs. So let us take a look at the six key steps I have used to show how you will be climbing the investment staircase as you travel through life.

> The question is, who needs to invest?

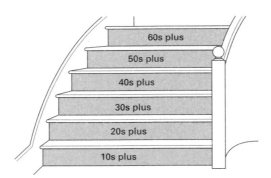

Six Stairs to Financial Success

Stair No.1 is the very first step on the investment staircase, where ten-year olds plus begin to take an interest in money because they want to buy comics, toys, sweets, games and other exciting goodies. Children are accustomed to handling small sums of money if they are given pocket money, but it is never too early to start teaching your children and grandchildren good money sense when they are very young. Teach them from an early age the value of money and why they should save it. Of course, you need to have a good grounding in managing money yourself before you can hand it on. But as you gain confidence after reading *The Money Maze*, I am hopeful that you will feel it is well worthwhile to pass on the basic facts you have learnt as soon as possible to members of your own family.

« *Blessed are the young, for they shall inherit the National Debt.* »
Herbert Hoover, President of the United States 1928–1932

Stair No.2 is the step on the route to adulthood for the twenty-plus age group. Young people should learn the basic skills of proper budgeting and saving as early as possible, especially as peer pressures may tempt them to want to buy designer clothes, CDs, evening entertainments and expensive items, like cars or holidays. Moreover, now that student loans have become a brutal fact of life, it is increasingly important that young people learn to be moneywise.

Many young people starting out in life have secret dreams of extravagant plans they would like to turn into reality at some date in the future. But for most, these will continue to remain elusive fantasies, unless the twenty-plus age group learn how to set about constructively trying to make their dreams come true. We should all be thinking from quite an early age about saving for the good things in life that we want to enjoy and of course, the older we get, and the higher we climb up the investment staircase, the more urgent this planning becomes.

Stair No. 3 marks the step when the thirty-plus age group embark on the great adventure of establishing their own families. When marriage and babies come along young families should begin to build their own tailor-made 'financial pyramid'. This consists of three essential building blocks to wealth which form the base of the pyramid: buying a house, building a long-term pension plan and using insurance-based savings. These can be highly successful schemes for protection and for starting to put aside regular savings that will accumulate over time. Those with young families need to consider making a **will**, to ensure their valued possessions go directly to the loved ones they leave, instead of being sorted out by the arbitrary rules of the public trustee. Today, in the UK, only 31 per cent of adults make a will, so many young widows and children face difficulties should disaster strike.

When they reach later stairs, young parents can build on their financial pyramids by adding **PEPs** (Personal equity plans) and **TESSAs** (Tax-exempt special savings accounts) in the short-term, although the Labour government plans to replace both of these in 1999 with the introduction of **Isas**, (Individual savings accounts). We shall cover the financial pyramid in greater detail in chapters 6, 7 and 9.

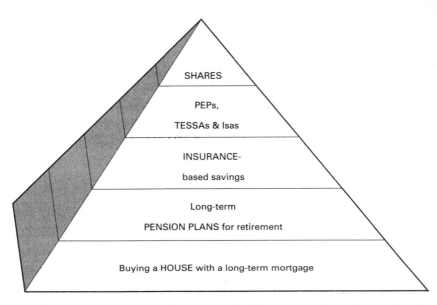

In addition, young parents with growing families need to know how to handle their debts successfully and manage them properly, so they can keep control of their finances as their family commitments rise.

Stair No. 4 heralds the age of the forty-plus. People in this age group now have the opportunity to begin accumulating **real assets** as career improvements occur, since these are usually accompanied by rising salaries. Of course, growing families can be even more expensive than young families, as demands can include putting youngsters through university or saving for weddings. However, people on step 4 should be aware of the big potential growth that can now be achieved, even when they face these large, often open-ended commitments to their growing offspring.

Stair No. 5 is where the fifty-plus stage begins. With your youngsters finally becoming independent, and major debts like your mortgage almost, if not entirely, paid off, this is the time when the serious business of planning for a happy future can really take off. Now is the time to start saving and investing in earnest, ready for retirement. Failure to take the key investment decisions at this stage can seriously affect prospects for a comfortable, financially secure retirement.

You might think that if you have arrived on stair number 5 without making sensible plans for retirement, you are too late to catch up.

Fortunately, this is not true. Although you will obviously have to work harder to get your money working properly for you from now on, the outlook can still be rosy, if you know what you should be doing to turn

Find where you are

on the investment

staircase and start

planning your

financial future

the money tide in your favour. And often, those aged fifty-plus have more experience behind them and extra time to allocate to this task, with the children, at last,
mainly off their hands.

Sadly, most of us have only limited financial resources. What we have to
realise is that to make the best possible use of them, we should all be considering putting some of our money to work in **real financial assets,** like companies
listed on the London **Stock Exchange.** But it will only be safe to do this
when we know a great deal more about how this type of investment operates.
It is a well known fact that in America the largest group of savers and
investors currently is the so-called 'baby-boomers'. This is the age group who
were born at the end of the Second World War in the late 1940s. Now in
their early fifties, a whole post-war generation of millions is saving like crazy
through stock market-related investments, to set themselves up for a secure old age.
They will probably begin retiring early in the next century, from around the year
2000 to 2015. Interestingly, there must be a similar generation of 'baby-boomers'
in Britain, since a record one million babies were born in 1947 alone, but they
do not seem to make the same attention-grabbing headlines over their saving habits
for retirement.

Stair No. 6 is where the sixty-plus age group begin to face retirement. In the UK,
life expectancy rates have risen astonishingly over the past thirty years or so. A man
can, it is hoped live to 72 and a woman to 78, but when you reach the sixties age
group, these figures become too conservative. At the age of 60, life expectancy
increases to 79 for men and 84 for women.

In June 1997 the Distressed Gentlefolk's Aid Association published a survey to
celebrate their centenary. They observed that 100 years ago there were probably
fewer than 100 centenarians, but by 1951 there were 271 of them. The number had
risen to 1,185 by 1971 and was 4,400 by the 1991 census. In 1997, the
estimated number of centenarians was 8,000 with a forecast rise to 30,000
by the year 2030. This remarkable forecast reflects the many beneficial
effects of our improving quality of life and the impact it is having on
longevity in particular.

The route to a secure retirement is to prepare your investment plan early and carry it out as you mount the investment staircase

So retirement can last for twenty to thirty and possibly even up to forty
years. Will you be financially ready for that? A study in February 1996
by the privately owned investment banking group Robert Fleming calculated that 10 million women will face a poverty-stricken old age because
they are not making adequate preparation now for their retirement.

Once you understand about the investment staircase you can start planning early to build your investments as you climb. This will enable you to
achieve your retirement nest egg by the time you reach the sixty-plus stair.

Save And Invest

It is never too soon to start saving and investing in earnest. In the following chapters we will consider in greater detail the actual steps you should be considering on each stair that makes up the investment staircase, and how these plans apply particularly to different age groups. But right at the outset, you have to sort out clearly the crucial differences between **saving** and **investing**, because many people tend to confuse these two related ideas, thinking they are broadly the same thing. This is not true at all.

Saving and investing are two distinct approaches to building a future nest egg. We have to know precisely what they both entail, so that we can make our financial plans accordingly and get the best possible results from our efforts.

Although we use the word investment to describe time or effort allocated to favoured activities or even in ourselves, when applied to money, an **investment** means putting a lump sum into possessions which offer us the prospect of increasing the size of our initial stake while at the same time providing a regular return. In financial jargon the original sum is called the **capital**, the regular return it earns usually takes the form of a **dividend** and the group of financial possessions which produce this ideal result are called **real assets.**

Think about growing your own nest egg: you'll be surprised how quickly you can make it grow

Investment = Capital + Dividend

Real Financial Assets

If this works out in practice, it seems too good to be true; it's our first example of money magic. You put your cash into a real asset and it produces an income even while the original sum is growing. This means that the best financial investments give you a double whammy. Like having your cake while you're eating it, your capital is growing at the same time as you are getting a rising return or income from it. It certainly sounds like magic. So how does it work?

There really is no trick. Real assets usually consist of two essential but separate parts: **capital growth** and a regular return or dividend. Added together, capital growth and the dividend income produce what is termed the **total return**. People are attracted to invest in these real assets because they *want* to have both elements; to take a regular and growing income at the same time as their capital is, hopefully, also growing. Naturally, as only a few possessions produce this remarkable combination they are usually highly prized and highly sought after. Moreover, anything financial that is in short supply will have a scarcity value, making it potentially more valuable.

6

The INVESTMENT *staircase*

Most of our possessions would fail to qualify as real assets because they start to

Capital Growth + Dividend = Total Return

lose their value as soon as we have bought them. A second hand car or boat, for example, will not maintain its original value and neither will most new furniture or carpets. However, antique furniture and hand woven carpets are examples of real assets because, regardless of their age or the numbers of previous owners, there are invariably new buyers wanting to own them. But these examples are not real financial assets, because they do not offer the unique combination of *capital growth plus a growing income.* Similarly, a painting, a rare silver goblet or a stamp collection might grow more valuable over the years, so although these will rank as real assets, like the antique furniture or carpets, they don't produce an income.

Real financial assets allow you to have your cake and eat it.

Most real financial assets that allow you to have your cake and eat it are based on stock-market related investments, although the same result can be achieved through running your own business or owning commercial property. A house is a good example of a real asset that can produce both capital growth and an income, although as prices tend to fluctuate considerably, the house may have to be held for many years, even decades, in order to obtain a worthwhile capital gain. However, as only a limited number of houses exist, especially in desirable areas, they do tend, over a period of many years, to rise in value. If you had bought a modest house in 1920, you might have paid around £600 for it. A similar sized house by 1970 would have cost about £6,000, and might have fetched around £180,000 by 1997. And if you wanted to earn some money as an income, you could have rented out rooms, or indeed the whole house, to provide a growing regular return right through that entire period.

|1920|1970|1997|

Real Stock Market Assets

Only a few real assets possess this special quality, the ability to grow in value while offering the opportunity of providing a rising regular return. Some, like housing, owe most of their astronomical rise over this century to the impact of inflation,

7

as we shall see in chapter 2. Most of them, however, are geared to the world of business and commerce. This is why the majority of people who want to own such assets have to rely on stock market investments. As they are not able to create their own businesses, they want to put some of their capital into existing businesses which are real financial assets.

An investment of £100

Some commentators differentiate between real assets that you can actually touch, like antique furniture, eighteenth-century French porcelain of a Picasso painting, and financial assets, like stocks and shares. As these are usually represented by a piece of paper, a share certificate, or increasingly today, simply a record in a computer terminal or on a printout, there is a tendency to imagine they are intangible. This impression is reinforced by the volatile way that prices can rise or fall, wiping out millions of pounds in value, or conversely, adding it back, almost overnight.

in Glaxo shares in 1981

would have grown to

£42,000 in 1997: now

that's what I

You should never be lured into thinking like this. When you buy a share in a **publicly quoted company** on a major international **stock market**, like London, New York or Tokyo, that is precisely what you are doing – *buying a share in*, that is, *an actual part of that company*. If you spent just £3,500 on

call *real growth*

your investment, you would admittedly only own an infinitely minute fraction of your company. But some huge investment fund managers, like Fidelity, Mercury Asset Management or Prudential, actually buy many millions of shares in British companies. So if the chief executive of Fidelity Fund Management went to visit the head office of a company where Fidelity had a major holding worth several millions of pounds on behalf of thousands of investors, he could point to a large number of items in the company, say office furniture, a bank of computers, some company cars or other machines, which this shareholding represented in terms of real physical objects.

« I'm not in Wall Street for my health. »

J.P. Morgan, American banker

It is a mistake to think that stocks and shares are simply pieces of paper that are traded to and fro on a stock market. Although you may have only a small piece of paper to indicate your claim on that shareholding, it represents a real claim to wealth. So conversely, when a company you have shares in goes bankrupt, this is a true loss of wealth. Its debts have wiped out all the value of the **ordinary share holders funds**. There is nothing illusory about the loss. It is a complete wipe out although some creditors with a secured interest may eventually get back part of the money the company owed them. Fortunately, very few companies fail totally so in general, your share certificate represents a real, tangible claim to your part in the company that you have bought a stake in.

The conversion of huge **mutual** building societies (owned by their members, who are savers or borrowers) to public company status as banks (owned by their shareholders) illustrates this point. If you received any windfall shares in 1997 when four of these major stock market flotations took place, you may have wondered where the money came from to distribute these 'free' shares. In all cases, the money had been accumulated as **profits** and **reserves** in the building societies' **balance sheets** over many decades because there was no proper mechanism in place to distribute the cash, although, in theory, this money did belong to the members. However, when these members were given free shares, they ceased to be passive owners of the mutual society. They now became shareholders. This made them active owners of the newly floated banks, entitled to participate in the company's affairs, for example, by voting on all the important issues discussed at the **Annual General Meeting** concerning the running of the company. The newly issued shares represented the new shareholders' claims to past profits (the company's reserves) and a claim on the future profits. This claim would be honoured twice yearly by a distribution of the company's earnings, as dividends.

In real financial assets, the combination of a rising income and capital growth is an ideal solution to taking care of future money requirements for most of us; it provides the capital growth of the original sum at the same time as we can draw a current return, the dividend. This regular payment can either be added to our original investment to increase the potential amount of the future capital growth, or it can be used now to spend as extra income.

Don't panic if you suddenly realise that you do not possess any of these remarkable real assets that allow you to have your cake and eat it. The whole purpose of reading this book is to unveil the mystery of money and guide you successfully through the money maze. We can all enjoy the rich fruits of our labour once we peel away the layers of mystique that surround this most misunderstood yet crucial commodity. But the priority has to be to familiarise yourself fully with the subject, before you make any drastic changes to the way you are managing or mismanaging your money right now. There will be plenty of time to catch up on making your money work well for you, but you must have a good grounding first.

Savers Keepers

If owning real assets describes investing, what is meant by **saving**? Money set aside for future use is saved. If you put it in a tin box on the mantelpiece it will just sit there until you decide to spend it. But if you put it into a bank or building society, you can earn a regular return, as **interest** from it. But there is no possibility of the capital growing, unless you leave the interest in the account to roll up without withdrawing it to supplement your income. The interest can be reinvested to make the capital grow, but if you do that, you forfeit the opportunity to take a regular income from it. With savings deposited in a bank account, you cannot have your cake and eat it at the same time.

Save to build your

nest egg: invest to

make it grow.

When you invest, you put your money into real financial assets to provide you with a regular return plus the prospect of growth in your capital. When you save, you are keeping money aside to pay for special occasions or cope with unexpected events for which you might need cash in a hurry, or for short term items, like paying for urgent repairs. This money will only earn a modest rate of interest if you put it into a deposit account.

Sadly, in Britain, most people keep almost all their accumulated capital in these types of savings accounts because they think stock market investments are risky, or because they have no idea how to set about learning the nitty-gritty facts about investing, as opposed to passively saving often right throughout their lives.

In Britain, we obviously have a savings account mentality, as in 1997 over £400 billion of our hard saved cash was held in bank and building society accounts. I feel sure that in part this attitude is due to a widespread ignorance about the great advantages that possessing real financial assets offer – the wonderful have-your-cake-and-eat-it bonanza.

Compare in excess of £400 billion in cash on deposit with estimates made in mid-1997 by Autif, the Association of Unit Trusts and Investment Funds. Their research showed only around £30 billion was invested in **unit trust PEPs**, (that is, Personal equity plans). PEPs were considered by independent advisers to be one of the most tax-efficient methods of saving in **collective funds**, which are funds run by professional managers for a large group of investors who pool their resources. Furthermore, funds under management in 1,694 **unit trusts**, (one popular form of collective funds), amounted to £149 billion in May 1997, held in 8.9 million unitholder accounts. Considering there are over 20 million deposit accounts in the Halifax alone, just 9 million PEP account holders indicates the huge improvement in education that is still needed. We will look more closely at unit and **investment trust** savings in chapter 7.

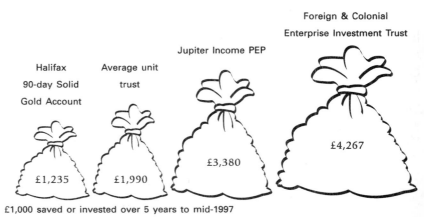

Foreign & Colonial
Enterprise Investment Trust

Jupiter Income PEP

Halifax
90-day Solid
Gold Account

Average unit
trust

£4,267

£3,380

£1,235   £1,990

£1,000 saved or invested over 5 years to mid-1997

According to Chase de Vere, the financial adviser, savers are missing out as equity investors gain. Their PEP-guide performance charts showed that £1,000 invested over five years to mid-1997 in the average unit trust PEP would have grown to £1,990. The same amount on deposit in the Halifax 90-day Solid Gold account would be worth £1,235. Five years is the minimum reasonable timespan for holding an investment. However, the difference between the savings account and the best performing PEP over five years is even more dramatic. The Foreign and Colonial Enterprise Investment Trust plan had turned £1,000 into £4,267, while the top-performing five-year unit trust was Jupiter's Income PEP, which turned £1,000 into £3,380.

So here in a nutshell is the secret of making your money work. By saving, you cannot have your cake and eat it; by investing, you can. It is obviously very important to recognise this elemental difference between the two activities.

I hope you can now see clearly that everyone needs both savings and investments. Saving is only ONE part of wealth creation. It provides vital, rainy day money to pay for unexpected expenses and cash we shall need during the next few weeks or months. It is also a tremendously useful way to build up funds ready for future investment. We will see in chapter 5 how this works in practice and in chapter 7 we will discuss in more detail how you can maximise on the opportunities to make your money really grow but without taking unnecessary risks. But saving is no substitute for investment in real assets. This is the key to achieving long-term growth for your money. Unless you own a thriving business or rent out property, the best route for the majority of people to take is through stock market-related investments.

Seeing Is Believing

You may think that a five year comparison is not sufficient evidence to clinch the argument that investing in the stock market is the best route to creating long-term wealth. So let us examine the claim in greater detail. Every year BZW, the global investment banking arm of Barclays Bank produces an Equity Gilt Study, which compares the long-term performance of three main asset classes: equities, (that is, company shares), gilts (fixed interest British government bonds or loans made by individuals to the government) and cash. This study goes back to 1918 and tracks the real return (that is, after deducting for inflation) over various periods. The 1997 figures show that with gross interest added (that is, interest before the deduction of tax) an investment of £100 into equities in 1918 would have been worth £710,556 by the end of 1996.

By comparison, that £100 invested in gilts would have grown to £8,917, while £100 left in cash deposits would have grown to £6,101. These figures have not been

Investing is the best route to creating long-term wealth

adjusted for the impact of inflation, which has made a huge difference to returns on savings, especially since 1940.

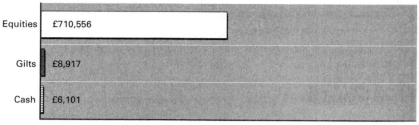

£100 invested in 1918 in equities, gilts and cash

We shall come back to this study in chapter 2, to consider the adjustments we must make for inflation, given the adverse effect it has on our savings. We shall also consider how, and why, reinvesting the dividends helps our nest egg to grow much faster as the years go by. But even without adjusting these figures for inflation, it is plain that investments in gilts and cash are left far behind equities in the race to build real wealth. If we look at the period since the end of the Second World War, the story of the rapidly growing difference between an investment in the stock market and in government gilt-edged stock and cash deposits is repeated. This is clearly seen in the chart below, which compares building society returns with equities from 1945 to the end of 1996.

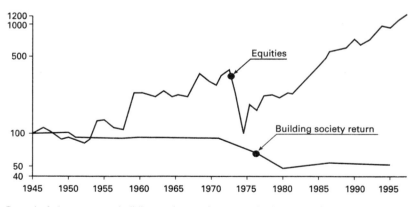

Record of shares versus building society savings over the long term from 1945 to 1996

Source: From BZW Equity Gilt Study

The BZW study certainly provides convincing evidence that saving in bank deposit and building society accounts doesn't build real wealth. A sum of £100 was a large amount in 1918. It might have been a whole year's wages for a skilled worker.

Recalculated into 1996 terms, it would have provided a decent middle class living standard. By contrast, growth in a deposit account amounted to only £6,101 by 1996. This is way below 1997's average annual income of £20,000 before tax and would not provide a decent living standard for anyone in work. The savings figures for building society accounts are even more depressing once they are adjusted for inflation, a point we will return to in the next chapter.

In chapter 2, when we discuss money magic, we shall look in greater detail at the puzzle of why investing in the stock market is able to create real long-term wealth, while an investment in a savings account lags so far behind. Here, I want to focus on publicly quoted companies, that is companies quoted on an international stock market, and suggest an explanation for why stock market investments tend to grow so well over long periods of time.

Growth In The Economy ...

Essentially, the secret lies in the long stretch of peace the world has enjoyed since 1945. This has allowed all the major economies and trading areas worldwide to concentrate on manufacturing consumer goods and services, instead of building bombs, guns, tanks and other weapons of destruction. The result of this prolonged period of global peace is the marvellous long-term improvement in living standards we have seen through rising national growth on almost every continent, except, sadly, for eastern Europe and much of Africa.

Are we going to allow

ourselves to become

seriously poor because

inflation is eating away

at our savings?

Although regional peace has been repeatedly interrupted by pockets of local conflicts, in the main this extended fifty years of general peace has allowed the levels of prosperity to rise in America, Australia, Japan, South-East Asia, Latin America and most of western Europe. Many of these countries have seen growth occurring consistently in their economies for years at a stretch, often in the order of around 2.5 to 3 per cent a year. There have also been irregular short bouts of recession, with growth hiccups. At these times, growth came to a halt, or there may even have been a short period of sliding backwards. In Britain, since the end of the 1990–92 **recession**, growth in the economy has been positive in every year, rising to a peak in 1994. This can be seen on the chart on page 14.

And On The Stock Market

Most people think of the stock market as a rich man's club, run like a swanky casino in the South of France. In reality, however, there is an exceptionally strong link between how well the stock market performs and the behaviour of companies that run all the important shops, businesses and factories in Britain, including companies that are household names for us all, like Rank, EMI, Marks & Spencer, Barclays and Boots. When there is growth in the economy, it is not an intangible thing: it is achieved by the expansion of thousands of separate firms and businesses, all improving their profits and performance at the same time. Obviously, some companies will not join in the improvement; some may simply stagnate or get taken over, while others may even cease to trade or go out of business entirely. This is the risk all companies run.

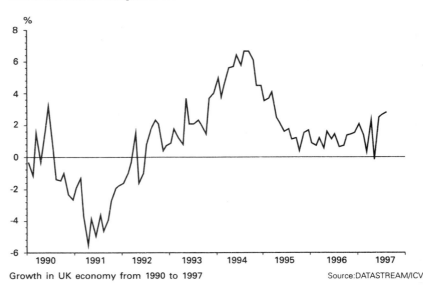

Growth in UK economy from 1990 to 1997   Source:DATASTREAM/ICV

But when the economy is growing positively, it reflects the profitable growth of the majority of the companies and firms who make up the entire manufacturing, industrial and commercial heart of the country. In Britain, this growth is principally reflected by the expansion of thousands of small, privately owned businesses as well as by companies that are publicly quoted on the stock market. There are well over 2,000 public companies. They are clustered into several groups, based on their size – huge, large, medium and small. Many of these companies are included in a series of stock market benchmarks, known as **FTSE indices** which represent the whole gamut of quoted companies of each size.

« *Although wealth may not bring happiness the immediate prospect of it provides a wonderfully close imitation.* »

HMS Surprise, Patrick O'Brian

This group of FTSE indices provides a measure of the long-term progress of UK public companies. The FTSE indices play a central role in how investors view company prospects. They also reflect how the general economy is performing. They are used by all professional fund managers and institutional investors in Britain and abroad, as a yardstick for measuring the performance of their funds against each other and against the performance of the stock market itself overall.

Growth in the economy helps to pay for the welfare state

Over time, as private companies expand and prosper, they tend to float on the stock market to improve their public image and gain easier access to new funds for further expansion. The entrepreneurs who create and build these companies are often driven by their vision of success in promoting the products that they make or the services they provide. The proposed flotation of Formula One during 1997 was an example. Formula One, an internationally known company, was built up from almost nothing, to have a value of around £1.5 billion by the vision of one man, Bernie Ecclestone. If you back owner/managers like him, when they bring their companies to the public market at fair prices, you are hoping to enjoy their future growth, sometimes over many years or decades.

This strong urge to 'go public' means the number of publicly quoted companies tends to rise although this rising number has to be offset by companies that leave the market because they have either been taken over or gone out of business. In 1996 alone, 232 companies were introduced to the London Stock Exchange.

The most prestigious of all the FTSE indices is the **FTSE 100 index** which is made up of the one hundred largest publicly quoted companies by value in Britain. Among them are all the major firms who are household names to everyone, such as Next, BP, Tesco, ICI, Halifax, Prudential, British Aerospace, Railtrack, British Gas and BT. The value is recalculated every minute of every working day. It is the number of **ordinary shares** in circulation multiplied by the share price at that moment. This value is called the company's **market capitalisation**. Although this really does mean you cannot count your money out to the nearest penny or even pound on working days, this is not a problem. I think it is only misers who need to count their money; financially secure people do not need to know exactly how much money they have on any particular day.

Share price x No of shares = Value of a company

The FTSE 100 index was introduced at 1000 in 1984 and, as can be seen from the chart on page 16, from 1984 it had risen to 5330 by October 3 1997. This is a superb increase of over five-fold growth in thirteen years from its starting level. The index registers the rise in the share prices of its constituent companies. This is purely a measure of the capital growth. It ignores any dividends which are paid out to shareholders as a regular 'income'. What does this rise mean for investors? Ignoring the costs of buying or selling shares, for the moment, if in 1984 you had put £1,000 into a wide spread of FTSE 100 companies, like those mentioned above, and if they had all managed to keep pace with the rise in the FTSE 100 index itself, your £1,000 would have grown to £5,330 by October 3 1997. In practice, however, this may not have been possible as some of the companies listed in the FTSE 100 in 1984 were no longer in it by 1997.

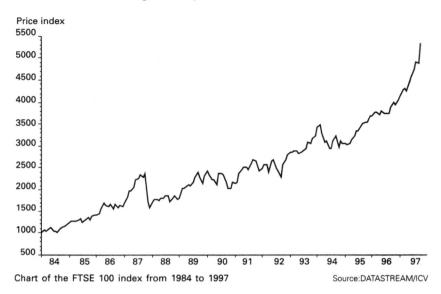

Chart of the FTSE 100 index from 1984 to 1997   Source:DATASTREAM/ICV

But in addition, you would have received dividend cheques twice every year from the companies you had invested your money in. If we assume a **dividend yield** of around 4 per cent (which means a return of 4 per cent on your initial £1,000 invested), you would have obtained around £40 in dividends in 1984. Assuming the dividend yield stayed unchanged at 4 per cent every year until 1997, your actual dividend cheques would have risen in line with the rise in the index to 5330, because over the years, as companies make larger profits, they tend to distribute more of them as dividends to their shareholders. This is one of the great attractions of owning company shares – the prospect of dividends rising as the years pass. So, for 1997 alone, therefore, you might have received almost £200 in dividends. Overall, during the entire span of thirteen years, the twice-yearly dividends would have amounted to about £900 in total.

One piece of good news can transform a company's growth prospects

You can now see that by investing £1,000 into some FTSE 100 shares in 1984 at a cost of around £60, and holding onto them until autumn 1997 you would have obtained a total of £5,330 capital growth, plus £900 in dividend income, to produce what professional investors call the total return of £6,230. Holding on, right through the October 1987 crash and the recovery that followed would have been an anxious time for you as a long-term investor, but it would have kept the costs of buying to an absolute minimum of around £125, a tiny expense when compared to this splendid outcome.

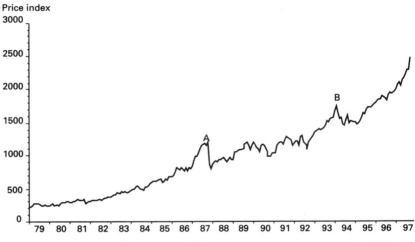

The FTSE All-Share index from 1979 to 1997   Source:DATASTREAM/ICV

Another key index, more broadly based, is the **FTSE All-Share index.** It embraces a larger group of companies, over 900 in total. It has shown a remarkably consistent rise stretching back over the past eighteen years. This is seen in the chart above, where the upward trend of the index appears to have coped amazingly well with several short term setbacks. Some of these assumed major significance at the time. They include the global crash of 1987, (A) on the chart, and a drastic collapse in confidence in early 1994, when American interest rates began to rise again after five years of falls (B). While these events seemed highly traumatic to millions of investors at the time, over the long term they appear of far less importance. They now seem like small blips on the remorseless rise of the index. Through this eighteen year period, the FTSE All-Share index has risen over 10-fold, from 200 in 1979 to 2492 by October 3, 1997.

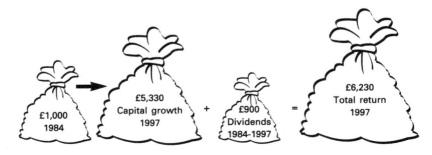

All Change On The Index

One important reason for the rise in the indices therefore, is that as the record of the past fifty years shows, over time the economy has continued to grow. This growth is based on the continued success and expansion of most of the major companies that produce the bulk of the goods and services we all use. But there is another important underlying reason why the FTSE indices continue to march steadily higher, despite periodic bouts of weakness and falls. Surprisingly, this reason depends on the fact that the **actuaries** who compile the indices treat them somewhat like football league tables. Promote the new winners; relegate the old losers. The result is that in essence, the indices measure UK company excellence while ignoring failures.

Periodically, some companies that are included in these indices hit a bad patch. Problems may crop up in a whole raft of areas: poor management, outdated products, a slump in the market, a failure to innovate. If any of these or other serious problems surface, growth will be affected by a drop in the company's sales. This will have a knock-on effect on profits. If profits suffer, confidence in a recovery takes a beating and investors sell their shares. If the recovery is delayed for too long, these unsuccessful public companies will either get taken over or go bust. According to figures published by KPMG, the accountants, in 1996 a total of over 35,000 companies collapsed as a result of bankruptcies and voluntary or compulsory liquidation. When publicly quoted companies go under, they will disappear from the relevant index, being immediately replaced by up-and-coming, more successful companies. This procedure, of removing the losers and installing more successful successors, happens four times every year for the FTSE indices. So, over a period, the failing companies are continually being eliminated.

> To build real wealth savers must turn themselves into investors.

What does this mean for investors? In general, even if you lose some money in a company that goes bankrupt, as long as you have a wide spread of other investments, the rest of them should not be affected and will, hopefully, continue to grow. On the bright side, once a company has gone bankrupt, no new investors can buy its shares, so this is a small safeguard for novices. Moreover, the possibilities of choosing successful companies is greatly increased if you are willing to spend some time developing a system for selecting your investments. This move alone will shift the odds more heavily in your favour. How I did this for myself is covered in *The Armchair Investor*, but the way for novices to learn about the rudiments of investment planning is discussed in chapter 4.

Many small successful UK growth companies expand to become monster businesses employing vast numbers of people with subsidiary branches all around the world. For the 100 companies in the FTSE 100 index, over 40 per cent of their turnover is sold as exports, reflecting their global reach. Many of them have

When you buy a share

in a UK company you

are buying a piece of

Britain

expanded consistently for decades, growing into major international companies with an important presence in countries all around the world. Companies like BP, Marks & Spencer, Glaxo Wellcome, Zeneca, Vodafone and Reuters spring instantly to mind. But ten years ago Vodafone, for example, was a developing part of Racal Electronics, the defence, radio and data communications company, and Zeneca was an integral part of ICI, the chemicals giant; neither company had yet emerged from the parent to acquire an independent existence, and neither was therefore included as a separate company in the FTSE 100 index. I like to think of my shareholdings as a family of investments. Every family has good sheep and perhaps one or two black sheep. This applies to companies as well. You can see almost at a glance, from the charts for Vodafone and Zeneca below just how successful these offspring have been since they finally parted company from their parent businesses.

Pictures Tell The Story

Charts are extremely useful for showing us the overall performance of a company or an index. They reveal a quick snapshot of difficult times (usually when prices fall) and booming times, (when prices rise). For both Vodafone and Zeneca, we can instantly see what a good rate of growth in their share prices they have enjoyed since they were floated as new companies in their own right on the stock market. This rise in the share price reflects the continuing success of both companies. If their expansion began to falter, investors would worry and begin to sell their shares. This action would cause a drop in the share price, which would register as a falling line on the charts.

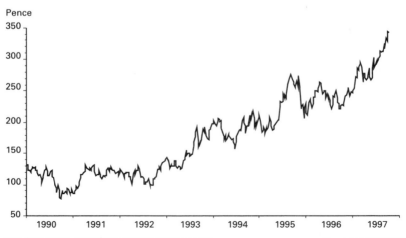

Vodafone share price from 1990 to 1997 weekly   Source:DATASTREAM/ICV

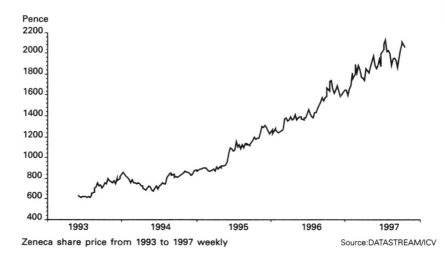

Zeneca share price from 1993 to 1997 weekly   Source:DATASTREAM/ICV

In 1997, when the major building societies of Halifax, Alliance and Leicester and Wool-wich plus the insurance company, Norwich Union, gave up their mutual status, to become publicly quoted companies on the stock market, several other companies were evicted from the FTSE 100 index to allow them to enter its ranks, as they are all extremely large and valuable companies worth many billions of pounds. The Halifax, for example, ranked as the eighth largest company in Britain on the day it was floated in June 1997.

« In a slow-moving economy, growth is not going to pop up
conveniently in your portfolio. You are going to have to seek it out
– and weed out the dogs. »

Barry Riley, *Financial Times*

Important events, like the flotation of mutual companies, are regularly mirrored in constant changes in the FTSE indices over the years. There is therefore nothing static about the composition of the key FTSE indices, as they undergo periodic revisions every year in their memberships. For example, in September 1997, five companies entered the FTSE 100 index – Billiton, Norwich Union, Sun Life and Provincial, Woolwich, and Williams – while five others were ejected – Burmah Castrol, Hanson, Imperial Tobacco, Mercury Asset Management and Tate & Lyle.

Nothing
succeeds like
success

It is important to realise that over the long term, therefore, all these main indices are continuously being updated to mirror company success and ignore company failures. As the indices act as the key benchmarks for the general stock market performance, their concentration on major success in business life gives an ever upward slant to the whole market. Essentially, these indices continually monitor only the surviving successful companies. This is a powerful reason for expecting stock market success to continue. There will always be some relatively unsuccessful companies as well as outright failures. They are the proverbial black sheep of the whole family of publicly quoted companies. They will be replaced by more successful companies in the all-important stock market indices benchmarks.

Why Not Buy A Piece Of Britain?

I have spent some time explaining why the stock market has shown such a spectacular rise over the past fifty years, compared to other savings methods, because there is such a widespread distrust and misunderstanding of how this growth occurs. People find it difficult to identify with the stock market. It is hard not to think of it as a greed-ridden casino rigged in some way, for the benefit of insiders. But most people own pension and insurance policy plans where the contributions they regularly make are primarily invested in the stock market for them by professional fund managers. How many of us ever stop to think that this market consists of thousands of major companies which play a huge part in our daily lives; companies where we shop for food, clothes, petrol or entertainment, or rely on for a multitude of important services, every week of our lives?

When I met Mike Blackburn, the Chief Executive of the Halifax, in April 1997, just before it converted into a bank, he gave me his thoughts on why we do not have a proper shareholding democracy in Britain as they have in America. In spite of the fact that we have the third largest stock market in the world and an army of millions of novice shareholders after the big mutual societies converted in 1997, most Britons are wary of the stock market and want nothing to do with it. Mike Blackburn thought one reason for this was:

« *Americans celebrate success. We envy it.* »

I agree that investing in publicly quoted company shares can be risky, but we will cover the topic of risk in chapters 3 and 4, where I shall hope to dispel many of the myths associated with stock market-related risk. In America, one of the slogans used to persuade people to buy stock market investments hits just the right note. I think we could profitably import it over here. They say, 'When you buy shares in an American company, you are buying a piece of America.'

I strongly believe that this message also applies to the majority of British companies. We have so many highly successful companies. We should want to share in a small part of that success. It is a well-known fact that the Anglo-Saxon version of **capitalism** that dominates corporate thinking in Britain and America puts pressure on company bosses to deliver shareholder value. Whether this is a worthy goal or not, the effect is that many company directors strive to improve their company's image through promoting shareholder value. If you own shares in companies with that philosophy those managers have your interests at heart. And when they personally own a large shareholding, these directors also enjoy the boost to their company's share price that springs from their inspirational financial flair and entrepreneurial skills.

Follow The Great Entrepreneurs

The example of Sir Ernest Harrison, the founder and long-serving chairman at the head of Racal Electronics, illustrates what can be done. Sir Ernest has achieved a remarkable record of creating value for shareholders. From humble origins in the 1950s, Racal was used by Sir Ernest to create Vodaphone, the mobile telephone company. By mid-1997, the combined market values of Vodaphone and Racal were almost £10 billion, over £9 billion of which was in Vodaphone. But this was not all he achieved. In 1984, he paid £170 million in a takeover of Chubb, the security company. By mid-1997, as an independent company once more, Chubb had a market value of £1.3 billion. In the process of creating these three important companies, Sir Ernest acquired large holdings in them all: 1.68 million shares in Chubb, (1.68m x £4.46) worth £7.49 million, 2.2 million shares in Racal Electronics, (2.2m x £2.36) worth £5.19 million and 1.09 million shares in Vodaphone (1.09m x £3) worth £3.27 million (all at mid-1997 prices).

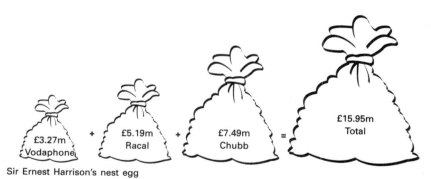

Sir Ernest Harrison's nest egg

Over his working lifetime, associated with Racal Electronics and the two companies he **demerged**, or split off from it, Vodaphone and Chubb, his personal worth has grown to almost £16 million (£15.95m). Not only has he generated wonderful returns for his faithful shareholders, he has enjoyed the fruits of this success himself. When small investors find British entrepreneurs of such outstanding ability, they are backing the management when they buy shares in their companies.

Build A Cash Cushion

All the evidence shows that once you have mastered the areas of risk, it is really never too soon to begin building up a nest egg for the future. It would be wrong to think that saving for retirement is the main goal of building that lump sum, as you might need some of it long before you ever reach stair number six. A lump sum could be a godsend to see you through an unexpected period of unemployment or ill-health when you cannot work. At such times, relying purely on state benefits provides only the most frugal support. Currently these benefits are hedged around with tight limitations and restrictions; they amount to around £49 per week for unemployed people over 25, for a limited period, and about £62 per week for long-term incapacity benefit. Of even greater importance is the reality that we can no longer take state funded assistance for granted as the government is perpetually seeking ways to restrict future entitlements.

Once you know the secret, money magic can work for you

Moreover, governments are constantly changing the financial structure of personal and company affairs, in a never-ending effort to balance the books for the welfare state. All our careful plans can abruptly become outdated if they introduce unfavourable measures, such as cutting interest relief on mortgages or withdrawing the tax relief on dividends in existing tax-exempt schemes, like Personal equity plans or personal pensions. We cannot know in advance what changes will be made, but we need to keep in touch with the government's actions, so we can adjust our plans, in spite of detrimental changes, to keep on course to achieve the money targets we have set ourselves. Nor is this all. During the past decade it has become glaringly obvious that financial security for those in work is a fragile advantage that can be unexpectedly snatched from our grasp without any previous warning. Even if we think we have the safest job in town, it would be unwise to take it for granted. More people increasingly find themselves job-hopping throughout their working lives – not from choice but necessity. Nowadays, lifelong employment over a forty-year time frame has become a relatively rare luxury available only to a very fortunate few. It is certainly no longer guaranteed for the majority of us.

« *Fancy giving money to the government! ... Ten to one they'll start another war.* »

A.P. Herbert

If you can begin steadfastly to build a nest egg from a very young age, even as early as ten or twelve, hopefully you won't wake up with a shock to discover on your fortieth birthday that you haven't even begun to put money aside for a rainy day emergency, never mind planning for a secure and comfortable retirement which is still at least another twenty years over the horizon.

And why, you might ask, should an early start to saving for this big nest egg make such a difference? The answer sounds like a fairytale rather than something in the hard-nosed world of money and finance. But truth in this case is definitely stranger than fiction. Because once you discover the secret mechanism whereby the money you save or invest can grow more money, you are on the way to financial bliss. And this happy state is attainable for everyone because it depends solely on the magic of geometric growth which we will explore in chapter 2.

« *I'm not opposed to millionaires, but it would be dangerous to offer me the position.* »

Mark Twain

Key Points To Remember

1 Six stairs to financial success.
2 Have your cake and eat it with real financial assets.
3 Own shares in a UK company and you are buying a piece of Britain.
4 Invest to make your money grow.
5 Save to put some money aside for future use.
6 Growth in UK companies reflects growth in the UK economy.
7 FTSE indices measure the stock market performance.
8 FTSE indices, like football league tables, promote the winners and relegate the losers.
9 Follow the great UK entrepreneurs.
10 Build a cash cushion.

CHAPTER 2

MONEY
magic

Before going out, the sorcerer set his apprentice the task of sweeping up his workshop. The apprentice, feeling lazy, used one of the sorcerer's spells to get the broom to do the work for him. Unfortunately, he used the spell incorrectly, and instead of sweeping the water up into the bucket, the broom multiplied itself and the bucket many times over, spilling out the water, which rapidly rose in the workshop.

Disaster was finally averted when the sorcerer returned, brought the misused spell under control and restored order.

Ignorance about money is like the story of the sorcerer's apprentice. When you have no idea what you are doing, managing your money is really more a matter of luck than judgment. Relying on luck is not a sensible way to prepare for the future. To ensure your own financial success, you must focus on two key points. First, you need to become much better informed so you have confidence in your ability to take important financial decisions. And, second, you should prepare a proper plan, a blueprint, which will help you to stay on course for reaching your financial goals. We will discuss how you can set about improving your success rate in later chapters. It would be pure chance for anyone to achieve financial success by relying on luck alone. Such an approach is most unlikely to produce a happy outcome: as in the story of the sorcerer's apprentice, the unplanned consequences of running amok in the money maze can be dire.

Spellbound On Money

Money is one of the most peculiar commodities we have to deal with. We can compare it to the sorry story of the apprentice's magic spell. He accidentally conjured up new brooms a-plenty with growing numbers of water-filled buckets, until he was literally drowning in the water they were pouring out onto the floor around him. In a similar way, in a modern society, it is almost as if money has a life of its own. It doesn't necessarily follow the normal rules that apply to other commodities, like ordinary brooms and buckets. As we shall now see, money can actually appear or disappear, whether or not we know how this bizarre event has happened.

Nowadays, bankers are closer to the sorcerer's apprentice than you would

> It is easier to
>
> make money
>
> than to keep it

imagine. They can literally create money out of thin air simply by crediting your account with a loan. This is purely a paper transaction in the bank's accounting system, but it allows you to treat that loan as real money jangling in your pocket. For you it is not purely a paper transaction. You can immediately go out and spend your loan. It can be used to pay for real objects, like a new greenhouse or a second-hand car. This loan of money has now become real even while it still counts as a paper entry for the bank. And that is not the end of the matter, for two different consequences can now arise.

In Two Places At Once

First, although you have spent it, the bank continues to count your loan as a paper entry in its records. At the outset, the cash belongs to two different owners at the same time – you and the bank. Naturally, the bank is hoping you will repay your loan in due course, to eliminate the debt. But suppose you don't, or can't, repay it? What if you are suddenly made bankrupt, get ill or lose your job and cannot afford the repayments? Abruptly, this money becomes a loss in the bank's accounts. Effectively, if for whatever reason you never repay the debt, the loan money the bank was counting on has disappeared without trace.

Or has it? You may still have your second-hand car. So although the money no longer exists, the real object it bought still does. But now let us look at the second consequence that follows as soon as the bank creates your loan and you have rushed out to spend it. The money has assumed a double life, belonging to both you and the bank. When it becomes hard cash that you have spent on a second-hand car, it has found its way into the circulation of money in the wider community. You hand your money over to the seller of that second-hand car; he now has your hard cash in his pocket which he can go out and spend on that new greenhouse. So this sum of money has led a very busy life! It is still recorded in the bank's accounts, but it has been used to buy a second-hand car and a greenhouse. How can this be? The total pot of money in the wider economy and what it will buy, is growing, rather like those extra inches of water in the sorcerer's workshop.

« *Money should circulate like rainwater.* »

Thornton Wilder

At times when money is cheap because interest rates are low, it becomes much cheaper for borrowers to repay their loans. When people realise this fact, more of them decide to borrow and the whole business is ratcheted up another notch. More loans create more paper records in the bank's accounts, giving borrowers more money to spend on more second-hand cars and greenhouses. This effect was seen in June 1997, when consumers appeared to be enjoying the mini-Clarke boom that the Tories must have hoped would help to get them re-elected in the May General Election. By mid-summer, retail sales were growing strongly, rising at an annual rate of 6.5 per cent, the highest level since July 1988, at the height of the last major boom. Bank lending to individuals and businesses hit £9.2 billion for the month of May, up from £4.4 billion in April.

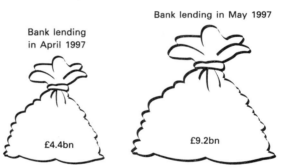

Bank lending in April 1997 — £4.4bn

Bank lending in May 1997 — £9.2bn

The government also monitors figures for the amount of money circulating in the economy. This is the money we were tracking that leaped from the bank ledger into your pocket then into the pocket of the chap who sold you that second-hand car, and on into the tills of the local garden centre where he bought a new greenhouse. Financial analysts, stockbrokers, economists and the government track this money-go-round by watching the 'money supply' which is a measure of the amount of money circulating in the economy. We have seen how quickly money can pop up in several different places almost at once, so it should not surprise you to learn that tracking the money supply is more of an art than a precise science.

One of the government's favourite measures is called M4. It measures the cash in circulation plus bank and building society accounts. This measure rose by 1.3 per cent month-on-month in May 1997. It had risen by 11.8 per cent on a year-on-year basis by July, the highest level since July 1990. We can see in the chart below how the annual rise in the M4 money supply has grown from around 2 per cent a year in 1993, as we came out of a very severe recession, to almost 12 per cent a year by mid-1997. The rise from a yearly growth of 2 to 12 per cent in four years is giving an indication of the growth in activity within the economy. Fortunately, you don't have to keep an eagle eye on figures like this, although hopefully the authorities are doing just that. But it is an important part of your general background reading, if you notice how these statistics are changing and better still if you read the accompanying comments in newspaper reports when the figures are announced. You should try to stay informed because figures like this matter to all of us, as they reflect rises in the amount of money that the banks are creating, mainly though widespread increased borrowing.

Relying on luck is not a sensible way to prepare for the future

Growth in the money supply from 1992 to 1997   Source:DATASTREAM/ICV

The mid-1990s rise in M4 illustrates how, in a very short time, the economy can begin to boom. If you can take note of changes of this magnitude in the money supply, you will not be surprised to find that people are suddenly beginning to feel a little richer, since more money has started to slosh around the system. This situation is really not very different from the rising inches of water gathering around the feet of the mystified sorcerer's apprentice when he lost control of his spell, although I doubt if economists would appreciate the similarities. They would claim that the governments and central bankers know what they are doing and are able to keep the expanding system well under overall control. As cynical money wizards keen to protect our hard-earned cash, a little scepticism is a healthy response; it is safer to be wary rather than taking everything on blind trust.

Good As Gold ...

Two centuries ago, people paid for all the goods they wanted to buy with gold or silver coins. If they had no money, they could barter; a second-hand suit of clothes for a new porcelain tea pot is known to have occurred in one instance, and some people were paid in essential supplies, like firewood or candles, instead of money. Most people who had no precious metal coins would have bartered for the goods they wanted. It is quite obvious that coins made of gold and silver, being desirable, precious metals in limited supply, have a value in their own right. And their circulation would prevent bankers from creating paper money a-plenty because the money supply was backed by gold. This system was known as **'the gold standard'**. Today, no one uses precious metal coins. We pay for the goods we want to buy with copper coins or paper – either as notes, cheques or entries in our bank accounts, like standing orders and direct debits. And, increasingly, we pay for our purchases with plastic, either as debit or credit cards. None of these commodities has any value of its own, at least not in comparison to the value of the items being bought.

« *A cynic is someone who knows the price of everything and the value of nothing.* »

Oscar Wilde

The statistics for plastic usage in Britain alone are astonishing. In May 1997, £3.66 billion was spent on debit cards with another £4.55 billion on credit card purchases. The latter, of course, are yet another way of conjuring money out of thin air, especially since the statistics show that over 70 per cent of the credit card accounts are not paid off within the interest-free period, so adding to the level of loans outstanding in the country.

Credit card spending May 1997

Debit card spending May 1997

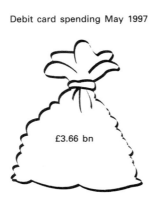

£3.66 bn

£4.55 bn

Or ... Maybe Not!

By now you may be thinking, 'Wait a minute. There must be something wrong here somewhere. It sounds too much like a money make-believe world'. It may come as a complete shock to you to learn that the whole complicated modern banking system is simply based on confidence and trust. It is rather like the story of the little boy and the emperor's new clothes. When he was watching the emperor riding in a grand procession the young lad suddenly exclaimed aloud that the emperor was completely naked. All the adults in the crowds watching the event were convinced their ruler was wearing his full royal regalia, because they had been told that he was. As the little boy had not heard this version of what the emperor was wearing, he was simply relying on what he saw. You may be amazed to think that when it comes to handling money in a modern democracy like Britain, France or America, the old adage 'seeing is believing' no longer strictly applies.

The only glue cementing the whole apparatus of our global money system together, now that we are not linked any more to a gold standard, is our confidence and trust that our money has a value and that it is safe in the places where we have chosen to put it. This is the primary reason why we should be very careful indeed with safeguarding our personal finances. Every now and then, confidence becomes exceedingly fragile and takes a really hard knock. People suddenly panic that their money may not be safe at all. Then, there may be a run on the bank, a crash on the stock market or a sudden collapse in a big institution that we thought was reliable and which, unknown to us, had been inflating the value of its funds in one way or another until disaster struck. In all these shock horror financial calamities, thousands, sometimes millions, of people are abruptly confronted with a bizarre reality: money they thought they owned has literally disappeared into thin air – as if by magic!

I hope, like me, you find this behaviour absolutely incredible. It hardly seems to fit with our image of the tough financial world of banks and city slickers where we thought smart money management took excellent care of all these complex issues. It seems more like a fantasy Disneyworld if bankers can create money out of nothing with a paper entry in their accounts. And a sudden knock to confidence can whisk it away, vanishing into space, almost as quickly. Does it make your hair stand on end to think that our intricate financial system should be built on such precarious foundations? Could the whole shaky structure come crashing down in a horrible, unforeseen disaster? We cannot know how the future will unfold, but I do not see it as a problem we should lose too much sleep over. My father had this wonderful saying for coping with shock horror situations. He used to say,

« *Don't worry about the things you can't change. Worry about the things you can change.* »

Money Is Not What It Seems

We certainly can't control the way central bankers create money, nor can we stop governments allowing too much money to come into circulation by letting an economic boom get completely out of hand. But you can look after your own finances more constructively, purely by beginning to realise that money is definitely not what it seems. It has an unexpectedly curious way of behaving. You should understand the enigmatic way that it can sometimes behave if you are to have any chance of taking and keeping control. You must try to become a sorcerer, knowing how the spells work and putting them right when things go wrong. You certainly have to avoid being a muddled apprentice who does more damage than good because you are uninitiated about how to use the spells that come into your hands. You can become a sorcerer in charge of the spells simply by getting to know how money operates in our society. If you only learn how to avoid the pitfalls waiting to trap the unwary, you will be far better off than most. Then, applying a little more effort will certainly allow you to enjoy a greater success when making your savings grow.

Money can actually appear or disappear without us understanding how this trick is done

Having seen some of the strange ways that money operates, we are now ready to explore the weird magic in the way money accumulates. And, like all magic tricks, insiders know exactly how it is done, while outsiders merely gape in baffled amazement. Understanding the enigma of money growth is the vital starting point for building a sizeable nest egg. Moreover, just as in the sorry tale of the floundering sorcerer's apprentice, what we find is that money magic is similarly a double edged sword. You can make it work *for* you (through the mystery of **compound growth**), but, equally, this same magic can work *against* you (through rising **inflation**). So you absolutely need to know in some detail how this money magic works.

Growth Is Good

Remembering what we learned at school we assume money behaves like any other object when it grows: one plus one equals two. There is certainly nothing mysterious about that. So if we start buying weekly gardening magazines to build a collection over one year, the consequences are obvious: if we save them all without throwing any away, our magazine collection will be growing linearly – adding one more every week to the existing total until we have 52 copies in all. This is an easy idea to grasp because it fits with our everyday experience. And there are plenty of ordinary examples all around us to prove the point. A young tree that grows one foot every year or a lawn that grows by half an inch every week in summer are other familiar examples of **linear growth**.

So let us see what happens to a ten-year old schoolboy who finds a lovely vase that costs £5 which he wants to buy for his mother as a Christmas present. We'll suppose he decides to start saving on July 1st by dropping a one pound coin into his moneybox on the first day of every month. If he continues to save one pound every month, he will achieve his £5 total by December 1st and can buy the gift. His money is growing **arithmetically**. In other words, it grows by a constant amount in a constant period.

« *Among the things that money can't buy is what it used to.* »

Max Kauffman

Growth On Growth

But suppose instead of saving the cash in his moneybox, he deposited his pound coins in a special bank account that paid him the marvellous sum of 10 per cent interest on his accumulating fund at the end of every month. By December 1st, as you can see from the table on page 33, his savings will have grown to £6.71. This may not seem a very large bonus, but the increase is over 25 per cent more than he would have accumulated if he had simply kept the money building up arithmetically in his moneybox. For the added effort of opening the bank account he has made an extra £1.71, which gives him enough money to buy a Christmas card and pretty wrapping paper to go with the new vase.

In money terms, although the additional £1.71 doesn't seem a huge prize, even for a ten-year-old, as a percentage of his total £5 saved, a 25 per cent gain in six months is not to be lightly dismissed. Instead of simply adding one extra pound every month in an arithmetic progression, his money is now growing **geometrically** and he has made a happy additional gain. By holding his savings in a deposit account, the interest he is earning at the end of each month will itself be earning interest in later months. *It is the ability to earn interest on existing interest which allows his savings to grow geometrically.*

« *I think money is on the way out.* »

Sayings of the Week, *Observer*, June 1956

This means the sum he can save will be far greater than if he simply carries on piling up coins in a moneybox. The calculations for these two five-month savings plans, in the moneybox and in the savings account, are shown in the tables below.

Saving £1 per month for five months in a moneybox

month no.	end of month	money saved £	new money £	total £
1	July	....	1.00	1.00
2	Aug	1.00	1.00	2.00
3	Sept	1.00	1.00	3.00
4	Oct	3.00	1.00	4.00
5	Nov	4.00	1.00	**5.00**

Saving £1 per month for five months in a deposit account

month no.	end of month	money saved £	new money £	total £	interest £	total £
1	July	....	1.00	1.00	0.10	1.10
2	Aug	1.10	1.00	2.10	0.21	2.31
3	Sept	2.31	1.00	3.31	0.33	3.64
4	Oct	3.64	1.00	4.64	0.46	5.10
5	Nov	5.10	1.00	6.10	0.61	**6.71**

The two examples in the table show the difference that can begin to develop when money grows geometrically, as in the case of the deposit account, instead of arithmetically, as in the moneybox, even in as short a period as five months.

But, you may be asking, so what? It is hardly mind blowing to conclude that if you put money in a deposit account that pays interest you will have more than if you put it under the mattress. The point is that if you continue saving you will soon discover that money magic really begins to get into its stride. After a short additional period, the differences between the two ways of saving become considerably more significant. So let us see what will happen if the schoolboy goes on saving. You would think that his 25 per cent gain in five months would produce a 50 per cent gain after ten months (25 + 25 = 50). But that's the trick! You would still be thinking in terms of arithmetic growth, when as we now know, his money is growing geometrically and therefore even faster than before.

After another five months the £5 cash in the moneybox will have grown to £10. But in the deposit account, another five months of saving will increase the interest not by another 25 per cent but by another 50 per

The sooner you jump on

the geometric savings

bandwagon, the sooner

your savings have a

chance to really grow

cent. At the end of ten months the deposit account will have earned £7.52 in interest overall, which is an amazing 75 per cent of the total £10.00 saved. The calculation is shown in the table below.

Another five months of saving in a deposit account

month no.	end of month	money saved £	new money £	total £	interest £	total £
	Total	6.71	5.00		1.71	
6	Dec	6.71	1.00	7.71	0.77	8.48
7	Jan	8.48	1.00	9.48	0.95	10.43
8	Feb	10.43	1.00	11.43	1.14	12.57
9	Mar	12.57	1.00	13.57	1.36	14.93
10	Apr	14.93	1.00	15.93	1.59	**17.52**

£6.71   £17.52

Geometric growth in money saved. After five months, money grew by 25% (£1.71 gain). After ten months money grew by 75% (£7.52 gain)

Think about this! After five months, the interest gave the schoolboy an added 25 per cent on his money. But after ten months the interest he will have received will have grown to 75 per cent. Doesn't that look as if the magic is starting to work in a big way? The reason for this accelerating growth is that, as we noted earlier, the interest he is getting every month is, in its turn, earning interest in the later months. And because the interest is piling more interest on itself every month he keeps saving, his cash hoard will soon be growing by leaps and bounds. Without putting any figures to the idea it is not easy to see how big these leaps and bounds can become. So we are using the examples to show how rapidly your savings can grow once you get started, even if like the schoolboy, you merely continue to save a modest £1 every month.

Double, Double

And so, astonishingly, only three more months of saving at that current rate will produce £26.96, which is now over double the £13 our thrifty schoolboy will have saved. In only thirteen months, as we can see below, he has actually more than doubled his money. His nest egg has produced just over 100 per cent of interest. This sort of result explains precisely why everyone should start saving, even modest amounts, at the earliest possible date. The sooner you can jump on the geometric savings bandwagon, the more interest you will have to go on earning more interest for you without involving you in any extra effort.

Savings after thirteen months in a deposit account

month no.	end of month	money saved £	new money £	total £	interest £	total £
10	Apr	14.93	1.00	15.93	1.59	17.52
11	May	17.52	1.00	18.52	1.85	20.37
12	Jun	20.37	1.00	21.37	2.14	23.51
13	July	23.51	1.00	24.51	2.45	**26.96**

And suppose our ten-year old saver was able to carry on saving at the rate of £1 per month at the same high rate of 10 per cent interest every month, his money would seriously begin to pile up, because it will be more than doubling itself with every year he saves. By the time he had doubled in age to twenty, he would have saved a terrific nest egg of over £13,000, of which his contribution overall would only have been £120. All the rest is pure interest. Put like this, the figures look staggering, because we are now talking about money that doubles in amount over a certain period. This bonanza is only possible with money that earns interest which in turn earns its own interest.

It sounds too good to be true. Are you looking for the snag? Well, of course we know no high street bank or building society is going to pay a thumping interest rate of 10 per cent every month. And as a general rule, both savers and

When it comes to

building your savings,

every little helps

investors should remember the time honoured adage, 'the greater the return the higher the risk you run of things going wrong'. This means no major national savings institution is going to pay out exceptionally high rates of interest on your savings. It looks as if we have simply used an example that is terrific on paper but cannot be achieved in practice. I wouldn't blame you if you have already jumped to that conclusion. But that jump would be too hasty, because only the example chosen is unrealistic: the basic ideas always apply. Later in the chapter I shall show you where this superb doubling result has been found repeatedly, on numerous occasions in the real financial world. To find it, however, we have to know where to look.

Add More Interest

Very few of you reading this page will be ten years old, so by now you might be thinking, sadly, that you have missed the opportunity to benefit from this golden bonanza, because you are too old. It is true, unfortunately, that very few of us will have

The greater the return the higher the risk

known the wonderful secret of geometric growth that can produce such spectacular returns on our savings when we were young enough to take the greatest advantage of this knowledge. But if we carry on with our imaginary tale of savings where the interest is earning interest to keep the money piling up, we can look at how the money might grow when, as adults, we were able to save larger amounts. So let's suppose we were saving £100 a year in a deposit account that gives a rate of interest of, say, 25 per cent paid once, at the end of every full year of saving.

The numbers are deliberately kept simple so the arithmetic is easy to follow. In practice, for most people £100 a year is far too modest a savings target, while 25 per cent interest every year is, again, way above what most safe savings accounts will offer. However, although this rate of interest is far beyond the bounds of possibility in a safe bank or building society, there are other real financial assets which can and do grow at this level, or even higher, as we shall discover a little later in this chapter.

« *These are few ways in which a man can be more innocently employed then in getting money.* »

Samuel Johnson, 1775

£100 saved over ten years at 25 per cent a year

end of year	money saved £	new money £	total £	interest £	total £
1		100	100	25	125
2	125	100	225	56	281
3	281	100	381	95	476
4	476	100	576	144	720
5	720	100	820	205	1,025
6	1,025	100	1,125	281	1,406
7	1,406	100	1,506	377	1,883
8	1,883	100	1,983	496	2,479
9	2,479	100	2,579	645	3,224
10	3,224	100	3,324	831	**4,155**

Note: these amounts have been rounded up or down to keep the calculations simple

For the purpose of this illustration we must bear these precautions in mind as we repeat the calculations again using £100 saved each year at 25 per cent interest per year. The results are given in the table on page 36. What they now show is that a saving regime of £1,000 over a ten year period with a consistent rate of return of 25 per cent at the end of each year, produces the impressive sum of £4,155. Overall, the money saved has grown more than four-fold: a tremendous £3,155 of it is purely interest. This interest earned is actually 215 per cent of the total £1,000 cash that was invested. As you can see from the figures above, the amount of interest earned is itself growing faster with every passing year. So while the interest is only £205 in year five, by year ten it is £831, which is 83 per cent of the total £1,000 that will be saved.

Can Money Grow This Fast?

The arithmetic is so surprising that you may still be sceptical and think it is purely hypothetical or perhaps, again, just money magic, which in a way it is. Certainly this level of growth cannot be achieved through normal savings or deposit accounts. As we saw with the BZW Equity Gilt Study in chapter 1, equities won by a huge margin in the handicap stakes for creating real wealth. If we look now at the average **real rate of return** (after adjusting for inflation) on all three classes of assets used in the Study, equities, gilts and cash on deposits, bought for £100 in 1918 and held to the end of the year 1996, the figures are as follows: the equities would have produced an average yearly real rate of return of 7.9 per cent. The annual return on gilts over this period was only 1.97 per cent, with cash on deposit still trailing, at a lowly 1.48 per cent. Over the really long haul, even the very bad spells get ironed out. During the inflation-prone 1970s and 1980s, both cash and gilts produced negative returns, that is, below the levels of the prevailing inflation.

If you want to make

£1 million, first get to

£999,000 and then be

very, very careful how

you invest your money

Equities 7.9%

Gilts 1.97%

Cash 1.48%

Average yearly return after inflation for equities, gilts and cash on deposit

We saw in chapter 1, that the FTSE 100 index of Britain's leading 100 companies grew over five-fold in thirteen years, from 1984 to 1997, showing that doubling time is not a vague, unrealisable idea. My own experience with investing in the stock market between 1990 and 1997 only reinforces my conviction that these are not just games we can play with interest rates. High returns are achievable in the real world of money making. But we must be prepared to spend some time and effort learning how to become well informed and how to manage our money properly and invest it for the kind of growth we have been illustrating here.

Never say 'never'; and never say 'forever'.

In broad outline, my experience reflects what it is possible to achieve. When I set out to rebuild my tattered finances in 1990, I thought in terms of money doubling over time. But I had the modest hope that I would be able to double my starting capital of a few thousand pounds in five years. However, as I learned more about the market and developed a system to help me spot good growth companies in their relatively early stages of growth, I found I was able to far exceed this initial ambition.

I lost some of my capital in the early months, about 7 per cent, but by the time the market hit a temporary peak in February 1994, my capital had grown by 238 per cent in four years. After the market declined over the next twelve months, and I had to withdraw around 20 per cent of our funds to pay for building repairs, by autumn 1996 the total funds had returned again to the amount they had reached in February 1994. There was a great upward surge for many of the world's main stock markets, including Britain, that continued well into the autumn of 1997. This strong market increased the size of my portfolio, so that even after discounting the money spent earlier on the building repairs, by October 1997 it had grown to around 360 per cent of the original sum I had started out with in February 1990. And if I add back all the money I have spent over seven years on foreign holidays, big furnishing items for the house, plus the building repairs, then the overall increase by late-1997 was in the order of 420 per cent.

During the seven years I was trying to rebuild the family nest egg, I tried not to withdraw any money from the capital and always reinvested all the dividends as they were paid out. In the BZW Study, Michael Hughes, the editor, was convinced that reinvestment of the income over the long run is the great secret for building real wealth. As he pointed out, since 1918, the capital value of equities had grown by 2.7 per cent a year. With income reinvested net of the maximum rate of tax, the annual return rose to 3.9 per cent. But if the income was reinvested gross – that is, without paying any tax, as was still the case in 1997 for PEPs and possibly for the proposed Isas, to be introduced in 1999 – then the average annual return leaped to almost 7.9 per cent.

« *I didn't know what capitalism was but retrospectively I learnt that it worked.* »

George Bain, Principal of the London Business School

Professionals often talk in terms of 'total return', that is, the dividend income added to the capital growth. While you are saving, this may be a good way to view your performance, especially if you reinvest your dividends, but at retirement, a different way of thinking is absolutely essential, a point we will return to and discuss in chapter 5.

Michael Hughes calculated that over the long term, about two-thirds of total return (capital growth plus income) comes from the reinvested income. But we have already seen this calculation in action. We have seen in the tables on pages 33, 34, and 35, that interest grows geometrically, as the months or years of saving go by. Substitute dividends reinvested for interest in our examples, and we can see how equities might grow by a real rate of 7.9 per cent over the very long haul, even after taking inflation into account.

Prizes For All

I am sure many investors will have easily beaten my investment record because the 1990s proved to be an excellent period for stock market investment. But I don't see making money for myself or my family as any kind of race where there is a first prize waiting to be handed out. Of course, I think there are prizes, and I would see them as huge benefits. The comfort of feeling financially secure is the greatest return I personally get from the time and effort I expend on caring for my share portfolio. Then there is the pleasure of giving, to family and charity, plus the bonus of paying for big ticket items, like changing the car or travelling abroad without having to borrow. And how can you put a value on the feeling of being in full control of your money, ready to face whatever new financial hurdles life might suddenly confront you with?

If you have money, making money is easier. It's getting started that is so difficult

All of these advantages add up to the return I have made for the hours I have spent in making myself as well informed as I can be over how to invest successfully and manage my money in a carefully preplanned way. And these results are not unique to me. I sincerely believe that anyone can repeat them starting, as I did, almost from scratch. And the purpose of this book is to share this secret with you. I have found the way to escape from the money maze. I hope I can get you thinking that you can repeat what I have done, or better still, even improve on it, because all you need is the essential know-how to give you the map. Then you too can exit from the maze and start on the right road to financial freedom. But you must also have the desire to continue along that route, so that you too can turn some of your money dreams into reality without having to win the National Lottery.

What we have been talking about in examining my investment experience, is using geometric growth to increase the value of our savings. Instead of the slow drip, drip of money added, sum on sum, in a linear fashion, like piling up tins on a grocer's shelf, geometric results are produced by growth on growth. And the higher the *rate of growth*, the faster it grows. Later in this chapter we will look at how some publicly quoted companies in business have managed to grow geometrically so that directors in these companies, as well as other investors, have been able to grow their money geometrically as their shares rose in value. We can compare geometric growth to blowing up a balloon. With every breath, the whole balloon gets bigger. It is expanding in all directions at once, growing larger overall by a constant percentage of itself as we continue to blow more air into it, that is with every breath. This means it is growing by a set percentage of the whole over a constant period. It differs from arithmetic growth, where the growth is by a certain amount over a constant period without the whole sum growing larger by this percentage at every stage. Arithmetic growth is simply *add-on growth*. Geometric growth is *growth on growth*. The difference between the two cannot be overstated. In money terms, it might be the difference between misery and comfort in old age.

Live for today but save for tomorrow

Doubling Time

A helpful way to think about geometric growth is in terms of doubling time. This is the time it will take for the growing quantity to double in size. When you are trying to build up your capital, this is an excellent way to think. In the schoolboy example we have seen that doubling can apply to money saved in a deposit account, but in that illustration we were adding extra money on a regular basis to what was already accumulating in the savings pot. To show how doubling works in practice we shall now look at how money doubles if we just begin with a lump sum and don't add any more to it as we go along. This is the kind of situation that a young man in his twenties might consider when he wants to put away a small lump sum of money, say £1,000 to start his pension fund growing geometrically. Again this situation will apply to adults when they reach stair 5, the fifty-plus age group. The children have left home, there are some savings, and now is the time to learn how to make those savings double themselves a few times over during the next ten or twenty years.

« *Money is like a sixth sense without which you cannot make a complete use of the other five.* »

W. Somerset Maugham

We will begin with an easy example not related to money, to explain the idea of doubling. It comes from a small volume called *The Limits to Growth*, a report by the Club of Rome, published in 1972. This Persian legend about doubling time illustrates just how rapidly growth can occur, often from very small beginnings.

MONEY *magic*

A cunning courtier presented his king with a magnificent chessboard. In return, he asked the king to give him one grain of rice for the first square on the board and to double up the number of grains for each succeeding square. The king readily agreed, because at a quick glance, this request seems very modest, even though there are sixty-four squares on the full chessboard. However, the mathematics of

one tiny grain doubling up for each square on the board are amazingly unexpected. The figures go like this: the second square requires the king to part with only 2 grains, the third takes 4 grains, the fourth another 8 grains, the tenth square needs 512 grains and the fifteenth takes 16,384. By the twenty-first square the king must give the courtier over 1 million rice grains and this had risen to a million million (known as one billion) by the 40th square. Indeed, the king's entire rice store was completely exhausted before the 64th square was reached. If one tiny grain seems like an innocuous request, the entire store is a valuable gift, which clearly the king had no original intention of giving away. The story demonstrates what a curious phenomenon doubling can be, because it often starts with a minute number but within a surprisingly short time it begins to generate enormous numbers.

Take each day as it comes, but prepare for tomorrow

Think about the way disease-carrying bacteria can multiply in your body. Each cell might divide into two cells once every minute or perhaps even faster. The cells are therefore doubling in number or growing by 100 per cent, say, at least once every minute. After two minutes, there will be four and after three minutes, eight cells and so on, until there are so many bacteria circulating in your blood that you will very soon be feeling terribly ill.

The unexpected suddenness with which doubling occurs, as with the rising pile of rice grains or the growth of bacteria that abruptly cause disease, is illustrated by a French riddle, again related in *The Limits to Growth*. You have a water lily on your pond which is doubling in size every day and you know it will completely cover the whole pond in thirty days. Were that to happen, all the other life forms in the pond will be smothered. In the early days of its growth, the lily looks very small so you don't feel there is any rush to cut it back. But when it has covered half the pond, how much time is left before the lily overruns the entire pond? The answer is just one day, because on day 29 the lily will cover half the pond, but it is still doubling in size every day.

Doubling Time Is Not Just Legends

Doubling time can be applied to savings in a similar way. Money growing in a deposit account at the rate of 10 per cent interest a year will double in amount in seven years. If our schoolboy had only put £1 into his account in his first year, and it was earning 10 per cent every year, it would have taken seven years for his £1 to grow to £2. Because he kept adding more money to his pile, our earlier example was more complicated than this and his cash grew much faster.

Doubling time is really good news for savers and investors. From tiny beginnings wonderful big nest eggs can grow

But there is a simple relationship between the growth, or interest rate, and doubling time of a quantity like money, if it is left to grow by a set percentage of itself in a constant period. This relationship is given by a formula: the doubling time is approximately equal to 70 divided by the growth rate. Money growing at 1 per cent a year will take 70 years to double, at 2 per cent it will take 35 years to double. At 5 per cent the doubling time is 14 years and at 10 per cent it will double in just 7 years.

When financial experts talk about savings growing through the addition of interest, they rarely talk in terms of geometric growth or doubling times. Their preferred term is *compound growth*. This is just another way of discussing any sum of money where the interest itself is earning interest and the money pile is growing geometrically.

I prefer to think of money growth in terms of doubling. My reason for this is that in Britain I believe we are already far too closely wedded to the idea of saving in cash deposit accounts, where compound growth works well. We need to think more actively about doubling our money through geometric growth, because when we are making plans for our financial future, this is a far more realistic yardstick to work with for creating real wealth. Most of us will not have a whole lifetime available in which to save and invest, and we must therefore get our money working for us as fast as we possibly can but we also want a high degree of safety. So we need the idea of doubling time, because it is a good measure of how fast we are able to grow our funds safely. We must ask ourselves how long it will take for our savings to double themselves, say from £5,000 to £10,000, or £10,000 to £20,000. We need to judge this doubling time in a sensible and practical way when we are planning for a secure financial future.

Growing Our Money

We talked, in chapter 1, about the way companies grow and collectively, when the majority of companies are doing well, the economy will also grow. It should come as no surprise now to find that this growth is also geometric. Individual companies can grow geometrically, if they have a good product to sell or operate in a niche market. The phenomenal rise of Microsoft from its flotation on the American stock market in 1985 is one of the most spectacular examples this century. It was just another small high-tech company in 1985, but Microsoft's financial strength stems from its monopoly over the development of

Something that costs nothing is usually worth nothing

the Windows computer operating system. By mid-1997, its Windows 95 software application had sold 77 million copies since its launch late in 1995. But Microsoft is not unique. In America, the same incredible growth has occurred in many other companies that now operate internationally; McDonald's, Coca-Cola, PepsiCola, Disney, Gillette and Intel, to name but a few. Similarly, there are plenty of successful, strongly growing British companies, and we will look at some of these shortly.

The UK economy follows an average long-term growth path of about 2.25 per cent. Then, if it grows by that amount this year, in the following year it will grow by 2.3 per cent of the total, which now includes the 2.3 per cent of growth that was added to the economy last year. The economy grows like blowing up the balloon, as we discussed earlier. However, when things are bad and there is a recession, the economy declines, which again may follow a geometric path if it continues for more than one year at a time. This stark reality actually occurred in many countries during the 1930s when unemployment rose grimly, economic activity fell and year by year the depression continued remorselessly to deepen.

How this works out in practice can be seen in the chart on page 44, which shows the annual percentage changes in **Gross Domestic Product (GDP)** over thirty-five years. Gross Domestic Product is used as a measure of the amount of goods and services produced in the economy in one year by all the firms and companies who manufacture these goods and services in the UK. It therefore gives a good guide to whether or not the economy is growing in real terms. As you can see from the chart, GDP rises in more years than it falls, but every few years, there is a growth pause (A on the chart), or an outright reduction in overall output (point B). It is useful for savers and investors to know that these growth cycles occur, because you want to be fully alert to the opportunities for making your money work more vigorously by joining in at an early stage when the next growth phase arrives.

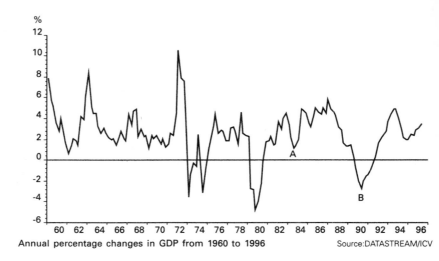

Annual percentage changes in GDP from 1960 to 1996   Source:DATASTREAM/ICV

Money Millions

Recalling the Persian legend, just think how much money will pass through your hands if you spend forty years working. Hopefully, in your job your salary increases by a modest 2 or 3 per cent every year. As we have seen, your income at age twenty-five would grow geometrically over forty years if you could save it all without spending a penny. You would probably see over one million pounds in earnings alone, without adding on the interest that you might get over that long working lifetime. That million could double itself several times over to many millions if it were all saved over a forty-year period in an interest bearing account. Clearly, living costs will take a very large bite out of your earnings. But after paying out all your living expenses, year by year, how much of that fortune will you put aside to enable you to fulfil your future spending plans?

« *All the money we dealt with was unreal: abstract numbers which flashed across the trading pit with a flurry of hands.* »

Nick Leeson

We have seen in detail the mechanisms whereby money, even in modest amounts, can increase substantially in value when saved over a long period in the right investments. You can now appreciate, therefore, the findings of the BZW Study, which showed how equity investors did far better than cash deposit savers over the long term. This is true not just for one lifetime, but over the course of centuries. A 1990s study puts spectacular money growth into an even longer term context, with figures to show that equities have no serious challengers. They carry off all the prizes.

MONEY *magic*

Centuries Of Compound Growth

A Californian economist, Bryan Taylor, investigated the UK stock market performance by looking at what a £1 investment made in 1700 in both shares and gilts would have been worth by the end of 1995. Clearly, £1 was a fair sum of money in 1700. It might have been a year's salary for a farm hand. By leaving it to grow for the next 296 years, without deducting any taxes, the £1 invested in equities would have grown to a staggering £51.5 million. The £1 invested in gilts increased to a modest £630,000. This study showed that the returns on shares really stormed ahead during this century as this is the period in which inflation has drastically eroded the capital value of gilts because they are fixed-interest investments, while most real financial assets have grown faster than the constant depreciation of the currency.

At the end of 1995, after 295 years, although the gap between the annual long-term return on gilts was only 1.6 per cent (with gilts returning 4.6 per cent a year while shares returned 6.2 per cent), gilts were trailing by a shocking £50 million behind shares. This monumental chasm was mainly due to the ravages of inflation during the twentieth century, a point to which we will soon return.

You can now see why it is important to teach children how their savings can grow and encourage them to get started right away by putting a little of their pocket money or birthday gifts into a safe savings pot. Doubling time is really good news for young savers and for investors of all ages.

« *Invest in inflation. It's the only thing going up.* »

Will Rogers

From modest beginnings, worthwhile nest eggs can grow. Of even more importance, you will know that your own future dreams and plans can indeed become reality if you take your saving seriously. Put some of your money to work in a constructive way and continue doing that while adding to it regularly over the very long term.

Inflating Our Money Away

Indisputably, therefore, we can get geometric growth to work for us, by compounding the money we are accumulating. This is the positive side of doubling time that we have been looking at so far. It is truly miraculous how, given enough time, money savings can literally explode in amount. But in the past sixty years doubling time, in money terms, has also shown vigorous signs of working against us through the insidious effects of inflation. To match the long term picture of growth in £1 saved since 1700, we can see how phenomenal has been the rise in inflation, just since the 1930s, by setting it in the context of the very

With inflation about, don't be lulled into thinking your capital is safe in gilts or a cash deposit account

45

long term. The full extent of this recent sixty-plus year rise is shown in the chart below, looking back over more than three centuries of British prices.

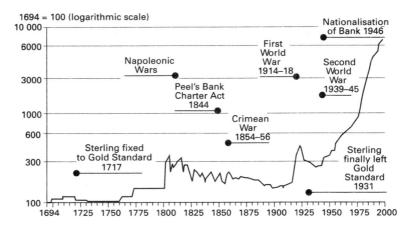

British Prices from 1694–1994, showing the geometric growth of inflation since 1930

Source: Bank of England

Inflation is the rise in the prices of goods and services in the economy over one year. It has been the greatest menace to personal wealth throughout the entire period since the Second World War. The reason is that once inflation establishes itself within the system, it is like the balloon; it grows bigger overall as it grows on itself. This year's inflation gets added into last year's inflation, so that the whole is growing faster with every passing year. It is a case of inflation adding to its own inflation, just like money growing with interest in the bank. However, the main problem with inflation is that as prices keep rising, your savings on deposit in the bank or building society will stay the same in terms of the numerical amount; they will not rise in tandem. This is the major snag that also affects all fixed-interest savings schemes, like gilts.

So inflation will eat away at the value of your savings. This means that if inflation is growing at 5 per cent, £1 today will buy less next year. It is an example of geometric growth in prices; with price rises feeding on more price rises every year. But the way people relate to inflation is through the indirect effect these rises have on their savings in deposit accounts or on their incomes, if they do not keep pace.

Inflation is truly an example of money magic. As it rises, the value of your savings, or even the money in your pockets, falls at an equal rate. It is the first of many examples we shall meet of what I call money seesaws. You can see how the inflation seesaw works in the diagram. As inflation rises, the spending power of your cash falls.

Value is such an airy-fairy idea that it is hard to grasp what is really going on. If you have £3,000 in a savings account, ignoring the interest, you can be reassuringly certain that it will stay at £3,000 for as long as you leave it there. It may take years of rising inflation before you realise when you come to spend it that this same amount of money, £3,000, will now buy less goods. Few of us track the prices of goods as they rise over the years, so you may not remember or even be aware that your £3,000 would have bought more goods some years back. Like a white rabbit hidden in a magician's top hat, inflation is a concealed tax on your savings. If ever there was a magic method of spiriting money away from right under our very noses, but without us realising what is going on, then inflation is the best candidate around for allowing that to happen.

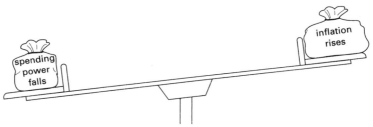

The inflation seesaw

Money Illusions

The main problem with inflation is that few people realise how it works because it is not a simple process to understand. It is far easier to think of money in terms of its nominal value, that is, by measuring the straightforward numerical size of prices. When applied to a savings account on deposit, the number 3,000 is readily understood; it is more than 2,990 and less than 3,050 and this would be true if the amount were there as pounds sterling, US dollars or French francs. Confusion between the nominal (numerical) and real (inflation adjusted) value is very widespread. It is as if people have a blind spot when it comes to thinking about

« *People react to changes in the cash value of their incomes or the prices of goods without taking full account of changes in the average level of prices that affect how much each dollar or pound will really buy.* »

their spending power. This oddity has been given a name. It is called **'money illusion'**. People understand money counted in numbers, but they seem unable to relate that directly to how much any amount of money will buy last year, this year, or next year.

A study carried out in America in 1997 showed how widespread money illusion is. Passers-by at Newark International Airport and two shopping malls in New Jersey were asked to judge a hypothetical case. Two students, Ann and Barbara, graduated from the same college one year apart and both took similar jobs. Ann started on a yearly salary of $30,000. In her first year, there was no inflation and at the start of the second year she received a pay rise of $600, or 2 per cent. Barbara also started with a $30,000 salary but during her first year there was 4 per cent inflation, and at the start of her second year she got a rise of $1,000, or 5 per cent.

« *Gullibility may be an amiable failing in some departments of life. The sucker may be afflicted by nothing but an excess of faith, hope and charity.* »

Richard H. Rovere

One group of passers-by was asked which graduate would be happier embarking on her second year of work – 64 said Barbara, 36 said Ann. Another group was asked which woman they thought most likely to move to another firm. Here, 65 chose Ann and 35 chose Barbara. The majority in both groups were obviously more impressed by the numerical value of each salary, rather than by how much each salary would buy. Ann's salary only rose 2 per cent, but it was a real rise, as there was no inflation. Although Barbara's salary rose by 5 per cent, the real rise was only 1 per cent, after taking 4 per cent of inflation into account. The details of how people misunderstood the real situation on Ann and Barbara's salaries are shown in the table below.

Money illusions on Ann and Barbara's salaries

	first year's salary $	second year's salary $	real rise in year 2 (%)
Ann	30,000	30,600 (2% – no inflation)	2
Barbara	30,000	31,000 (5% – but 4% inflation)	1

public reactions	happy in year 2 (%)	move to a new job (%)
Ann	36	65
Barbara	64	35
Total	*100*	*100*

MONEY *magic*

The 'Money Illusion' Red Herring

It is essential that you recognise the difference between real values and 'money illusion', which, by ignoring the impact of inflation is, sadly, nothing but a red herring. 'Money illusion' is the scourge of our age. It can delude you into thinking you have made wise savings decisions when, all the while, your capital sitting in a deposit account is shrinking in terms of what you can buy with it when you finally come to spend it.

No one doubts that stocks and shares fluctuate constantly; the risk here is obvious for everyone to see. Unfortunately, a widespread lack of knowledge and understanding of how these risks can be managed means that for over eighty years almost the entire UK population has been denied access to the best route for creating long-term wealth. Millions who save conscientiously with banks and building societies out of fear that they will lose money if they invest in equities have failed to enjoy the benefits that can be derived from equity-based investments. I think this lack of attention to financial affairs is one of the greatest failings in the current UK education system.

Consider this illustration: we all know that fire can be an uncontrolled hazard, a serious danger to life and property. Yet equally, we realise the enormous benefits that fire has brought to mankind. Life in some cold regions of the planet would be quite impossible without it. Similarly, in a modern industrialised state, like Britain, money is a vital component in everyone's lives. So learning to manage fire risk effectively is a very good example to compare with learning to manage financial risk efficiently.

When you have reached the point in this learning process of understanding that 'money illusion' constitutes as much of a real financial risk as buying stocks and shares, you will be more in command of the vital facts you need to handle your affairs in such a way that you reduce the risk of loss to the lowest possible level you can reasonably achieve. I hope that when you have digested the contents of *The Money Maze*, you will feel ready to put your newly gained knowledge to work.

Punch Drunk On Inflation

The prevalence of 'money illusion' means we need a different way of thinking about the impact inflation has on our spending power. I like the analogy with wine. If you drank a whole bottle of a good quality red wine, perhaps a vintage Beaujolais, you might feel pretty tipsy by the time you had drained the bottle. But suppose you diluted the whole bottle with the equivalent of another bottle full of water. Now you have double the wine, but it would be far more time-consuming to drink two bottles so if you did not finish them both you would get less drunk. And you certainly would lose the full fruity flavour of the wine in this diluted version. By diluting the wine, you need to drink a great deal more of it before you begin to

49

feel drunk. This is exactly what happens to money when it is subjected to persistent inflation. After decades of this dilution, you have to pay out much larger numbers of notes, simply to buy the same amount of goods that you bought previously with far fewer of them.

It is an illusion to think you have a secure nest egg of £3,000 in the building society savings account if the rate of interest you are earning is 2.5 per cent after tax, but inflation is growing at a rate of 5 per cent every year. In this situation, you are losing money at the rate of 2.5 per cent a year. Money in an interest-bearing account is not guaranteed to hold its value if there is inflation.

As we saw from the calculation on doubling time, if inflation persists at a rate of 5 per cent a year, prices will double in 14 years. If you withdraw all the interest you are earning on your savings each year to supplement your income, but just leave the £3,000 lump sum on deposit, with 5 per cent inflation, your money will have lost half its value over those 14 years in terms of what it will buy.

The result of such a continuing leap in prices will mean the collapse of many of your well intended plans. A once-in-a-lifetime cruise that costs say, £3,000 this year might cost double, or around £6,000, after another 14 years, but the money you have in the deposit account will have stayed stuck at £3,000 leaving you with a huge shortfall and your dream holiday will be out of bounds. Against this example, however, we should note that many new technologies have brought the costs of some products crashing down. Personal computers which cost £3,000 fourteen years ago would now be obsolete, but that same £3,000 would today buy a far more superior product. However, on the whole, most prices for large items like houses or cars, have risen considerably over that period.

Between 1947 and 1997, bread prices had risen 40-fold, vehicle licences 144-fold and Sunday newspapers around 100-fold.

Inflation Shockers

When in 1994, the Central Statistical Office celebrated eighty years of cost-of-living surveys, it published a range of comparisons with 1914, the year official price monitoring began. Over that eighty-year stretch, prices had risen more than fiftyfold. The 1914 pound was then worth two pence and by today would be worth even less than that! The table shows how Prime Ministers and ordinary MPs fared over this period. Clearly, modern Prime Ministers are a bargain, but MPs have become far more expensive.

Over the full eighty years, prices rose on average by 5 per cent annually but this long span smoothed out the uneven variations. Between 1918 and 1939, prices doubled, but between 1945 and 1994 they had increased more than twenty-fold. The last year in which prices fell (by 0.8 per cent) was 1960, but from 1974 to

1994 inflation averaged 9 per cent each year. The record yearly rise was almost 27 per cent in 1975. What dismal reading these statistics make, especially since inflation in October 1997 was still moving ever upwards, at 3.7 per cent, a two-year high.

Changes in salaries for parliamentarians from 1914–1994

	Prime Minister's salary £	MP's salary £
1914	5,000	400
1994	78,292	31,687
in line with inflation	250,000	20,000
Result	*underpaid*	*overpaid*

Anniversaries provide a good opportunity to review the full horror of cost of living rises. In August 1997, the government celebrated fifty years of compiling the Retail Prices Index. The impact of inflation over this time frame is truly awesome. The value of the pound had shrunk twenty times since 1947. This means, in 1997 it would cost more than £20 to buy what £1 would have bought in 1947. However, weekly earnings for the average manual worker had risen over sixty-fold, from £6 to £385, making him over three times better off.

Shopping basket
1 loaf of bread; 6 eggs; 1/4 lb tea; 1 lb butter; 1 lb sugar; 1 lb beef

	1947	1997
total cost	27p (5s 4d)	£6
time taken to earn the basket of food	2 hours	less than 1 hour

Back in 1947, when rationing was still in force, Parliament approved an extra 100 clothing coupons for Princess Elizabeth to buy a wedding dress to marry Prince Philip.

We discussed the BZW Equity Gilt Study in chapter 1 and earlier in this chapter. Now is the time to examine the figures it revealed for the real return on the three main classes of assets, that is, after adjusting for inflation. The real value of £100 invested in equities since 1918 to the end of 1996 would have been £36,528, after taking inflation into account. But £100 invested into government gilt-edged stock over that same period would have produced a mere £458. If this seems horrific enough, the wooden spoon for failing to keep up with inflation goes to cash on deposit, for that would have returned a minuscule £314.

These figures are truly shocking, because they reveal the full extent to which inflation is eroding our savings over the long term. Without allowing for inflation, equities returned £710,556, so the difference before and after adjusting for inflation is a thumping £674,028. This is a staggeringly huge loss, which explains why inflation is a hidden tax on savings. Although in numerical terms the losses on the gilts and cash are lower, they repeat the same story of how inflation has whittled away at our nest eggs over the past sixty years. Gilts, before

Inflation, like poverty, is always with us

adjusting for inflation returned £8,917. The loss to the saver due to inflation was £8,459 (£8917 – £458). For the cash on deposit, the rise without allowing for inflation was £6,101, so the saver lost £5,787. Although these latter two losses are smaller overall, they leave you even worse off in absolute money terms than if you had invested in equities. Continuing inflation is a horrendous prospect for everyone who is saving over a working lifetime to build a special nest egg. Plans you are following to make a wedding, travel around the world or prepare for a comfortable retirement will all be thrown off course at a time of high inflation unless you fully grasp the impact it will have upon your savings. The recent history of the course of inflation gives grounds for thinking it may at last be slackening off,

Equities — £ 36,528

Gilts — £ 458

Cash — £ 314

Real return after inflation for equities, gilts and cash on deposit

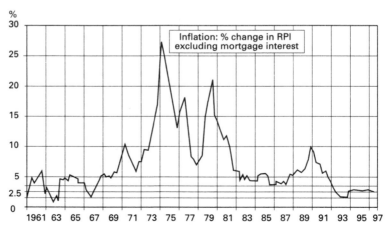

Inflation: % change in RPI excluding mortgage interest

The course of inflation since 1961

Source: Bank of England

Inflation is a hidden tax on savers

as can be seen in the chart. And although experts are divided on whether or not the levels of high inflation that were commonplace in the 1970's will return in the future, I think it would be unwise to consider the inflation dragon as now totally dead. He may just be slumbering in his lair, waiting to awake and play havoc with your savings at some future date.

You need to be aware of how you can protect yourself from the ravages of inflation if it were to return. Learning how to manage your money is the best form of protection against future bouts of inflation. As we have seen, there is no secret here. Investing in real assets that can outpace inflation is the only way to beat this hidden monster at his own game – the game of money doubling time.

Recognise The Risk

If inflation is going to diminish the value of your savings, you will need to find a method of saving that will beat inflation hands down, so that your money funds continue to grow. We have seen that investing is the route to making your capital grow at the same time as you are earning a regular income, or dividend from it. I call this having your cake and eating it. So now we will look at how you can achieve this utopia by investing some of your capital in the stock market. First, we must dispel the claim that stock market investing is risky. How do you rate risk if you watch the value of your capital in terms of what it will buy, diminish by half over 14 years while it is sitting in a 'safe' deposit account? Stock market investing is only risky when you do not know what you are doing. You have to reduce the risks by learning how to avoid losing situations and how to act cautiously as a beginner. We will consider the various ways of coping with risk in chapters 3 and 4. I explained earlier in this chapter how I was able to grow my money several times over by choosing the stock market route. Although it can be risky to the uninitiated, this is no longer a worry once you learn how to manage risk in order to improve the chances of making your money grow.

Doubling Time For Real

A few spectacular real assets, most often in the stock market, occasionally do produce this doubling type of astounding growth. They manage to grow so rapidly that the doubling time is achieved within a matter of months, rather than years. Many public companies that are quoted on the London stock market have grown in this exciting geometric way.

Money has a nervous disposition. It is always looking for security

As an example, consider the case of the Halifax Building Society. This is a massive company, worth over £18 billion in 1997. It was valued by the company's advisers at 390p per share about eight weeks before it floated itself on the stock market as a bank on June 2 1997. But when dealings began for the newly issued shares, they were quickly changing hands at 775p, a remarkable increase of 97.4 per cent in just about two months. Savers who were allocated free shares at the conversion and managed to sell them within the first half hour of trading would have obtained that price although this high level was not maintained for more than about half an hour. However, the price had recovered to 778p again by June 20. This type of rapid gain is not a unique example. It occurs for the shares of many publicly quoted companies.

Stock market investing is only risky when you do not know what you are doing

Look at the growth in the size of the company, Abbey National, the first building society to convert to a bank in 1989. The shares were floated at a price of 130p and were issued free to all eligible members. Over the years since its conversion, Abbey has expanded into a much larger business by acquiring several other financial companies and diversifying its operations to become more of a financial supermarket, offering a wide range of products to its customers. Since it became a public company, almost 50 per cent of its profits are now earned in other areas not related to mortgages and savings deposits.

« I forget what I was taught. I only remember what I've learnt. »
Patrick White

As you can see from the chart of Abbey National, the share price had risen from 130p at launch to 960p by October 1997. This is a doubling of two and a half times over eight years. And when it comes to having your cake and eating it, Abbey has provided this wonderful growth of capital to its shareholders and also given them dividends on a rising scale twice a year over the entire period that it has been operating as a publicly quoted bank. By mid-1997, the net amount of dividends paid out (after deducting tax), amounted to £116.80 and if the shares had been held in a Personal equity plan, allowing the dividends to be paid out free of tax, the gross amount would have been around £140. But suppose you had been given 100 free shares in Abbey National at the time of its conversion to bank status and had promptly sold those shares and put the £130 capital back on deposit in the newly converted bank. Today, your capital would still be worth just £130. This is less than the gross dividends you would have earned on your shares over eight years. Moreover, whether £130 would buy you what it would have bought in 1989 is a moot point. Although you would have earned interest throughout the whole period, the interest would not have amounted to more than around £250 before tax, depending on the account the money was held in. The interest, added to the £130 capital, is way below the figure of £1,100 you would have gained from capital growth and gross dividends obtained by holding onto your shares. This example is a perfect illustration of the difference between saving and investing, as it can be seen within the same company, Abbey National operating as a building society and Abbey National as a publicly quoted UK bank.

Abbey National share price from 1989 to 1997 weekly   Source:DATASTREAM/ICV

When I was giving a talk to novice investors in June 1997 someone asked me when was the right time to sell and I told the story of my investments in Airtours, the tour operator and travel company. Using the first version of my FASTER GAINS formula for spotting stock market winners, (discussed in detail in *The Armchair Investor,*) I bought 4,000 Airtours shares at 46.5p in March 1991. At that time, the market was rising on hopes the Allies would win the Gulf war. I spent £1,860. Within six weeks the shares hit 92p. Thinking they had risen too quickly, I sold out in three lots of 1,333 shares as my money had almost doubled. As a novice, I was nervous I should lose some of these amazingly rapid gains if I held on to the shares. This is a common mistake that novice investors often make.

But Airtours carried on rising while I watched from the sidelines. So I bought them again in August at around 178p and sold them in February 1992 at around 285p. I made very good profits, but on the day I gave my talk in June 1997, I had noticed Airtours crossing my Market Eye screen (for information on Market Eye, see address on page 238) at around 1120p and I was no longer holding any shares. This observation only registered when someone asked me about selling at the right time. My answer to that questioner was to do a rough calculation of what Airtours would have been worth in June 1997 if I had not sold them in 1992.

On a quick calculation, I worked out that if I'd just held onto my original 4,000 shares from March 1991 until June 1997, my £1,860 would have grown to £44,800 in six years. This is a doubling of four and a half times. What a fabulous rate of growth, and a great chunk of it happened in just eighteen months, from December 1995 (point A on the chart) to June 1997 (point B), as you can see from the long term chart of Airtours. When I first invested in Airtours, the company was tiny and had a stock market value of under £100 million. But in October 1997 its value had grown to over £1.7 billion, a huge rise in just six years, reflecting the long term success of this business and the brilliant managerial skills of David Crossland, the entrepreneur who runs it and still has a large personal shareholding in his company.

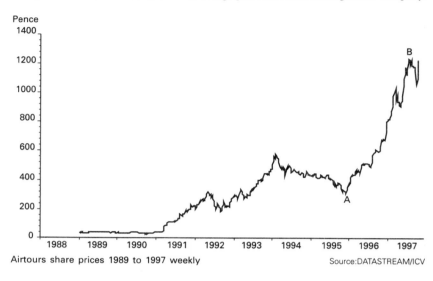

Airtours share prices 1989 to 1997 weekly   Source:DATASTREAM/ICV

A similar success story occurred with the clothes retailer Next. As can be seen from the plunging share price at (A) in the chart, this company hit hard times in the late 1980s when there were problems with management and stock selection. But from 1992 the company began to put its affairs in order and the recovery continued so strongly that Next was admitted into the select band of 100 top UK companies and became a constituent member of the FTSE 100 index of leading shares in July 1996. The chart of Next's share price over ten years of decline and recovery reveals how the share price has mirrored the revival of the company's fortunes. From a low of 11p in 1991 (at B), the share price has doubled six times over. The great rises in the share price are easily seen on the chart. In three years the share price rose from 25p (at C) to 250p (at D) a ten-fold rise. The price then more than doubled again from 250p to 600p in just two years.

Of course, doubling share prices can work in reverse for companies that run out of success. We must not think that affairs will run smoothly all the time for every company. Some manage to turn themselves around after hitting a rough patch. The charts of Airtours and Next show how this can be done. Other companies have been less fortunate. The recent history of Laura Ashley illustrates how things might turn out if recovery proves to be too elusive.

Laura Ashley was floated on the stock market in 1987. As a fashion-oriented clothing and furniture retailer it began to lose its way during the 1990's after becoming a quintessentially English fashion company in the 1980's. It experienced a prolonged period of poor trading until a new chief executive, Ann Iverson, was appointed in 1995 when the losses were £31 million. Through 1996 the share price rose strongly and profits were made for that year. However, problems with over expansion in America again hit profits and the share price in 1997. The Laura Ashley chart on page 58 illustrates the plunging share price that greeted the bad news.

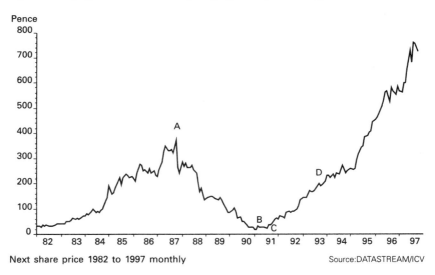

Next share price 1982 to 1997 monthly   Source:DATASTREAM/ICV

When we buy shares in popular companies trading on the stock market we must follow their progress so that we stay with them when the news is good but are prepared to part company with them if the growth story falters. Our prime objective has to be to take care of our own financial needs, which means staying with these companies while the growth is there but abandoning them, however reluctantly, when the problems arise. This happened to me when one of my favourite small growth shares, Telspec, ran into difficulties in 1996. The profits collapse saw the share price dive from 1048p in November 1995 to 200p by September 1996. I sold out most reluctantly at 770p and watched the company's fall from grace from the sidelines.

Perhaps one of the saddest corporate stories is the saga of Eurotunnel, where, once again, the collapse in the company's fortunes can be seen to be mirrored in the chart of its share price. On July 10 1997 the 720,000 private shareholders voted on the £8.9 billion refinancing 'debt for equity' rescue package, which would seal the company's future fate. Any one of those small shareholders who had been aboard the century's most ambitious engineering feat from the outset in 1988 has seen a dreadfully steep loss in their investment. An original outlay of £3,500 to buy 1,000 shares was worth less than £700 by June 1997, ahead of the vote. This is a capital loss of almost 80 per cent in nine years.

Laura Ashley share price 1992 to 1997 weekly   Source:DATASTREAM/ICV

The roller-coaster ride of Eurotunnel share price 1988 to 1997 weekly

Source:DATASTREAM/ICV

We have seen that the concept of doubling time is a powerful idea for helping to focus on how your savings are growing. It is very useful to apply the notion of doubling your savings in tandem with climbing the investment staircase. We all need to see our money growing to take care of future needs. You know now that it is possible to achieve your ambitious financial targets if you invest your money in the right real assets. But you are nowhere near ready to take that plunge yet. There is more to managing your finances than ploughing a lot of money into a few shares. So let us move on to chapter 3, to consider some of the nitty-gritty aspects of why you need to take control of your finances in a positive way.

« *Half our life is spent trying to find something to do with the time we have rushed through life trying to save.* »

Will Rogers

Key Points To Remember

1   Circulating money can lead a double life.
2   The modern banking system relies on confidence and trust. It is not as good as gold.
3   Arithmetic growth is add-on growth, but geometric growth is growth on growth – for money this means existing interest earning more interest.
4   The FTSE 100 index grew five-fold from 1984 to 1997.
5   Equities with gross dividends reinvested would have given a real annual return of 7.9 per cent since 1918.
6   Doubling time is the time it will take for a given quantity like money, to double in size.
7   The doubling time rule is given by 70 divided by the growth rate.
8   Since 1700 there have been three centuries of compound growth in UK stock market performance.
9   Inflation is geometric growth in retail prices.
10 Inflation is a hidden tax on savers.

CHAPTER 3

MONEY
matters

'In the UK around 17 million people (over half the adult working population) face a poverty-stricken old age because they are not making adequate provision for their retirement.'

Report by Robert Fleming, investment fund manager, February, 1996

Learning how to manage money properly is a skill, like any other. You can't reduce your golf handicap unless you spend time practising those all-important swings and you certainly won't master a Mozart piano concerto if you don't practise it regularly, until playing it becomes as familiar as walking down the street.

Similarly, acquiring money skills may come naturally to a few lucky individuals, but for the majority, if you don't make a conscious effort to grasp the basic essentials, you will constantly find yourself floundering in the money maze, when you grapple with your financial affairs. But once you have learned how to take a firm control over managing your money, thrilling new vistas will beckon enticingly. You may be able to afford a new set of expensive golf clubs, join that trendy golf club or buy that wonderful Steinway piano once you have put yourself in the driving seat for making your money work properly for you.

From Cradle To Grave

Clearly, you have recognised this exciting possibility as that is why you are reading *The Money Maze*. But surely, you may be thinking, wasn't the welfare state designed, way back in the 1940s, to look after us all, as the poet Shelley famously said, 'from the cradle to the grave'? As someone who grew up in the 1940's while the welfare state was in its infancy, I have a great admiration for the concepts of equality and fairness for all that it sought to implement, right throughout society.

« *The future is the most expensive luxury in the world.* »
Thornton Wilder

But over the fifty years since its inception, society itself, and with it our expectations of what we think the state should provide, have changed quite dramatically. Neither society nor technology is the same now as in the 1940s, when the welfare state was conceived. Then, the average income was about 30 per cent of its 1997 level, after accounting for inflation. Britain still had a nineteenth-century social pattern, with a small middle class and a very large working class which could not afford to pay for its own health care, education, housing or pensions. Today, the situation is completely reversed; the middle-income group amounts to around two thirds of the population.

The welfare state was a brilliant twentieth-century idea. But as we head rapidly towards the new century, it is patently obvious that the system is creaking under the burden of the obligations we are all demanding of it. Sweeping changes will be needed so it can cope more adequately with the new social conditions we now face. A major overhaul of how it operates is long overdue, but in the meantime, evidence accumulates all around us in our daily lives that the ideals on which it was founded are no longer proving entirely realistic in practice.

National Health Disservice

If we look at the operation of the National Health Service, for example, we spend less per head in Britain on our health than many other major nations. In 1998-99, for example, total UK spending on health, including private provision, is forecast to account for 6.9 per cent of national income against 14.2 per cent in America, 10.4 per cent in Germany and 9.8 per cent in France. And although the efficiency of our system is comparable to some others in Europe, increasingly, health provision is becoming more of a lottery. It depends crucially on where in the country we live, as to what services our local authority will and will not provide. Some areas offer post-operative physiotherapy under the National Health Service, but it was not freely available in my locality in 1992, for example, when I needed it. When Aneurin Bevan introduced the National Health Service in 1948, he was convinced that free medical care at the point of demand for all who required it would create a fitter, healthier population as the years passed. In that respect, his vision of the future was certainly right. But, he also thought that this higher level of health in the population would in turn ensure that the system would become increasingly cheaper to run in the fullness of time.

On this point, however, the exact opposite has happened. Over the years, health care costs have become ever more expensive. The service is gobbling up as much money as the government is willing to allocate to it and yet the endless waiting lists never shrink, and increasingly people are turning to private provision out of sheer frustration with the lengthy delays that can be experienced in the state service. By mid-1997, waiting lists for non-critical operations had risen 13 per cent in one year. At 1.2 million people waiting, this was the largest yearly rise in forty-nine years, in fact, since the National Health Service had first been introduced.

« Everyone expects the welfare state to do its duty. »

(with apologies to Nelson for misusing his quote!)

Sadly, Aneurin Bevan's original projections for a decreasing expenditure over time failed to anticipate the rise in people's expectations of how much more extensive health care provision would be possible as the system matured. Our demands are rising way beyond the bounds of what the service is funded to provide. And the incredibly rapid advance of medical technology has only added to the never-ending funding crisis. Demand has mushroomed on all fronts as rising expectations and technology advances continue, leading to a permanently cash-strapped service where unless a thorough and drastic reform of the service takes place, demands can only be met by imposing an arbitrary, and highly uneven, system of rationing of the scarce resources.

But the example of a severely over stretched health service is not unique. It is steadily being repeated in several other areas of national life. Many of the essential services we have come to take for granted as being available for us in the years ahead will run into these same financial buffers as the sums for unlimited provision in every area of social life no longer add up.

Home From Home

So we are naturally shocked to read that every year, around 40,000 elderly people are forced to sell their homes to use the proceeds to pay for nursing home or residential long term care. But why should we be shocked if people who have independent means, from a property, for example, are asked to sell in order to pay for their own long term provision?

You may think that it is only reasonable that one's lifetime's assets should be sold to fund one's own particular nursing requirements. However, we should remember that elderly people today have lived through the entire period that the welfare state has been in existence. They were precisely the young voters who were constantly reassured through successive decades by every government that state welfare was everyone's inalienable right. And now, suddenly to discover at a time of

The sums for unlimited provision for everyone by the welfare state no longer add up need that this option has been peremptorily withdrawn has left many feeling confused and betrayed. A contract of obligations extending back over fifty years is being reneged upon because the sums are impossible to meet. And no amount of indignant rage will change the inevitable arithmetic. Moreover, once again, on this issue, there is a lottery depending on where you live. In some areas, you may not be required to sell your home to fund your own long term care.

University Fees – Who Pays?

This type of financial shock to the elderly is now rapidly filtering down the generations. It is increasingly becoming the fate awaiting parents who are planning college education for their youngsters. Local authority university grants are dwindling in size. Rumoured talk of students having to pay some fees towards their own tuition became a stark reality in the summer of 1997, when the newly elected Labour Government decided students should pay up to £1,000 of tuition fees for each year of their course, in addition to major contributions to their living costs. Like all big debtors down the ages, the government might return again to extract more money from this source. So this proposal, due to start in September 1998, could easily pave the way for even higher contributions in a few years' time.

A survey by Barclays Bank in 1997 revealed that most parents were already helping their children to fund university education. The survey found that 37 per cent of the 875,000 students in higher education cited their parents as their main source of income. Overall, nearly three-quarters of students in the survey were receiving some financial support from their parents towards their expenses. Evidence suggested that even prior to the introduction of compulsory contributions to fees, most students were leaving university at the end of a three-year course saddled with debts in excess of £3,000 before they even began to earn a regular salary.

A little saving can buy a lot of choices

So the prospects are rapidly rising that parents will be required to pick up a larger proportion of these tuition and living costs. If substantial student loans become the norm, within a few years young people leaving college with a degree will find themselves saddled with a much larger debt. This could be in the order of, perhaps, around £12,000 to £15,000. It will have to be repaid during their working lives. However, learning how to budget sensibly and save to repay such sizeable debts is still rarely included in the routine college curriculum for students preparing to cope with adult life.

But the problems of self-funding are not confined to Britain alone. In America, the famous 'baby boomer' generation, the population bulge of 1945-50, has acquired a new name. They have been dubbed the 'sandwich generation' as they are caring financially for their aging parents while forking out college fees for their children. As a group, 22.4 million American families are spending about $2 billion (£1.25 billion) every month on caring for elderly parents while over 10 million students are enrolled at universities with the average cost of a four-year degree course ranging from $39,000 at a state university to $82,000 at the Ivy League, higher end of the scale. The unusual situation of the sandwich generation simultaneously paying out cheques for their children's college fees and their parents nursing home bills, has prompted the quip that they are the first American generation to have 'more parents than offspring'. Shall we begin to follow this pattern in the near future?

Pocket Money Pensions

Nor is this all. For what then, is the future for state pensions? The history of its sad decline over the past eighteen years makes depressing reading. In November 1980, the state pension for a single person was equal to 22.6 per cent of average earnings. By October 1997 this had fallen to 16.2 per cent of average earnings. And estimates suggest by the year 2040, the state pension will be equal to only about 7 per cent of average earnings. The state pension in Britain, a universal pension for all, is withering on the vine.

In Britain in November 1997, the weekly state pension for a married couple was £92, less than one-quarter of the average wage packet of around £385 per week. This was woefully below what our French and German neighbours were currently enjoying, as their pensions were approximately two-thirds of the average wage. Not surprisingly then, with Dickensian parsimony in vogue here, within the European Union British state pensions ranked among the lowest.

However, we should not envy the fat pensions our European partners enjoy, because as in Britain, this magnanimity cannot continue indefinitely. Every European nation faces the same financial crisis; the figures for providing substantial state pensions do not match the reality of how they can be funded, year after year, even for the next thirty years.

British politicians recognised this problem much earlier than their continental colleagues. UK legislation was passed in 1980 to link pensions provided by the government to the rate of inflation rather than average earnings. This change has dropped the value of the weekly pension since this measure became law by a considerable margin as average earnings have tended to rise faster than inflation. For example, in July 1997, inflation rose by 3.3 per cent but in the same month, average earnings rose by 4.25 per cent. In this month alone, therefore, pensions linked to inflation, through the Retail Prices Index, lagged average earnings by 0.95 per cent. Although multiplied over a whole year that lag only amounts to £45.45, that sum is still significant because it actually represented almost half the average week's old age pension of £92 for a married couple.

Everyone wants to live to a ripe old age, but no one wants it to be a miserable descent into poverty

Such modest pensions amount to hardly more than a supplement to private pensions, providing they have been planned for during one's working life. But evidence in the late 1990s suggests that 90 per cent of people retire on less than the maximum pension of two-thirds of final salary allowed by the Inland Revenue, with about one third of current pensioners receiving the state benefit of income support because they had no private income provision. On present levels of provision, future pensioners, especially women, face an equally bleak outlook. In September 1997, the Trades Union Congress warned that millions of women face poverty on retirement. Only one in four had joined a pension scheme through work and over 3 million were receiving less than the maximum state pension, which, as we have seen, is, on its own, insufficient to survive on.

Your Pension Targets

Financial advisers calculate that to enjoy a comfortable retirement you need an income of around 70 per cent of the gross annual income you received while working. With the average annual income at about £20,000 therefore, you would need to plan for an annual pension of around £14,000 to meet this criterion if you were retiring today. In 1997, the married couple's state pension of £4,784 leaves an enormous shortfall of £9,216 on these calculations. This is a considerable shortfall if the state pension is supposed to be serving as an average income. It gives a measure of the lack of adequate provision available with the current state pension. Even when relying on the added sums of income support, today's pensioners seldom have ready cash to pay for little luxuries or major items, like holidays.

Now you understand about money doubling, you can start thinking about your own pension provision. Your salary might rise around three-fold over a full working life of forty years. Assuming you remain in work throughout, your income will probably more than double from its current level, if you still have twenty to twenty-five years up to retirement at around age sixty. On current average income this means a rise by the year 2022 to roughly about £40,000. To achieve a decent income replacement you would then want an annual income of at least £28,000 (£40,000 × 70%) to retire on. To build a reasonable pension you must be ready to invest a significant slice of your income. One rough rule of thumb would be to make premiums that are a percentage of your earnings equal to about one third of your age. If you are forty on a salary of £30,000, you should be putting aside at least 13 per cent of your income, that is, £3,900 (13 × £30,000 ÷ 100 = £3,900). The state actually allows you to pay in more than this, but for most people, paying in the maximum allowable amount would probably prove too big a financial burden. But buying pensions with low charges can improve your savings.

For a thirty-five-year-old man saving £100 a month, a regular premium with-profits pension plan growing at around 9 per cent a year, might create a fund of around

£200,000. On current annuity rates this produces a pensions annuity of about £20,000. On present projections the state pension is expected to continue falling as a percentage of average earnings to around 10 per cent in 2022. This would only provide an additional £4,000 annually, but on the change in legislation of 1995, the pension would not be paid for either men or women below the age of sixty-five. If you would like to retire at sixty, therefore, you will have to manage on your own resources for the first five years before the meagre state pension kicks in to provide an income 'top-up'.

Today, the level of the state pension on its own falls below the definition of poverty. There are more than 10 million people living on state pensions. For many of these elderly people, who were young adults when the welfare state was first introduced, the huge shortfall in the actual pensions they receive compared with the current average wage has created a population where over around 3 million people are desperately poor. Sadly, they failed to foresee how the state pension provision would operate in real terms for them. Having been nurtured throughout their working lives on the ideal of an all-benevolent state system that would cater for their major financial needs throughout life, the reality has been exposed as being far short of that ideal.

« *And don't rely on the state – why do people trust this manifestly untrustworthy institution?* »

Paul Ham, *The Sunday Times*

Vanishing Provisions

My great worry now is that people in their forties and fifties will in due course face a similar rude awakening when they discover that promises of welfare provision turn out to be precisely that – promises that cannot be met because the funding simply is not there. In Britain, weekly average earnings almost doubled between 1986 and 1996, rising from £163.80 to £301.10. Of course this is very good news, but, as we all know, it is far easier to become accustomed to living on a higher income than it is to adjust down again to a lower one. These rises in average earnings could foreshadow increasing difficulties for people who are climbing stairs number 3, 4 and 5. Many of them not only spend every penny they earn, but run up loans or debts as well and have not yet begun to make sensible long term plans. A 1997 survey by PensionStore revealed that current levels of contributions into personal pension plans by these groups are abysmally low, at around £100 to £129 per month. The projected pensions at age sixty-five were as low as £5,500 for the thirty-five to forty-four age group and £1,600 for the forty-five to fifty-four age group. In 1997 calculations suggested it requires a fund of £150,000 for a woman (£135,000 for a man) to buy an annuity at age sixty representing two-thirds of average earnings. But with average earnings at around £20,000, two-thirds would only provide £13,330 before tax, leaving a sum of around £10,000 to live on after tax. That amounts to a weekly income of only £192.

The good news is that we can all read the warning signs. They are clearly visible to those with eyes to see. We know we are climbing the investment staircase, and for most people it is not too late to learn how to take control of your own financial affairs, so that if the state fails to provide, you have made yourself secure enough not to have to worry unduly over any broken promises.

Today we can see that on many fronts, the welfare state is in retreat. With the harsh facts of financial necessity apparent right across the range of services we routinely take for granted, the chances are increasing that many more of us will find ourselves facing welfare promises which cannot be met. Whether we like it or not, we shall be required to provide for more of our financial needs in the next century. And if we fail to respond to this demanding challenge, our futures could be as bleak and uninspiring as that facing over 3 million poverty-stricken pensioners today.

A Mean Means Test

David Rough, investment manager for the mighty Legal & General Insurance Company, with £40 billion of funds under management in November 1996, told me that he thought state pensions would be means tested within a decade. If that were to happen, the bulk of the population would have to take a more

What will you do if direct control of their financial futures and provide for their own pension requirements. He thought means testing was an inevitable outcome to

promises of welfare the dilemma of growing demands on the public purse, while the tax paying population to support the provision of state services is set to remain

provision for you static or even decline in absolute numbers. According to the 1997 annual report by *Social Trends*, by the year 2016 people over sixty-five will

turn out to be just outnumber those under sixteen for the first time. Apparently, this crossover will initially ease the burden of state spending, but this will

that – promises? prove to be only a temporary effect.

If there will be fewer people in the working population in the coming decades to provide for the ever growing needs of the sick, the unemployed, the young and the old, their long-established benefits will become even more of a hostage to fortune. And this tally only covers the most obvious calls on public funds; it fails to mention the costs of defence, public transport, road building and law and order. Nor does it include prison facilities, which are an escalating demand on tax-payers' resources. In 1997, every person in prison cost the state around £23,000 a year, while the prison population is forever rising, and stood then at over 63,000 people. I saw a caption in a newspaper cartoon recently that read: *'On these chart projections, by the year 2800 the whole population will either be retired or in prison!'*

Fend For Yourself

The message is clear, as the table below illustrates: in the future we will be forced by the government to provide more of the services we now look to the state to provide, be it university education for our children or long term care for our parents. And if we want a comfortable retirement, we are going to have to fund it for ourselves or simply go without many of life's little pleasures.

The Welfare State cash crisis

public service	state cash problem	result for the public
NHS	longer waiting lists	operations delays or go privately
university fees	part-payment of fees	parents contribute or students take out loans
university living expenses	reduction in grants	parents' subsidies or students work part-time or run up debts
long-term care	rationing of places by queuing	forced sale of assets, including homes
pensions	linked to inflation not average earnings	pocket money pensions. 3 million poverty-stricken pensioners. Public must provide for themselves

Nor is this the end of the grim news: the City bank, UBS, produced a report which claimed that many costs in Britain are far higher than elsewhere in the western world. Their findings suggest London hotels and rail travel in Britain are both the most expensive in the world. Buying a medium-sized car in Britain costs more than in any other country outside the Far East; £17,000 in London against £10,800 in Paris and £9,550 paid in New York. If a basic need, like travel, is so highly priced in Britain, this leaves everyone with even less money to pay for other everyday expenses.

In chapter 2 we discussed the report by Robert Fleming which arrived at a figure of 17 million people who will be seriously impoverished in retirement, because they are not making adequate provision now for their old age. The study calculated there were only four regions, London, south-east England, the west Midlands and Scotland, where more than half the people of working age were due to receive adequate pensions income. Sixty per cent of men, still considered the main breadwinner, earn below the national average and only one in four makes any extra pension provision. In 1997, the Low Pay Unit calculated that 14 million, a quarter of the British population, are 'poor' now, while 10 million live below the Council of Europe's 'decency threshold'. This threshold provides enough cash to buy the absolute basics plus a few items they term 'essential luxuries'. A television and holiday would be included among these.

Definitions of what constitutes poverty vary widely. According to the Low Pay Unit, you are poor if you earn less than half the average wage: less than £193 a week in 1997. The Council of Europe will consider you 'poor' if your income falls below their 'decency threshold' but this figure would amount to £243.66 a week on mid-1997 figures. Under the regime of a minimum wage fixed, perhaps, as the British Trade Union Congress hoped, at around £4.61 an hour, whole groups, including bar staff, waitresses and hairdressers, are instantly slotted into the poverty bracket. Although the official government level of income support lifts the basic weekly payment to a minimum of around £110, there is evidence that, even today, over a million pensioners are living on amounts below this basic level and have not been informed that they are entitled to extra help.

« *You never know what is enough until you know what is more than enough.* »

Barton Biggs, head of global strategy at Morgan Stanley Dean Witter

Facing these unpalatable facts raises some uncomfortable questions. Are you destined to be one of the 17 million who Robert Fleming's report suggests will be desperately poor in the coming decades? Are you clued-up sufficiently to avoid that fate? Do you know how to take control of your own finances so your future can turn out advantageously?

Does a gloomy view of the future rouse you to action or simply leave you unmoved? One way to shake yourself out of a monetary inertia is to try getting by for just one month on one or another of the sombre scenarios I have been painting. How does this work out in practice?

A Short Sharp Monetary Shock

There are several ways to invigorate your thinking about what financial hardship really means on a daily basis. We will consider them each in turn shortly. They are the monetary equivalent to the short sharp shock treatment for prison offenders. But if it helps you to face some of the facts about coping with poverty, these mini-experiments will have served a useful purpose. If you can try to persevere with each experiment for one month, you will get a general feeling for what financial restraint can really mean. And if your resolve cracks and you cannot keep up the experiment for at least one month, just think, this is a trial run. It isn't for real. But if you cannot sustain a frugal regime for thirty days, how would you manage if you had to implement it for a year or two, or, perish the thought, for the rest of your life?

1. Pretend to be poor for a month

You can try to imagine what life would be like if you had to live on unemployment or incapacity benefit for a month. Allocate yourself just £65 a week and budget for that level of expenditure for the full month. How will you divide this princely sum up each week to cover your needs? Will you spend it evenly at the daily rate of £9.29 until the second week's £65 becomes available, or will you spend £8 for six days and have an extravagant fling of £17 on Sunday? What about rent, heating, the phone bill or gas to cook with? People with no other financial resources must go through the rigours of applying for income support benefits to pay for some of these essential items. Try this harsh regime and see how easy or difficult it is to cope. Living on the equivalent of state benefits, what goodies will you have to forego? Theatre visits, weekend breaks, eating out or buying new shoes?

« *If you have ever been poor, the stratagems of poverty come back to you like old friends when it looks you in the face again.* »
Mrs Jordan's Profession, Claire Tomalin

Another easy experiment to try out for living on very modest means is to deny yourself absolutely everything you would consider as a non-essential or luxury, again for one month. Live only on the pure essentials. Everyone will have a different idea of what they include as luxuries but in general it would mean cutting out such items as new clothes or shoes, books, magazines, cigarettes, sweets, chocolates, imported fruit, wines and spirits, cinema or theatre visits, even perhaps, renting a video. When everything has to be boiled down to the barest essentials, the available choices will be very restrictive indeed. It might just be manageable for a month, but it could be impossibly miserable if you had to live like this for long periods at a time.

A less demanding alternative to experimenting with a low-income lifestyle might be to try to manage on only half your weekly income. Again, you might have to ignore such large regular items as paying the mortgage, but the more realistic the experiment, the quicker you will come to understand how crucial the lack of money can be when this sort of penny-pinching routine is forced on you. It should open your eyes to the vital need for better money management.

2. Budget vigorously for a month

We shall look at budgeting in chapter 5, but here we can consider the idea of budgeting for one month to find some money to save. Figures produced by a Direct Line survey in 1997 make depressing reading. There is a widespread apathy about handling mundane financial matters which is costing Britons dearly. Around 48 per cent of the 1,000 adults interviewed did not check their change, while 44 per cent did not count the cash withdrawn from cash machines. Only 55 per cent checked bills and receipts while 57 per cent regularly checked bank and credit card statements. Just over half of those surveyed thought they were good at handling money, compared to 61 per cent in 1989. These abysmal figures suggest Britons are losing £4 billion a year by failing to keep a watchful eye on routine money matters.

If you have never tried to budget, this can become an all-consuming task, if you take the trouble to record every penny you spend, to see where all your weekly cash is actually going. When you have read up in detail the section on how to budget in chapter 5, you could try this experiment for one month, to see if it helps you to manage your money more effectively. An added bonus will result if you are able to find some money to save for your future.

3. Teach yourself the value of money

Instead of stressing the downside of low incomes and the hardship that goes with them, here is a fun way to learn the value of money. Begin collecting something which we would consider as a modern antique – an antique of the future, sometimes called 'collectibles'. This would include any small item of modern manufacture that might acquire a rarity value in the future. The key requirement is that they should all be reasonably cheap to buy today. The list of suitable items is extensive. You might like to collect beer mats, matchboxes, table mats, hat pins, tea spoons, small pottery jugs, book marks, miniature cottages, pottery animals. Hunt for your chosen collectibles in boot fairs, antique fairs or flea markets to build your collection and you'll soon discover that when you find one piece that is exceptionally cheap compared to the prices you usually pay, you can get quite a buzz from finding a bargain.

With the right frame of mind, you will see the big picture

Get Sorted

Even if you have already decided you should do something positive to improve your financial position, you might immediately realise that two major obstacles seem glaringly obvious. First, where should you begin? How should you start to plan for this financially secure future that you want? And second, what about the risks? It is common knowledge that investing in the stock market is fraught with difficulties, so how are you going to cope with the risks of losing your hard earned cash? These are both serious and sensible concerns which we should address straight away, to ensure you are ready to take advantage of the good opportunities that are around to produce the exciting financial gains you hope to achieve. In fact, all the following chapters will tackle the various strands of information, planning and risk control that are essentially at the heart of these two paramount issues.

Attitudes Matter

Where to begin and how to get started rest primarily on one crucial idea. Right at the outset you should try to ensure you have adopted a positive attitude. This may

The optimist thinks his nest egg is half full. The pessimist thinks it is half empty

sound trite, but it is the vital jumping-off point for everything else you do. If you think making your finances secure is an impossible task, the chances are, it will prove to be so. If you feel beset by horrendous money worries which you think will never be resolved, your negative frame of mind might actually be the one obstacle that prevents you sorting the problems out and achieving a successful result. An unconstructive frame of mind is very counterproductive. It can become an insurmountable hurdle to climb. I recently attended a lecture where the speaker described positive attitudes as 'positive illusions'. This is a neat positive turn of phrase to set alongside the negative idea of 'money illusions' we discussed in chapter 2.

Cultivating the right attitudes sounds simple, but for people who have a naturally pessimistic outlook, this may be the most difficult task they have to face. Once you have realised that your ultimate success depends heavily on your own determination – desire, perhaps – to make your financial dreams come true, you are almost a quarter of the way towards making the good things happen.

Work Smarter Not Harder

To get at least halfway there, you have to do some proper preparation. Even this is less tedious than you might suppose, but only when your mind is set to make positive illusions, so that the preparation doesn't seem an enormous imposition; this is the negative way of thinking. It is better to see all the preparation as the route you are going to take to help you succeed with the *least possible effort*. We all know people who spend a huge amount of time and effort tackling something that needs to be done. But in spite of all their fuss and fury, things go wrong, get delayed or seem to be unendingly complicated. Even if these people are well intentioned, their preparation obviously is far short of ideal.

Making your money grow can be one of the most rewarding of your hobbies

You want to achieve your financial goals with the minimum trouble and effort. Of course, some time and energy will have to be allocated, or your plans will never get off the drawing board. But there is no need to become obsessive or a slave to your financial commitments, unless you really want to be that greatly involved. You should realise before you start that what you are aiming to achieve is to become financially aware through a process of careful preparation and continuous monitoring of what you are doing to ensure you stay on track. In chapter 9 we shall look more closely at how to get started, but now we will turn to the other great hair-raiser – the notion of **risk**, which in financial terms means the possibility of losing money.

Become A Know-All

I believe the worry over losing money on risky investments is the principal reason why people avoid stock market-related investments. They are scared they may take the wrong decisions and end up facing losses. One way of looking at risk is to consider it as a type of cautionary warning to prevent us making hasty or reckless decisions. This, after all, is why we teach children safety first in the home and kerb drill for how to cross the road.

Risk, however, must be seen in a relative context; I believe it is linked to the fact that we live in an unpredictable world where events are rarely guaranteed or certain. Almost every day, it seems, we learn of another food product that has been shown to contain some unexpected health hazard, or we read of a terrorist bomb alert or a fatal aeroplane accident. Common sense tells us that we have to make balanced, informed judgements about such risks. Failing that, then we should hide ourselves away at home and never venture out, for fear of being run over whenever we cross the road or being struck down by an unidentified flying object. Managing risk is all about weighing up the probabilities of something adverse happening.

« *If you risk nothing, you win nothing.* »

Napoleon

Although many savers do not realise it, *even the most innocent-seeming financial decisions can involve the risk of loss.* Every day your money sits in an investment, it is exposed to the risk that it might lose some, even all, of its value. As we saw in chapter 2, in a savings deposit account, although the money amount of your original capital stays the same, it is only the face value of that sum that is unchanged when inflation is present. The real value of your capital, in terms of the amount of goods it will buy, is actually falling after you have made an adjustment for inflation. This means that, over time, the goods and services you want to buy will cost more, relatively, while your savings stay static and are not keeping pace. This kind of risk is called inflation risk.

If you find a money-making scheme that sounds too good to be true – it probably is

Because the face value of your savings stays intact, and the deceptive nature of inflation is difficult to grasp, people tend to ignore its impact. If the balance on deposit remains unchanged, they imagine, wrongly, that their savings are 'safe', and not exposed to risk. The idea behind building up your savings in a deposit account is easily understood, while other forms of saving seem too complicated to grasp or undertake. Yet when the consequences of inflation are fully recognised, these 'safety first' savings accounts are patently shown to be an inadequate way of protecting your cash from a creeping devaluation. Risk of loss, therefore, may be incorrectly judged if you are not in complete command of the true facts. The evidence of the BZW Equity Gilt Study, spanning almost eighty years, shows unquestionably that the savings methods which appear to be the safest are actually producing consistent losses in your purchasing power. Indeed, they are continuously the subject of a concealed risk.

We cannot simply take it for granted that our money is safe on deposit; it may be losing its value, as the idea of the inflation seesaw suggests.

The Risk Seesaw

So we need a different way of thinking about riskiness. I like to use the idea of the 'risk seesaw'. The greatest way to overcome the element of risk is through acquiring a sound level of knowledge in what constitutes good money management and value for money. One of the quickest routes to making mistakes is to rely on inadequate or ill-judged information. The more knowledge you can gain, the higher your confidence will rise. Conversely, the less knowledge you have, the greater the chances of you being wrong and losing money into the bargain. Every time this happens to you, your confidence about handling money takes another beating. Along with the financial loss you will carry the memory of your mistake. Then, when the next money crisis begins to unfold, you will probably feel even less competent than you did on the previous occasion. One glaring consequence will be that you are even more unwilling to get personally involved in solving your latest problem.

Managing risk is all about weighing up the probabilities of suffering an adverse outcome

This, therefore, is the basis of the risk seesaw: very low knowledge is a recipe for higher risk; much higher knowledge can result in lower risk. Again, the diagram below seems obvious, but it is there to underline this very important message. We met our first money seesaw concept in chapter 2, when we noted that higher inflation meant lower spending power for your money. Interestingly, there are several more occasions in the book where the seesaw concept is useful for understanding an important aspect of managing money.

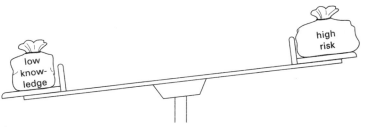

The risk seesaw

The last thing you want is to lose some of your precious money resources. Therefore you should always try to keep in mind this picture of the risk seesaw. If an idea for an investment looks tempting, or if someone is trying to persuade you that one special scheme will be perfect for you, pause to recognise the risks by asking yourself two key questions: 'Do I *know* how safe my money will be if I make this move?' 'Have I paid enough attention to any possible losses I might suffer?' The more you know, the greater your level of security will be. The less you know, the lower your security will be. And this is true wherever you place your money; in a higher rate deposit account, in a pension or insurance-based savings plan, a UK-based unit trust or in a publicly quoted company.

Weigh The Risks

There are numerous ways to assist you to avoid losing your hard-earned cash. We are really considering loss avoidance right throughout the book. But here, in summary, is a short list of ways to consider reducing the risks of losing money when you are planning to put your cash into an investment:

i   read carefully through *all* the relevant information provided before making any decisions.
ii   do not make a hurried decision, even if an adviser tells you there is a time limit on what he wants you to do.
iii ask the right questions when taking out a plan through an adviser. (We shall return to this crucially important point in chapter 6).
iv   join an investment class to get more expertise.
v   join a local investment club to pool your ideas and funds with other like-minded people.
vi   use collective funds to spread your risks and to learn about stock market-related investments.
vii save regularly through monthly plans to avoid poor timing when buying your investments.
viii never put all your funds into one scheme. Spread the risk as widely as possible until you know exactly what you are doing.
ix   Learn from your mistakes so you don't keep repeating them.
x   stay flexible: if you are losing money on one investment, consider selling it, but allow the profitable investments to run, so you get the full benefit of the growth as it occurs.

Get Into The Driving Seat

In these and all other cases of financial decision-making, careful preparation is the other great boon for reducing risk. Again, this works by providing you with increased awareness and knowledge about all the differing aspects of any one situation, before you enter fully into it. Being right not only breeds increasing confidence in your ability to handle your own financial affairs, but it also diminishes risk. Devising a proper investment plan is, without doubt, the key element in careful preparation

Early lessons in

risk management

pay off

that allows you to be right on more occasions than you are wrong. Without a plan, you are at the mercy of your own whims or ignorance and a far easier prey for a well informed, highly trained salesman to sell you the product he is offering rather than any other that might be better suited to you, but which he isn't selling.

Designing a tailor-made investment plan is the greatest weapon in your investment armoury. It will be your blueprint to enable you to stay on course to reach your investment targets. It will be a unique plan, special to your particular situation, to reflect where you are on the investment staircase, the time frame for your savings, the size of your family and number of dependents, and, perhaps most crucial of all, your attitude towards achieving your goals, either cautious or aggressive. Having a sensible investment plan is indispensable to your financial security. It is your road map to charting out how you are going to reach your savings targets and ensure you do not get lost for ever inside the money maze. In short, it is the main tool you will be using to manage your financial risks. Although you may feel impatient and ready to get started, there are several crucial topics to discuss before you will be ready to prepare your investment plan. This is such an important item it is the final topic covered in chapter 9. By the time you reach chapter 9, you will hopefully be fully briefed and ready to begin putting your new knowledge on managing your money into practice.

It may seem daunting to state that higher knowledge is the key to reducing the level of risk to which you are exposed. But there are several quite simple methods of managing risk to keep you firmly in control. Knowing how to manage risk is crucial to successful money management. So we will return to it again in the next chapter, to look at the wide variety of ways in which you can reduce the chance of things going wrong. Controlling your risks is one of the positive outcomes that derives from knowing all the general principles you need to grasp to improve your money management skills.

« *To carry one's eggs in a great number of baskets without having the time or opportunity to discover how many have holes in the bottom, is the surest way of increasing risk and loss.* »

John Maynard Keynes

Key Points to Remember

1 The welfare state is running out of money to fulfill all our expectations.

2 Promises of support 'from the cradle to the grave' cannot be funded, for health, education, pensions or long-term care.

3 For a comfortable retirement, reckon to have around 70 per cent of the gross annual income you received while in work as a pension.

4 17 million people in Britain today are not making adequate provision for retirement.

5 With the welfare state in retreat, we will be forced to make more financial provision for ourselves.

6 Have a trial run to face being poor in the future: pretend to be poor for a month; budget for a month.

7 Adopt a positive frame of mind to help turn your financial dreams into reality.

8 Work smarter not harder.

9 Move the risk seesaw from high risk/low knowledge to low risk/high knowledge.

10 Careful preparation and regular monitoring are the secrets of financial success.

CHAPTER 4

One STEP at a
time

'One has to establish a view about where the statistics are leading. One has to anticipate an uncertain future. Gut feelings and experience play a considerable role.'

Professor Charles Goodhart, London School of Economics

Money plays such a central, everyday role in your life it is almost inevitable that you should take its presence very much for granted. Yet this is precisely why it is often hard to appreciate that you need to understand how it works before you can ever begin to practise sensible money management. Handling your money efficiently is a skill, like any other. But unlike many other skills, if you are not adept in money matters, you run higher risks of making losses. All the elements of financial expertise that you need to know are centred on reducing your exposure to risk. Given the appropriate instruction, everyone can learn how to manage their finances more effectively and so take advantage of this newly gained ability to make dramatic improvements in their financial situation.

Just as it is essential to focus on the important first principles when learning any new skill, so it is with money. But as we have repeatedly seen, money has uniquely strange properties that mean you should be extra wary when applying your new-found knowledge, especially during the early learning stages. Fortunately, the points to pay special attention to apply to managing any new expertise. So if you are learning to play the piano or golf, some of these may already be familiar to you.

Grasp The Essentials

Many of the key elements that I consider are essential for novices to grasp apply mainly to equity-based investments. You might think this approach will not be suitable for you if you have decided, from long experience of avoiding this type of investment, that you definitely do not want to go in that direction at all. However, as we saw in earlier chapters, equities are undoubtedly the best route to take for creating wealth. Even if you never buy a share in a publicly quoted company, it may surprise you to learn that you probably hold a lot of equities, but at one step removed. When you pay premiums on pension plans or endowment policies, or if you buy regular savings plans or unit trusts, you are indirectly investing in equities, as this is where the professionals managing your money will put the majority of it. So in order to build a strong financial position, learning something about stock markets and investing in them is important. It cannot be avoided. It is the fundamental basis for all your planning and for your future financial security.

There is more to managing your money than plunging a lot of it into a few company shares

Above all else, you should aim to build your investment skills through careful planning, which is the first priority. In chapter 6, when we look more closely at building your financial pyramid, we will address the stages of your planning in greater detail. But now, we will concentrate on an outline of the principal elements that you need to grasp to ensure you can begin to conduct all the various aspects of your own financial affairs with success.

Start Slowly

Perhaps the most important factor is to take one step at a time and not be tempted to rush on ahead too hastily. This is especially crucial in money affairs as losses arising from rash actions often mount with surprising rapidity. Whatever you plan to do, you should remember to start off very slowly. This will ensure you have time to think your actions through most carefully. Your main aim must always be to take the utmost care of your precious capital. Warren Buffett, the fabled American investor who built an initial $100 in the 1950s into a fortune worth over $8 billion invested in his share portfolio alone during 1997, was emphatic on this point. He had this pithy advice for investors:

« *There are only three rules on investing: first, never lose any money, second, never lose any money, and third, never lose any money* »

When I was reading lots of different books to sharpen up on my investment skills, I must confess I was puzzled for some years by the message in this simple idea. It didn't properly register with me until, with a sudden rush of comprehension, I finally saw that it was a sober caution on the inherent dangers of standing aside inactive while allowing your capital to disappear. It is crucial to learn this lesson as early as possible. Starting slowly and adopting a safety first attitude will help to ensure you do not fritter away any of your valuable capital before you have learned the details of how you can make it grow substantially through sensible saving and investing.

When novice investors act too quickly, they run the risk of making unfortunate mistakes. While working through the complications of skilfully managing money, mistakes usually lead to financial losses. However, even for the most informed and experienced investor, it is virtually impossible to avoid making some mistakes. The greatest bonus comes from accepting this inevitable reality and planning to learn from your mistakes so you won't constantly repeat them. If you can make a determined effort to learn from your early mistakes, you will reap large benefits as you progress. We will look more closely at benefiting from your mistakes later in the chapter.

Expert Alerts

Surprising as it may seem, a lot of so-called experts are really no better at managing financial matters than you can be, once you have set yourself the task of understanding what finance is really all about and learning how you can improve your own personal affairs. I believe very strongly that no one has a greater interest in safeguarding your affairs than you have yourself. When you take control, you will give yourself more confidence to deal with any nasty money surprises that might crop up.

When an expert handles your affairs, you have lost control

Indeed, you may just be keeping your head in the sand by relying on others to sort out your financial affairs because, unfortunately, the evidence of unreliable experts is very widespread. Even if you have escaped all the disturbing monetary disasters to date – and there are plenty of them – this alone is no guarantee that at some time in the future an expert in whom you now have complete faith will abruptly let you down. When your confidence rests on others, it can come as an awful shock to find yourself unexpectedly caught up in one of these financial nightmares. Suddenly, you are floundering in a complicated money mess or, most scary of all, facing a cruel loss where restitution of your funds, or even some compensation, looks uncertain.

Hidden Risks

In the late 1980s, thousands of investors were lured by promises of high returns to put money, through an independent financial adviser, into a Barlow Clowes offshore investment fund. They thought they were investing in gilt-edged stock. This is British government stock, termed 'gilt' because it is backed by the UK government. Throughout the nineteenth century when the British empire ruled half the civilised world, gilt-edged stock was considered 'as safe as the Bank of England'. It can be bought directly from the government's official **broker**, by filling in a form obtained from any main post office. But financial advisers earn their money either from client fees or, more commonly, from commissions paid when they place their clients' cash with professionally managed funds. However well intentioned, this arrangement may influence advisers' actions, giving them an incentive to use these funds rather than help their clients to fill in routine forms to buy gilt stocks directly. In fact, however, using professionally managed funds is often a far better route for many small investors because these funds give them a broader spread of differently priced and dated gilts. Investors would need to have much more capital if they wanted to purchase a broad selection of them all directly for themselves.

When the Barlow Clowes Company collapsed in 1988, with debts of £130 million, 11,000 retired investors discovered, to their horror, that they were actually putting their precious retirement savings into a dubious Gibraltar fund run by Peter Clowes. He was squandering their money to finance a lavish lifestyle, which included buying a luxury yacht, four personal jet-aircraft and a host of highly speculative investment schemes. In the Barlow Clowes case, all concerned – the authorities, the advisers and the investors themselves – were later to discover how misplaced their trust in Peter Clowes had been. Hardly any of the money they had placed with him had been invested in gilt-edged stock.

Lawrence Lever chronicled this story in a fascinating book, *The Barlow Clowes Affair*, which I believe should be compulsory reading for every small saver and investor. Although it tells the facts surrounding the events of the Barlow Clowes collapse, it reads like a detective story. The Barlow Clowes Investment Fund had an authentic licence from the UK regulatory authorities, allowing it to manage investors' money. But the dominant thread running throughout Lawrence Lever's account was the relaxed and unfocused way in which the authorities of the day handled this escalating fraud.

It would be a mistake to become complacent, merely because in this case the authorities *finally* agreed to pay compensation to around 11,000 victims. These people had to fight a lengthy battle to obtain redress, during which they surely suffered all the anxieties and trauma of an indefinite uncertainty. During the protracted enquiry, they had no idea what had happened to their money. Was it lost or simply frozen pending the final outcome? It took several years to win their case and throughout that long ordeal they received no regular interest payments on their squandered investments. Yet it was precisely in order to secure a highly attractive rate of interest during retirement that they had originally been advised to invest their money in the Barlow Clowes funds.

You do not eliminate risk simply by handing your financial affairs over to an expert

« *It is better to be certain of a good result than hopeful of a great one.* »
Warren Buffett

Scandals A-Plenty

Unfortunately, Barlow Clowes is by no means a unique example. Throughout the last decade, almost every year, so it would seem, another investment scandal hits the headlines.

This was the savage fate that befell thousands of hapless investors in Polly Peck, the Cyprus-based agricultural products distributor. The company had been a great success story of the 1980s, growing large enough to become a member of that elite band, the FTSE 100 index of giant blue chip UK companies. But the shares collapsed in value in the autumn of 1990, hit by rumours about the integrity of Asil Nadir, Polly Peck's chief executive and chairman. He was soon faced with a bankruptcy petition for £60 million and a string of criminal charges. The shares were eventually suspended in 1991 at a fraction of the price at which they had peaked in 1990. Several professional experts, among them BZW, which acted as adviser to the company, and Legal & General, one of Britain's most widely respected household insurance companies, lost several million pounds in this collapse.

Mistakes are only costly if you never learn how to avoid repeating them

In 1991, the fraudulent misuse of £400 million of pensioners' funds associated with the ailing business empire of discredited entrepreneur Robert Maxwell brought several years of misery and financial hardship to another group of retired people. Yet even the scale of this financial disaster was capped during the early 1990s, when the mis-selling of pensions to about two million unfortunate people during the late 1980s duly came to light.

This dreadful nightmare followed from the Conservative government's decision in 1986 to introduce personal pensions, to move more people away from state pension provision. The life insurance industry used the handing over of pensions to the private sector as a massive selling opportunity in which over £4 billion was diverted into these private plans. The selling was spearheaded by the direct sales forces of many of Britain's largest, most prestigious insurance companies. Collectively, the salesmen earned hundreds of thousands of pounds in commission, encouraging miners, nurses and other public sector workers to switch out of safe schemes with many in-built guaranteed benefits, and into new personal pension plans where the charges, in some cases, meant that very little of the new policyholders' contributions were invested during the first two years.

Hundreds of thousands of victims subsequently learned to their cost that they had been tempted out of their secure employer-related pension schemes and into far less secure personal pension plans. The total number of mis-sold pensions was estimated to be above 2 million, involving at least 41 different pensions companies. This huge, long drawn-out case alone is the perfect illustration of why everyone needs to wise up and know how to protect their own interests when it comes to dealing with the big financial institutions who make their money by selling us their products.

« *The world needs banking, not bankers.* »

Bill Gates, chief executive of Microsoft

By 1997, it was reckoned that 18,000 victims had died without receiving compensation. Figures from the Personal Investment Authority in September 1997, revealed that over £452 million in compensation had so far been paid to only 73,000 victims, an average of just over £6,000 per case. However, after years of wrangling, under the urgent naggings of the new Labour government's Economic Secretary, Helen Liddell, compensation to claimants suddenly took a great leap forward. If only one third of the total two million cases require compensation, the bill for the pensions and insurance industry could exceed £4 billion.

Periodic bank failures are yet another hazard savers might face. In July 1991, the Bank of Credit and Commerce International, BCCI, was closed by the Bank of England when fraudulent malpractices amounting to £17 billion came to light. This

'Safe as the Bank of England' – But is it?

was the largest fraud in history, at that date, and BCCI collapsed with debts to its depositors of $11 billion (£6.7 billion). Several thousands of shocked bank depositors saw their savings evaporate. The **liquidator,** Deloitte & Touche, whose job is to try and sort out the company's problems, pursued a claim for $1.7 billion against Ernst & Young and $3.5 billion against Price Waterhouse, **auditors** for the failed bank. These are two of the largest, most prestigious companies of auditors in the UK. By mid-1997, $4.5 billion had been raised, of which $2.65 billion had been returned to creditors. But the Deposit Protection Scheme had only paid out £78 million in compensation to the bank's depositors, while Deloitte & Touche were still attempting to claim $750 million (£500 million) plus interest from the Bank of England on behalf of 6,000 UK depositors.

Only four years later, in 1995, the enormous trading losses in Japanese options by Nick Leeson were revealed, and the prestigious Barings Bank became insolvent after more than 230 years of life as a reputable and independent British financial institution. When it failed, depositors who thought their savings were safe faced the instant loss of all their deposits. Subsequently, there were accusations that the Bank of England had failed in its regulatory role. The collapse was a staggering blow, as this group of savers would have had absolutely no idea that Nick Leeson's unsuccessful trading activities in Singapore could possibly have a detrimental knock-on effect on their bank deposits held in the UK.

Unfortunately, far too often savers misguidedly believe the authorities are offering an open-ended guarantee if an investment they acquire collapses or proves to have been mis-sold. Many investors take comfort from the idea that some institutions are 'too large to go under'. The failure of Barings Bank in 1995 illustrates how erroneous this view can be. No one can be sure such disasters will be averted in future.

Become Your Own Expert

These are all scary examples of experts who have recently failed their investors or savers. As a result, millions who thought their savings were safe have suffered major losses. You might be tempted to think that these sorry tales simply emphasise the fact that if the experts can get things horribly wrong, what chance is there that you will do any better? Naturally, it is comforting to find a reliable professional to hand all your money problems over to, but this catalogue of financial scandals provides a very clear warning. It suggests that most passive investors would be unwise to imagine there is no possibility that someone they have put their trust in will let them down very badly at some date in the future.

What you should recognise is that when an expert handles your affairs, you have lost control. You may be lucky in your choice of expert, but if you know almost nothing about managing money for yourself, how will you handle the awesome fallout if things do go horribly wrong? You should at least contemplate the possibility that you are rather like a loose cannon on the deck, simply waiting for the big accident to happen.

Tip the risk seesaw

decisively in your

favour

It is far better to recognise the dangers inherent in trustingly handing over your financial affairs to someone else. You do not automatically eliminate risk, simply by handing over your financial affairs to an expert. Become your own financial expert and learn to manage your own money. In the end, this has to be the best route, to avoid all the trauma and distress associated with being seriously let down over money matters.

However, avoiding a financial disaster is the negative side of learning to handle your own finances. The positive side is the wonderful exhilaration you can feel by making a success of your new-found knowledge and getting your money to work properly for you to put you firmly in control. This will give you the confidence to know that if something unexpectedly does go wrong, you stand a far higher chance of sorting the problems out for yourself.

Company Credentials

Astonishing as it may seem, when making financial decisions, people appear more ready to take another person's advice without questioning it too deeply than in any other sphere of life. It is crucial that you know how reliable the company is that you intend to entrust your money to. Talk to friends or colleagues, but don't just blindly accept their recommendation. After all, they may know very little more than you do yourself.

Consumers probably spend more time choosing the family car than they do examining the details of a pension plan. The car might be roadworthy for six to eight years, while the pension plan may make a contribution to your financial future right through the rest of your life. You should make a deliberate effort to pick the insurance company you want to trust your money to, and that applies equally to the product that you think will best suit you.

Your first task is to look at the wide range of major companies providing funds in the area you are interested in, say, personal pensions. Do not be tempted to invest in a small, fairly unknown group, as it may be difficult to follow

Even the best

investment

advice is not

infallible

the progress of your investment. Moreover, a small group may not have sufficient financial backing to escape a major disaster if it should occur. Even when companies appear to have substantial backing, some do run into difficulties. This was the fate that befell thousands of innocent savers in Barings Bank. Their deposits evaporated when the bank was declared insolvent. The problems may be compounded if the company you choose has a relatively small share of the overall market. We are extremely fortunate in Britain to have a large, sophisticated pensions and insurance industry operating in the public arena. We should all be actively working to secure the maximum benefit from that advantage.

When you decide to buy a policy, you may consult an independent adviser or a salesperson from a company, who comes to discuss your situation with you at home. Early in the interview you should ask about the credentials of the company he is either recommending or represents. You should not be satisfied merely to accept his verbal assurances; ask for written evidence about the company to support his claims, unless you are 100 per cent convinced that you have chosen the right company. In view of the long recent history of financial scandals, no one can really be that sure about that, especially a novice investor at an early stage of financial planning.

When you deal with a major financial company, you can check its credit rating with independent credit agencies, like Moody's and S&P. The best rating is a Triple A; it reflects the financial strength of the funds the company manages. You can ask the financial adviser or salesman about credit ratings and also about the size of the funds the company manages. You will want to know whether

When you lose your

own money, you

feel the pain

the company you plan to use has hundreds of thousands, hopefully millions of investors linked to those funds. This gives reassurance that it is highly respected in the industry and has solid and substantial resources to back its successful long-term continuation in business. Most major companies will have small booklets giving precisely this information for potential new policyholders.

For companies where you are hoping to take out a pension or insurance-based savings, you will also want to know if it has produced consistently above-average investment returns for its policy-holders, especially over the term of years you have in mind. This may be anything from ten to twenty-five years for an endowment savings policy and thirty-five to forty years for a pension. Consistent performance is vital if you are to achieve your financial targets. Here, again, ask to see written evidence to confirm any claims being made to you about 'excellent performance'.

Dealing With Experts

One of the most important lessons about handling money that you should try to learn at the earliest possible stage is to be extra-vigilant when dealing with experts. By all means listen to their advice, but never accept it totally on its face value alone. Try to get confirmation or another opinion from some other source, even if it is only from your own further reading, before completely accepting what an expert thinks you should do.

Give yourself time to make a proper assessment. Remember, he probably earns most of his income by giving clients, that means you, advice that you are willing to act upon. The best approach is to prepare yourself as fully as you can before the interview so you can act like a self-taught canny consumer. If you do not weight the odds in your favour, you will be an easy target. This caution is not made to denigrate experts, but just to alert you to how unequal the interview will be if you enter it totally unprepared while he, the professional salesman, is fully in command of where the interview will lead. Let me pass on to you the greatest lesson I was taught when I went through a selling training course: The person who controls the interview wins the argument or makes the sale!

This valuable advice applies to many areas of life, but when it comes to safeguarding your money it is absolutely indispensable. Some crusty old clichés are based on the bald truth, and 'Buyer Beware' must surely be counted among them. However, if you do your homework properly you have the greatest chance of staying in full control when handling an interview where someone is trying to sell you financial products in your home. After all, the salesman will not be expecting you to be well informed. This gives you the advantage, and should enable *you* to keep control of the interview. So how can you do that?

Enter The Salesperson

When a salesman comes into your home to sell you a financial product you should be alert to the fact that his objectives are completely different to yours: he wants to make a sale; you want to buy a product that closely meets one of your financial targets. Moreover, there is a huge imbalance in financial awareness between the two of you: he has been well trained for this interview. What preparation will you have had? You need to sharpen up your financial skills so that you get the product that you want rather than ending up with something he has to sell. Your choice of product is another vital priority where you must be wholly convinced you will not later regret the decision you have made.

All too often, sadly, *you* will have been chosen by a salesman. Thanks to his intensive training and undisputed selling skills, he knows exactly how to calm your fears about making a financial error. He also will be an expert in gaining your confidence, but that is not at all the same as selling you a product that will prove right for you.

The statistics tell the whole sorry story. Almost one quarter of all long term savings plans taken out are cancelled within two years. This is a colossal waste of savers' hard earned cash. The Personal Investment Authority produced figures to show that half of all the personal pensions sold are lapsed or transferred to another pensions provider within five years. These statistics illustrate to an alarming extent just how easy it is to beguile people into making the wrong financial decisions. It may keep the salesforce in work, but early transfer values for pensions and surrender values for policies after two years are both extremely low, because almost all the costs of the policy are paid for by *you* over that initial period.

You should buy the financial products you need, rather than allow a salesman to sell you what he has to offer.

Be Prepared

To put the interview on a more equal footing, you should be as fully prepared as he will be. There are laws now in place to ensure a salesman gives 'best advice'. This means he should recommend only a pension or insurance plan which is suitable, after proper enquiry. Both company salespeople and independent financial advisers now have to fill in questionnaires on your present financial situation to ensure they give you best advice. After a preliminary 'warm up' chat, this will be the first stage in any suggestions they offer you. However, you shouldn't rely on his skill alone.

You must attempt to be fully conversant yourself with your current position, so that you have all the relevant facts before you during a sales interview. Then you will be more informed to judge what policy you are being offered and the salesman can easily provide you with the vital information you need on how much you will have to save to realise your financial goals. When you have reached the end of *The Money Maze*, you should feel in a much more commanding position to tackle all the key financial issues for yourself, including the correct handling of interviews with experts.

There are several ways to keep in control. First, you should line up the list of questions you want answers to. Second, always stay alert to the reality that he is hoping to make a sale. Third, resolve firmly at the outset not to be tempted to sign any papers or hand over money, unless you are completely convinced the product, with all its various clauses, is right for you. Have an answer ready, however tame or contrived it sounds, to deal with any over-firm persuasion he offers: 'I'll think about that and let you know my decision next week.' You might even say, 'I have run out of cheques and I'm waiting for a new cheque book to arrive.' If you have any doubts, ask yourself, 'Will I still think this is a good product by next week?'

The best boost to confidence comes from being right

When working on your preparation for the interview, think about all the questions you should ask before making a big financial commitment. Always try to ask him the difficult but essentially practical questions: 'How much commission will you earn?' 'What are the penalties in this plan if I surrender it early?' 'Are there any small print clauses I should know about? Can you tell me what they are?' 'Show me the figures on the performance of funds which apply to this policy.'

It sounds rather mercenary, but even if the salesman comes from a friend with the highest recommendation, always think, 'What will he gain from this deal? What will I gain?' If you are too shy or reticent to ask him this outright, but are not sure about the long-term implications of this intended transaction, be willing to step back awhile, and give yourself time to do more thinking or investigating. This might be the right moment to bring out one of those lame excuses to prevent yourself from signing a contract you feel uncertain about and want more time to evaluate.

Ask Before You Buy

But how, you might be wondering, can you set about discovering what you need to know to become your own expert? Deciding something as complicated as choosing your own personal pension is obviously fraught with difficulties because there is such a vast selection and so much available information. How do you choose between perhaps one hundred different policies, all offering the same type of product?

« *It has taken thirty-three years and a bang on the head to get my values right.* »

Stirling Moss

Fortunately, this is not such a horrendous task as you might imagine. In fact, the essentials of how to choose between a welter of similar products apply to all investment products; for personal pensions, insurance-based savings policies, unit and investment trusts. There are three vital areas of information that you must evaluate whenever you are considering making an investment in one of these types of plans: first, the performance of the investment funds; second, the charges made by the managers and third, all the small print in the policy or plan which might affect the flexibility of your options at some future date. You should therefore not be afraid to ask the key questions regarding the performance, the charges and all the small print clauses. These are the three essential factors that will affect the long-term results of your savings plans.

Do not feel discouraged at this stage that you may never master the money maze. It may take a little while to get there, perhaps a couple of years or so. But the trek through to financial freedom is not too arduous if you work steadily towards it, always remembering just to take one step at a time. And the view from your position of full control is incredibly exhilarating. Not to mention the financial rewards that await you.

Be Your Own Adviser

The best antidote to fear of losses from faulty financial decisions is to decide to become your own financial adviser. This is far easier to achieve than you would imagine if you concentrate on the five main elements that will allow you to take your own financial decisions with confidence. These few essential points will guide you through the recurring panics and crises that invariably crop up from time to time. In addition, they are useful factors to add to your risk control kit. We will first list the five key elements you should focus on so you can become your own expert and then we will briefly expand on some of them to fill out the picture.

i   Take the simplest route.
ii   Be a long-term investor.
iii Prepare your own investment plan.
iv   Follow the market action.
v   Diversify.

If you can follow these five guiding principles, you will be far more capable of controlling your own affairs. So, first, whenever you face a new financial decision, always look for the simplest route to reach your objectives. This leads naturally to the second point, because, in general this means right from the outset you should aim to become a long-term investor. This is especially important if you are in your forties and fifties with large cash deposits sitting idly in the bank or building society. If you belong to this ultra-cautious group, now is the time to have a serious rethink on your finances. To switch track and become a long-term investor instead of a passive saver, you need to concentrate on the last three ideas.

Your investment plan is your safe route through the money maze

So on the third point, you should prepare your own customised investment plan to ensure you are always taking exactly the right course, that is, the one you have planned to take. Preparing your own investment plan is at the very heart of becoming more financially aware. So we will digress a moment here, to discuss it in outline.

The Investment Plan

Devising your own investment plan is really an open secret to achieving long-term financial security. It will become your personal blueprint to turning your plans into reality. It forms the essential route map to guide you through the tangled byways of the money maze to take you safely to a better financial future. There are many great advantages in preparing your personalised investment plan; it focuses on your long-term aims and gives you a well-thought-out scheme. This will allow you steadily to monitor your progress. Finally, by carefully laying out the route you are following, the investment plan is a wonderful method of controlling risk.

Think for a moment about that financial adviser or insurance salesman who comes into your home to help you make a decision about buying financial products. As we noted earlier, by law he is now obliged to fill in a complicated questionnaire about your current financial position and your future financial goals. In short, he is doing a quick, on the spot investment plan in outline for you to give you advice on your particular needs. In chapter 9, we will consider all the necessary steps involved in this, so you will be able to perform this vital role for yourself. You will find the Action Plan details laid out for you to guide you through the major points you need to cover to ensure you can be a competent adviser to both yourself and other members of your family.

Any method that gives you more control helps you manage the risks

As a foretaste of where we are now heading, here is the general outline of what you will be doing in order to prepare your own investment plan. The jumping off point is first to identify where you are on the investment staircase. You should then go through the essential preliminary stages, which centre around clearly setting out a list of your future money targets. You can then design your own financial pyramid. With all this under control, the essential kernel of your investment plan will be firmly in place.

Follow The Market

The fourth idea to becoming your own adviser also rests on being a long-term investor; with the long view in mind, you should try to hold your investments through the various short-term dips that often disturb the market. It is far easier to do this if you focus steadily on your long-term goals and follow the market action.

For novices to personal finance and investment skills, following the behaviour of the stock market through your reading is, in my opinion, time well spent. Some investment experts suggest it is pointless to watch the direction of the market because its movements are unpredictable and so cannot be accurately forecast. This advice suggests you can succeed with your money affairs even if you blithely ignore what is going on in the wider global economy and financial community. I am not of that opinion, however, for two key reasons.

First, on a personal note, I embarked on my investment adventure in the spring of 1990. In August, Saddam Hussein invaded Kuwait and stock markets around the world began to fall, in anticipation of the Gulf War. If I had paid more attention to these crucial global events, I may not have promptly lost 7 per cent of my initial capital within six months of starting to invest. Second, on a broader point, I have discovered that there are many useful signals you can pick up about timing your investments if you know what you should be looking for. It is precisely because investing money is not an easy skill to master, that small investors should use all the helpful signals they can find. This again is another useful way of cutting down the risks of being wrong.

For beginners in particular, I think it is even more important to know a little about the general markets and follow the market trends if you are planning to save through collective funds. It is sensible to follow the market so you do not put large sums into an investment when the market is riding very high after it has already enjoyed a long run up. At such times, statistically, history suggests it is nearer to a fall than a further rise. If you are patient and invest when prices have dropped lower, your money will go further. You will then be better placed to make larger gains. Conversely, if you invest at or near a market peak, your funds will buy fewer units or shares and you will be more poorly placed to make the large gains you are seeking.

« *I do the opposite to what I feel I should do. When I'm sick in my stomach, it's time to buy. When I feel great, it's time to sell.* »
Elaine Gazarelli, top Wall Street analyst for 11 years

Repeatedly, the records show that small investors tend to buy into the market when it is nearing a peak. This is the time when newspapers and the media highlight how well the stock market is doing. But it is entirely the wrong time to be investing as you will be paying very high prices for your purchases. At the market peak, there will be few bargains around. If the market then falls, it could be months or years before your investment shows a profit. At the peak, all the smart investors will have been fully invested for months. They will now be thinking about taking their profits. They are waiting for the fall-guy novices to pile on board so they can offload their highly priced shares and bank their big profits. Make sure they are not waiting for you. If you gain nothing else from your reading but a better idea of when the market is high and therefore offering poor value and perhaps more likely to fall, you will have saved yourself a lot of trouble, aggravation and, of course, money.

Diversify The Risks

The fifth idea for becoming your own adviser is to aim to diversify your assets right from the outset. This goal will naturally develop from your investment plan because when you are compiling that you will look for a wide range of investments, hopefully to cover all your future needs. Aim to create a family of investments in your overall portfolio, with each group having a different job to perform.

However, there is a price to pay for diversification. It is an excellent way of spreading risk. But while it certainly helps to reduce losses, it also dilutes the eventual gains. The greatest benefit you will derive from becoming your own expert is when you have assembled sufficient knowledge to move on and concentrate your growing portfolio into a few choice investments. This is the route to making substantial profits. But it is strictly the preserve of the well informed investor as higher potential gains carry higher risks. The best way to reduce these risks is by tipping the risk seesaw decisively in your favour with higher overall knowledge. You must know clearly at every stage exactly what you are doing.

Save As You Learn

If you feel your money awareness is rather low when you start, take plenty of time to acquire sound investment skills. There are several ways you can improve your knowledge about money matters. Reading books about successful investors is one useful idea to give you a flavour of how successful money managers set about their tasks. A basic primer on investment subjects is also helpful. A reading list for easy books designed primarily for beginners, plus useful journals, appears at the end of the book with some notes for guidance. If you do not want to buy any books, you can borrow them from the library.

Write little notes on investment ideas and thoughts that you think will be especially helpful

However, the majority of the available books mainly focus on stock market-related investments, especially all the important elements you need to consider when building a share portfolio. Do not be put off by this limitation. Some of the books make fascinating reading and offer excellent insights into making your money work. There is no ducking the real issue: if you want to become more financially secure, you will need to gain expertise on how to make money through the stock market-related route.

What I have found from my reading is that almost every book or article gives me yet another little nugget of knowledge to add to my growing collection. I like to write very short notes on the items which seem to fit in especially well with my own views on investing and the investment approach which I constantly use. I particularly like to read about different methods of investing, as some of these I can adopt myself as I go along.

Some references for managing your personal finances appear in the reading list. But apart from reading *The Money Maze*, the regular money sections of the daily broadsheet newspapers are good information sources. These include *The Times*, *Telegraph*, *Guardian* and, of course, the *Financial Times*. These papers often give up-to-the-minute facts on major issues of topical interest as they crop up from time to time. Periodically, in addition, they all produce useful specialist supplements covering one particular topic in depth, for example, unit trusts or pension planning. This is an excellent source of current information. It often includes advice from experts within the general coverage. Reading the weekend newspaper money sections is another good source to rely on for helpful information, because these papers tend to provide broad overview articles on important and topical subjects that often bear directly on the current issues. Here again, there is a wide choice, including the *Sunday Times, Sunday Telegraph, Observer* and the *Mail on Sunday*.

However, although the newspapers are extremely good reference sources for general details on individual subjects, I firmly believe that really to become the master of your financial destiny, you should try to polish up your money skills with a book that provides the guiding principles to managing money, as we are covering them here, in these early chapters of *The Money Maze*.

Read your way
to a more
profitable
future

Start as soon as possible to browse more seriously than you have in the past, through the recurring information provided by the daily and weekend newspapers, taking careful note of those areas that especially interest you, or apply to your situation most directly. It is helpful to compile a file of newspaper cuttings or supplements covering the key topics, so you can refer back to them at a later date. Be sure to date the cuttings as financial information is constantly changing so you need to know the date when the information was written.

On the journal front, I have used the *Money Observer* magazine from the outset of my investment career. It has excellent articles on many aspects of investing and is a minefield of useful statistics. It gives regular update figures on deposit savings rates and mortgage lending rates in addition to prices on company shares and unit and investment trusts over several different periods, from one month, six months and a year, to one, three and seven years. As a monthly journal the annual subscription at around £30 is quite small for the amount of wide-ranging information it provides.

Although more expensive, the weekly *Investors Chronicle* is also well worth considering. It can be read in most main public libraries. Even if you do not want to invest directly in company shares, it has excellent coverage of collective funds, both unit and investment trusts. It also includes a weekly section on personal finance. Furthermore, it regularly produces interesting articles giving a wide-ranging assessment of market activity, events and future prospects. These will look at what the markets are currently doing as well as where they might be heading. This coverage is especially valuable because it is truly global. In different weeks it might look in depth at one or two topical areas. These may include any of the following:

Europe, America, Japan, Latin America and South East Asia, in addition to the UK. *Investors Chronicle* is especially good in reporting what the major global brokers and analysts are thinking and advising their clients. This information gives the small private investor a useful insight into what advice the big institutional investors are currently receiving.

Every investment book you read will contain a few nuggets of useful information

While you are working through *The Money Maze* it would be a good idea to begin to read some of the pages in the financial press, to become more familiar with the most recent or popular news items or stories. Do not be too concerned if you only understand a little of what you read. By starting slowly and continuing on a regular long-term basis, you will find you are gradually learning more of the jargon and pivotal factors that you need to grasp to become more fully informed. The topics in general tend to be complicated rather than complex, so it is quite possible to educate yourself, but you must accept that it will take time.

Learn With Others

If you can interest your work colleagues or friends in brushing up on their money expertise, you can compare notes to expand your knowledge. You might try attending seminars and money shows, where many companies run stalls to display their products. At these venues, you can exchange ideas with other investors and ask questions at first hand from experts on the display stands. There will also be plenty of literature to take home and digest at your leisure. Follow up on this information by telephoning the company for answers to any questions that occur to you when reading through their leaflets. Many of the larger insurance companies and fund management groups now have Internet sites, so you can have immediate access to a lot of useful information from this source. You can also print this information out directly via your personal computer at home.

In order to be safe it is necessary never to feel secure

Increasingly, some local authorities or private teachers are running investment courses. You can check with your local library to see what is on offer in your area. Again, this is an excellent way to make contact with others who are interested in this vitally important topic and it will give you access to an expert to whom you can put all your questions directly, as they arise.

Know Yourself

Whatever investments you plan to buy, it is fundamental to your future peace of mind that you clearly understand your own investment psychology. People have different tolerances to financial losses, depending on several factors, including their age and how long they have in which to build up a large nest egg. If you are young, with a longer time frame to build your capital, a higher level of risk, with the

One STEP at a *time*

prospect of a greater return, may be quite acceptable. But this situation would probably be out of the question for a person during, or even close to, retirement.

Your risk tolerance may depend not just on how comfortable you will feel if you lose money on one of your investments, but it will also be affected by your basic attitude to money, saving and investing. Some people are more willing than most to take a risk, if they think the odds favour a profitable result. Others would have sleepless nights and never feel relaxed if they were worrying endlessly about the possibility of losses. Everyone must ask themselves this pertinent question. Am I nervous about losing money or willing to accept some level of risk so my capital can grow?

There are only two kinds of investors: the optimists and the pessimists

However, even if you think you are the most pessimistic, loss-averse person around, you should still keep an open mind. The aim of *The Money Maze* is to give you a good grounding on the inside information about what makes money work and how you can use that information to your financial advantage. Right now you may be sitting on the wrong end of the risk seesaw, very low in knowledge and therefore very high on risk. But after reading to the end of the book, you will begin to put your investment plans into action. All the new knowledge you will have acquired will, hopefully, transform your situation. When you are high on knowledge and low on risk, your whole attitude to investing will be changed out of all recognition from the way you feel now. Stay flexible in your approach and I feel sure this miraculous transformation could yet come about for you, in due course.

Benefit From Your Mistakes

One of the key reasons for starting slowly on your route to greater financial security is to ensure you make as few mistakes as possible. However, it is almost certain that some mistakes will occur. Small investors repeatedly make many mistakes which jeopardise their long-term financial interests. So as it is useful to know what some of the most common mistakes are, here is a short list.

i   Most investors confuse volatile conditions with risk. Long-term investors should aim to ride out the short-term fluctuations and focus on more specific risks as we are listing them here.

ii Investors try to find the 'lowest risk' investment without realising that by eliminating all volatile investments in favour of 'safer' deposit accounts they are actually increasing their exposure to another type of risk, that of inflation risk. We discussed this fully in chapter 2.

iii Many private investors buy their shares and unit trusts at a market peak. They suddenly get tempted to buy from noting the television news headlines or newspaper reports on how well the markets are doing, but they have not followed the big picture.

iv   They tend to sell after prices have fallen back from a peak. This is often the direct outcome of buying at the top of the market. When prices fall, small investors discover they are sitting on losses and decide to sell, rather than hang on and ignore the short-term volatility. However, it is important to bear in mind that when you buy at a peak, you may have to wait for years before prices recover to those that you initially paid.

v   Small investors tend to pursue fashions instead of looking for consistent long-term investment performers.

vi   They often focus on safe deposit accounts ignoring 'money illusion' by not taking inflation into account.

Risk Control For Beginners

We saw in chapter 3 that controlling risk is one of the key issues that you can actively improve upon by doing a tremendous amount for yourself, once you understand how that can be achieved. In essence, right through *The Money Maze*, we are covering the many different aspects of managing money. They are all guidelines centred on one idea: *controlling risk*. You should use them continuously to reduce the level of risk you face when you are making financial decisions. The really good news is that there are numerous sensible ways of controlling risk. The more you know about them, the more of them you will use and the lower your exposure to risk will become. We have already covered several important ways of reducing risk in the earlier chapters.

Money can buy you almost everything, but not common sense

The idea of the risk seesaw is central here. The more information you can obtain, the better informed you will be. If you can mix with other investors and share ideas, your depth of understanding will increase, again lowering your risk level while gaining the added bonus of making new friends and improving your social contacts. Reading suitable newspapers, journals and books is yet another way of increasing your knowledge and reducing your exposure to risk. Trying to follow the fortunes of the stock market through your reading is another helpful risk control idea. Articles on how, and perhaps why, the market is either soaring or plunging appear regularly in the daily or weekend newspapers and in journals, like *Investors Chronicle*. Attending investment courses, seminars and money shows is yet another avenue for enhancing your knowledge base to reduce your level of ignorance on money matters.

Pooling The Risk

In addition, there are several positive ideas that investors with a nervous disposition can adopt to minimise risk. One exciting thought is to copy the example of the famous American Beardstown Ladies and join an investment club in your area. Better still, find a group of like-minded friends or colleagues at work and set up your own club. Collectively, you can all learn the basic essentials by pooling your cash and expertise. Additionally, by sharing your experiences, you can dispel the loneliness of making important decisions on your own, while enjoying your investing adventure in good company and at the same time, expanding your social life.

It is tremendously good news that there are so many different ways of reducing risk.

Clubs usually meet once a month, in a local restaurant or pub or in a member's house, to discuss their portfolios and decide which investments, if any, they should buy or sell. Two books to consult on this interesting topic are *The Beardstown Ladies Common-Sense Investment Guide* and *Investment Clubs, the low-risk way to stockmarket profits* by Tony Drury. The details of both are included in the reading list at the end of the book.

In earlier chapters we have mentioned collective funds, which cover both unit and investment trusts. I talked about the topic of collective funds in *The Armchair Investor*, but in chapter 7 we will look at it in more detail, as part of the planning in building your financial pyramid.

I think putting money into a small range of unit trusts is a good jumping-off point for the savings of novice investors. It is yet another excellent route for pooling your risks. When you buy your shares in a company directly, you alone are exposed to all the possible profits. This is naturally wonderful news. However, the downside is that you are equally alone in facing any losses. Until you have gained more experience, this is clearly a risky route to take. You can reduce this risk by joining forces with other like-minded investors in a unit trust fund when you buy units in it. The fund manager has millions of pounds entrusted to his expertise and can therefore buy shares in numerous companies. He will use your money together with that of thousands of other investors to buy shares in a wide range of companies.

The secret for making money is to practice risk control

With millions to spend he can run a huge, well diversified portfolio.

When you buy units in a large fund invested in a big selection of varied companies you have spread your risk among all these companies even though you may only have invested a very small amount of money. If you put £1,000 into a fund which has shares in 100 different companies, you have £10 in each of these. This is clearly a minute sum of money which you could not possibly invest directly and economically in one company. Moreover, if you have £10 in each of 100 companies, carefully chosen, there is a possibility that some of them will do very well indeed, even if a few do badly. If you put your £1,000 in only one company, it may or may not rise in value over the next few months or years.

Buying a small stake in a large number of companies is an excellent route for novices to take. For example, if the fund you have chosen rises by 12 per cent in one year, your initial £1,000 will have grown to £1,120. And this result will arise even if some of the 100 companies fell while only a few of the others grew faster than 12 per cent. If the average of the rises and falls works out to give a 12 per cent gain, you will have made £120 in one year.

Peter Lynch, who managed the enormously successful American Fidelity Magellan Fund from 1977 to 1990, had this sound advice for small investors: 'If seven out of ten stocks perform as expected, that's good going ... but six out of ten is all it takes to produce a very favourable return.'

Another way of reducing risk is not to buy a full stake all in one transaction in case your timing is poor. It is always a disconcerting event to put money into an investment and then watch the prices fall immediately after your purchase is made. Instead, you should buy units in your chosen fund on a monthly basis. This evens out the times when prices are high, and your money will only buy a few units, with times when prices are low and the same amount of money will buy you many more units. Saving in a monthly plan is an ideal beginners choice for ironing out the short-term fluctuations in unit prices and thereby reducing risks.

Stay Flexible

If you stay flexible in your planning you will be more ready to deal with unexpected events as and when they crop up. Being flexible is yet another way of controlling the risks. It prevents you acting precipitately or dithering and doing nothing when decisive action might be a better solution. I have sometimes found it is better to make a decision, even if it proves to be wrong. You can often reverse a bad decision, but indecision usually stems from ignorance and is not a good formula for handling financial affairs. Of course, hand in hand with flexibility should go the sound preparation you have invested in making sure you thought all your actions were right at the outset.

Your Portfolio Family

During 1996, when we were filming the first television series of Mrs Cohen's Money, one of the researchers was terribly upset to discover she had bought an expensive **endowment policy** to repay her mortgage when she might have been better off repaying the mortgage and the capital during the course of the term on a **repayment** basis. I tried to explain to her that she should set these worries on one side and focus her energies on ensuring she chose more effective investments in the future. After all, no one makes only one investment through- out their life. As you move up the investment staircase, many different investments will need to be made. So, if you have a good portfolio of varied investments, one poorly performing plan is far less important to your overall chances of growing your capital effectively.

You have diversified your portfolio if it includes three or four different types of asset, each covering another area of investment. Having a whole collection with a variety of investments, therefore, is another way to reduce risk. The whole idea of building a financial pyramid is based on this important diversification principle. All the different blocks of your financial pyramid will play a different role in your investment plans, as we shall see when we consider the financial pyramid in detail in chapters 6 and 7.

Your portfolio family

I like to think of my portfolio of investments as a family. It includes our house and pensions, life assurance and insurance-based savings plans held either jointly or separately, for my husband and myself. In addition, there are all the stock market investments we hold, again, both separately and jointly. These include shares in UK companies, held both inside and outside of PEPs. As with every family, each member will be an individual. So it is with your portfolio of investments. Each one will be a part of a total collection to cover one aspect of your wealth creation plans. If they all have a separate role to play, if one turns out to be a poor choice, all the others may help to compensate.

In a family, there tends to be one, or if you are really unlucky, two black sheep. These in investment terms are the duds that are showing you losses. When you think of your investments as a family, even if you have made one bad choice, you do not have to put up with the black sheep in your investment portfolio for ever. Whereas you might be smitten with guilt if you tried ignoring a member of your family who was the chronic black sheep, this is definitely not the case with your errant investments. Everyone must expect to have one or two poorly performing assets which are employing money that might be providing a better return if they were sold and the proceeds reinvested in a more promising area. If you can extricate yourself from these black sheep without suffering too great a loss, that could be the best route to take. If not, then, as with my researcher friend, don't worry too unduly. Concentrate on choosing your next set of investments with even more care.

Cut your losses fast and run your profits slowly

An important investment rule that I try always to follow is to cut the losses early and run the profitable investments for as long as the story about them stays good. This is an excellent rule for controlling risk. Unfortunately, here again, evidence shows that most small investors do exactly the opposite to best practice. As they like to see some profits in the bank, they tend to sell their successful investments far too early. On the other side of the coin, they tend to hang on to losing situations, hoping that these will eventually recover. This rarely proves to be a sound method for managing the growth in your portfolio. It means you are being driven by emotion in your investment decisions, hoping for a revival that may never come, rather than by discipline which means you will set a target selling price to protect your capital and sell at around that price, without dithering on whether this is the right time, the correct decision or any other worries that suddenly make you hesitate to act.

Devise A System

Applying discipline to your financial decisions is sometimes difficult but it can make an immense improvement to your results because you, not your emotions, are firmly in control. As an extention of this idea, when you have devised a proper investment system you will be controlling the risks even more. Throughout the book we are working to slot all the pieces of sensible money management into a complete picture. By the time you reach chapter 9, all the separate essential elements for creating an effective investment plan will have been covered. You will then be ready to build the total plan that best suits your particular circumstances. It will provide your best route through the money maze. For example, working with a plan to build your financial pyramid can play a large role as part of your overall investment strategy. Devising an all-embracing plan, working with it and improving it as you go along is one of the most powerful ways to put yourself in control and thereby reduce risk.

Ensure you, and not your emotions, are in control

From this long list of items, you can see how much risk control lies within your own hands. Each and every one of these approaches can make a considerable improvement to managing your money with more skill and effectiveness. In this chapter we have covered a lot of ground in how you can move the risk seesaw more decisively in your favour. By adding all these elements to your knowledge armoury, you reduce the risks that your investments will let you down. And, the final bonus, you will become your own expert, relying more securely on your own advice. We are now ready to move on to chapter 5, where we will consider how we are going to find the money with which to buy all these mouth-watering investments.

« Our most important responsibility to the future is ... to attend to it. »
What Time is This Place? Kevin Lynch

Key Points To Remember

1 To build a strong financial position you must know about stock market-related investments.

2 Expert advice can result in losses.

3 Become your own expert.

4 Ask before you buy: What is the performance? What are the charges? What are the small print clauses?

5 Prepare your own investment plan.

6 Follow the market action.

7 Diversify.

8 Save as you learn.

9 Benefit from your mistakes.

10 Practise risk control.

CHAPTER 5

THE
money-*go-round*

'Well, since you're wanting to get people interested in the stock market in your country, we always say over here that ladies or girls, from birth to eighteen, they need good parents, from eighteen to thirty, they need good looks, from thirty to fifty, a good personality. But after fifty, you'd better have some good investments.'

Ann Brewer (one of the Beardstown Ladies) to Bernice Cohen, in Mrs Cohen's Money *on Channel 4, May 1997*

We have seen that during the average working lifetime, a vast amount of money will probably pass through your hands. It is really great news that most people can expect to earn a substantial sum through the forty years they spend working. The trouble is, earning it over such a long period is not the same as receiving it all together at one time like a giant jackpot. If today, you could put £1 million on deposit and earn a tiny 4 per cent interest on it every year, you would have an income of £40,000 to live on and would probably never want to work again. But when this same amount is dribbled out to you over a whole working lifetime, very little of it will be free at any time to be earning interest for you, since it has to cover all your living expenses. Nevertheless, as this mighty river of cash is flowing into and out of your hands, the big question is; how much of it will you put aside for *your future*?

In 1996, the Tory

Government coined the

motto:

'spend to save'.

But 'save to spend'

makes far more sense

Clearly, the need to pay for all your daily expenses is fundamental to maintaining a reasonable standard of living. The major part of your spending on a wide range of goods and services will usually be focused on providing your creature comforts. So you might argue, quite reasonably, that you are looking after yourself and getting the best possible return when you pay regularly out of your income for all these essential items. However, there is a downside risk in living up to the full extent of your income, year by year. Now that we live in a job-hopping era, how will you manage if you run into a bout of difficult times? Suppose your salary suddenly drops, or you are made redundant? As we saw in chapter 3, your options will be pretty dismal if you have no resources set aside to cope with precisely these unforeseen situations. It is hardly sensible to continuously spend every penny you earn, without giving any thought to how you will manage if your full income is suddenly reduced or completely cut off.

Pay Yourself First

We don't want to get obsessively concerned about what the future might or might not hold, but I was greatly impressed by the sensible attitude towards saving taken by the Beardstown Ladies in Illinois USA. Although many of these fourteen ladies are over sixty, they have run one of the most famous and successful investment clubs for over fourteen years, from 1983 to 1997. They made an average return on their money of over 23 per cent during that time, easily beating almost all the professional American fund managers. To run their investment club, they pool their investment cash within the club and develop their expertise together, to make their money grow. One of their favourite mottos is: 'Pay yourself first'. They

A pay-yourself-first

fund turns current

income into savings

or investments

suggest that every time you receive a salary cheque, you should take off a sum of money that you have decided you want to earmark for your future use.

This will be money that doesn't get spent on gas or telephone bills, paying the rent or bus fares. It is money for your future spending, either for unexpected events, or for some specific long–term goal. Pay-yourself-first money goes straight away into the special savings scheme you have chosen, so that you are sure to get the benefit of this growing savings pot at some later date. All the rest of your salary is then freely available to spend as is necessary or as you wish. In chapters 6 and 7, we will look at how to choose your special savings schemes for your pay-yourself-first money.

It may seem odd to think money you set aside for future spending is really paying yourself first, but remember the £1 million lump sum and the income of £40,000 it could provide, almost without lifting a finger? When you live on income that derives from a capital lump sum, it is called **unearned income.** This is surely an exact description of how we would all like to live: on money that is there for the asking, without having to work hard every year to obtain it. With a sizeable nest egg, the choices that open up to you are far more varied than if your money keeps dripping steadily into your hands and then straight out again. Paying yourself first is a sensible way of putting your priorities in the right order. The main objective of every savings scheme, until well into retirement, should be to build up a worthwhile sum of capital.

You may think it sounds a rather selfish attitude to put yourself first, when it comes to allocating priorities for your spending. But, think about this. If everyone knew how to swim, no one would drown trying to save someone who got into difficulties in the sea or in a swimming pool. Learning the value of saving

Live like a Lord on unearned income

is similar. If you run into financial difficulties, someone else will have to come to your rescue. However tiny the hand-out, someone will certainly be there to look after your essential needs. This someone may be a parent, a brother or another generous relative. But increasingly today it is the state that provides the lifeline. The world would surely be a poorer place if Vincent van Gogh's younger brother Theo had not made him a regular allowance so that he could continue to paint until his premature death, even though he sold hardly any of his paintings during his short lifetime.

Seen in this positive light, no one who is entirely self-sufficient financially will be a drain on the state. So, from that point of view, saving for your own needs to become financially independent is not selfish at all. It may help the welfare state to cope more successfully with those unfortunate people who hit a bad patch and really cannot provide for themselves.

Income To Spend

We have seen how important it is to know the difference between saving and investing, although this difference seems vague to most people. So it is equally important to understand that there is a subtle difference between **capital** and **income**. Your income is money from a reliable source that you receive on a regular basis. This regular income is then allocated for everyday living. The larger this slice

Capital is your passport to wealth

of money, the easier it will be for you to have a comfortable life. As we have seen, it can be earned or unearned, but unless you have total confidence in a source of cash, it would not be prudent to treat irregular payments, like dividends and bonuses, as if they were permanently guaranteed to continue.

By contrast, capital is a lump sum of money, however large or small, that you own over and above what you spend on everyday living. Your capital may take the form of money on deposit, an investment in a home or a business, or in quoted companies on an international stock exchange, like London or New York. These are all examples of real assets that can be converted into cash at a future date. However, some of these examples are considered to be rather **illiquid assets**, meaning assets that are not easy to convert quickly into cash, which is obviously the most liquid of all assets. When you have cash, it is there to be used immediately. If you own property, for instance, it can take a long time, perhaps six to nine months, to sell. Property is therefore an example of an illiquid asset.

The difference between income & capital

When you have acquired some capital, it acts as a valuable cushion to provide flexibility in your financial planning. If you amass enough of it, you might be able to retire early. A cash cushion can be invaluable in a crisis or for dealing with heavy items of expenditure. The London Stock Exchange requires company directors who are selling (or buying) shares in the companies they work for, to make these transactions public. The announcements show that directors often sell large tranches of their shareholdings to buy new houses, or a share in another business, to diversify their portfolios or just to pay large tax bills. At certain times in your life, you may need to spend part of your accumulated capital to pay for similar, major items, perhaps to help your children through university or to make a wedding. You might have to dip into your capital for large, unexpected expenses, such as house repairs or changing jobs.

Total Returns

As we saw with the example of the rising value of the building society Abbey National, after it had floated as a bank on the stock market, your capital can be invested in real assets which allow it to grow while providing you with a regular income. As the value of these assets rises, the income will rise, roughly in tandem. This is tremendously good news for investors. It means that they can leave their investments on automatic pilot for six to twelve months at a time, hoping for growth in the capital sum, while either reinvesting the dividends or using them as additional income, to supplement other sources of income for daily expenses. Adding the

Reinvesting your

dividends brings

many happy returns

dividends you receive to the growth in your capital produces the total return figure. This serves as a reference for how quickly your money is growing every year you are saving.

When handling large amounts of other people's investment funds, professional managers and pension fund actuaries tend to think in terms of a 'total return' on the real assets they are managing. Small investors can think like this while their nest egg is growing. If you regularly reinvest your dividends, as we saw in chapter 2, your capital will grow much faster than if you withdraw the dividends each year to supplement your income.

Vanishing Capital Means Vanishing Income

Pensioners, however, should definitely never think along these lines at all. Capital and regular income must be treated separately, because if they are not, you will rapidly find that you have spent capital as income and lost both of them in the process. If you confuse capital with income, this shock horror situation can arise much more easily than you would imagine. It is yet another example of money doing a disappearing act. No one should ever confuse capital with income, and to emphasise this crucial point we will look at an illustration, told by Max Gunther in his book *The Zurich Axioms*. It shows how quickly this crisis situation can steal up on the unwary.

Learning from other people's mistakes is far cheaper than learning from you own

He tells the story of an American woman he calls Paula. She spent her working life on the production line at Ford Motor Company. When her husband died in the late 1970s, Paula took early retirement and put all her spare money into Ford shares, hoping to live comfortably on the dividends. Ford was paying a dividend of $2.60 a share and she had 20,000 shares. This gave her a comfortable annual income of $52,000, although she did have to pay tax on her dividend. But added to a small early-retirement pension she felt quite secure with this arrangement.

Unfortunately, a recession was looming in 1979. There was a downturn in the US economy and Ford very soon ran into problems. It cut its 1980 annual dividend from $2.60 per share to $1.73. This dropped Paula's 1980 income to £34,600, but the auto industry's troubles got rapidly worse. In 1981, when the dividend was cut again to 0.80 cents, Paula's income fell to $16,000. Then disaster struck! In 1982, Ford paid no dividend at all.

Clearly, with her income disappearing, Paula's financial situation became desperate. In 1982 she was forced to sell 4,000 shares to survive during that bleak year, simply to cover her living expenses. To add to her woes, as a forced seller, she had to accept an appallingly low share price due to the prevailing pessimism in the stock market over Ford's trading problems. That meant she had to sell more shares than would have been the case when the market was booming and prices were high. By 1983 Ford was climbing slowly out of its difficulties and the directors declared a 50-cent dividend. But Paula had to sell another 2,000 shares to keep herself afloat. In 1983, her dividend income was only around $7,000 (14,000 × 0.50). Even when Ford increased its dividend again in 1984, her problems continued, because she only had 14,000 left of the original shares she had held in 1979. So the dividend pay-out of $1.20 only gave her $16,800 as income. This was a long way short of the $52,000 income she had received just five years earlier. Moreover, although Ford's fortunes did eventually recover, Paula's situation never could, as she no longer had 20,000 Ford shares on which to rely.

Paula's vanishing Ford dividends

year	dividend paid $	no. of shares	dividend Income $
1979	2.60	20,000	52,000
1980	1.73	20,000	34,600
1981	0.80	20,000	16,000
1982	nil	16,000	nil
1983	0.50	14,000	7,000
1984	1.20	14,000	16,800

Protect Your Capital

Max Gunther uses this story to point out the pitfalls of being inflexible in your long-term planning. He tells how Paula's broker had warned her in 1980 of Ford's looming problems, but she wanted to hold her shares as a long-term investment.

Capital is the seed corn to your wealth; treat it with care

This is a very sensible attitude for investors to take if it is part of a low risk strategy. Unfortunately there are very few rigid rules that always apply when you are planning your financial future. At times, taking the long-term view can prove to be the most unsatisfactory outcome, especially when you are relying on your dividends as a major source of income. Paula put her Ford shares on automatic pilot for five years at a time when she should have been taking a far more active interest in how this investment was performing.

Even so, Paula's long-term philosophy might still have had a happy ending, if she had not been relying exclusively on one company's performance to provide all her income. So we see that there are several lessons to learn from Paula's plight. She made a whole series of mistakes which are all typical examples of errors small investors make when they do not know about the important issues on how to plan for the future or how to spread their financial risks.

Paula's Investment Mistakes

We discussed the many different ways you can minimise risk in chapters 3 and 4. So now we can look at each of Paula's mistakes to see how you can profit from them.

i   Never keep to rigid investment rules.
ii   Stay flexible in your planning.
iii Never rely exclusively on one source of income from only one company share.
iv   Monitor your investments regularly, at least twice a year.
v   Make regular reviews of your entire financial situation.
vi   Plan to build yourself a good replacement income through a pension.
vii Never confuse income with capital.
viii Have a long-term investment plan in place to reduce the risk of things going wrong.
ix   Swing the risk seesaw in your favour to create a low risk strategy

Apart from being inflexible in her planning, Paula certainly should not have put all her precious capital into just one investment, however safe she thought it appeared to be. She should have been much more prepared to review her deteriorating situation long before the disaster of her vanishing dividends finally struck. For greatest security, a financial review should preferably be carried out at least twice every year. Again, she would have managed far better if she had been able to build up a respectable pension while she was working so that her Ford dividends were an add-on extra rather than being the main source of her income. We can see from our earlier discussions on risk that Paula clearly did not understand what we mean by the risk seesaw. Her financial planning was therefore high on risk and low on knowledge. All the errors she made are really the reverse side of a low-risk strategy.

However, I have related Paula's sorry story to draw attention to yet another lesson: she clearly did not realise the important difference between capital and income. Once your capital is spent, its valuable income-earning ability is completely lost: it simply disappears without trace, never to return. If you are retired, falling into this dilemma is terribly bad news. This is why you have to understand fully the special relationship between your income and capital.

« *Never get rooted in an investment because of the feeling that it 'owes' you something.* »

Max Gunther

Thinking in terms of a big lump sum to live on, as Paula did, can be quite misleading. In the 1990s, a quarter of a million pounds, for example, sounds like a big pot of money. So how would you manage if you had to live on a regular return from that capital sum alone? You might think you could live very well indeed on the income from £250,000, but a cautious view would suggest you should only reckon on receiving a return of around 4 per cent after tax, if that sum was placed on deposit. It is necessary to be cautious in calculating annual returns because rates of interest tend to fluctuate up and down rather unpredictably. At a 4 per cent yearly return, a lump sum of £250,000 will only produce £10,000, which was just about half of the average annual income in Britain in 1997. This certainly cannot be considered a substantial income that one could expect to live well on.

Pensions For All

With Paula's story in mind, when you realise the difference between capital and income, you can immediately see why everyone needs to save for a pension. When you reach retirement, the income you receive from work will cease. It is most important that you can replace it immediately with another form of regular income that is reasonably close in amount to the wage you are losing. This is precisely what a pension can provide if you have allowed yourself plenty of time to plan to achieve this replacement. If Paula had received a reasonable pension from Ford, to cover most of her living expenses, her Ford dividends would have been additional spending money, not her vital lifeline. So the collapse in her Ford dividend income for four years would have been a nuisance rather than a disaster. Of course, her total income would have fallen in 1982 and 1983 when her Ford dividends dried up so drastically, but with careful economy, she would at least have had her regular pension income to rely on. When Ford recovered from the 1980s recession, Paula's situation would also have recovered. Her extra dividend cash would simply have resumed again at its earlier level because she would have retained all her initial 20,000 shares.

Before you know it, you are living on your capital and heading for financial trouble

Pension planning is one of the three key planks to building your own financial pyramid which is part of your blueprint for turning some of your current income into future capital. But before we look in detail at how this blueprint will work for you, we absolutely have to know where this current income is coming from and how you are spending it now. The real heart of all your financial planning is to get your current finances into excellent shape; and the best way to do that is to learn about budgeting.

Budget For Buried Treasure

Doesn't budgeting sound like the greatest bore ever invented? Wrong. If you are thinking like that, you have completely missed the point. Budgeting is a treasure hunt, to find the missing money that will help to make your financial dreams come true sooner than you ever thought possible. Budgeting as a tedious hassle is how pessimists think; budgeting as a hunt for buried treasure is the optimist's approach.

Budgeting is a hunt for buried treasure

The whole purpose of budgeting is to find a tidy sum of money for you to pay yourself first. At present, that sum is probably hidden. The game comes in two parts: first, is to find your buried treasure and second, is to decide on the special place you plan to invest it in, where you can get both satisfaction and pleasure while you are watching it grow.

Budgeting serves several purposes. The first is to find out exactly how much money you are earning and spending right now. This is the secret to all successful financial planning; it puts you in control. The second purpose is to lay out your current monthly totals of income and expenses to see what the current yearly picture looks like in detail. The third aim is to find some money to save. This can be achieved quite easily if you write down all the income and expenses and discover that, with luck, you are spending less than you earn. This difference will be the money you can now put aside to pay yourself first. But suppose the expenses amount to more than the income? This leads on to the most important role that budgeting can now perform for you: it will make you more financially aware.

By knowing how big your overspend is, together with the detailed figures for how your monthly income is allocated, you can immediately begin to prune your spending and have a direct, hopefully better, idea of how you are managing your money. All your future progress stems from getting the budgeting to work *for* you rather than *against* you.

Advantages of Budgeting

i   To discover exactly what your current income and expenses are now.

ii   To find some money to start or increase your pay-yourself-first fund.

iii To find and reduce the 'black holes' in your spending.

iv   Compare your actual spend with the target spend to reduce your overspend.

v   Watch your cash flow.

vi   To budget your way out of debt.

« *It is better that a man should tyrannise over his bank balance than over his fellow citizens.* »

John Maynard Keynes

Time To Budget

To prepare your own budget you will have to use the figures you have to hand on all last year's income and expenses. However, all that money is either spent or saved and the outcome cannot be changed. The key objective now is to capture some of this year's money as it comes into your hands and before it is spent on a hundred and one different items, many of which you may be only vaguely aware of at the moment. If you begin to record the details of this year's income and expenses as you go along, day by day and week by week, you can monitor and, if necessary, modify, your spending pattern over the coming twelve months. By doing this you will be able to achieve the savings goal that you are now going to set yourself.

At the outset, you will have to make intelligent guesses about your expected income and expenses for the coming twelve months. It does not greatly matter if the figures turn out to be wildly wrong. The whole point is that during your routine monitoring, you can identify one or two areas where you decide, as you calculate the expenses totals, that your spending is excessive. Alternatively, even if it is not, you can find some items where you think, with some determined action, these are areas where you could economise so that you will have some money to save. If your spending is over budget putting you regularly into debt, you need a system for getting it back again under your control. What you are hoping to see, in the broadest terms, is if your current spending fits with what you are earning or if some drastic revision will be needed, even before your budgeting can begin in earnest.

Your budget can unearth money you never thought you had

To arrive at this decision you can use the prepared budgeting grids at the end of the book. You need a set of three budgeting grids: the first will be for your current, the second for your target, and the third is for your working budget. When I started budgeting, I first sorted out my annual current budget, and then I decided to work with three-month grids for my target and working budgets, all held in my personal organiser. You can use three or six months or yearly budget grids for both your target and working budgets. The way to set out the grids is shown in the budget in the table on page 112, although this only covers a six-months period, not one full year.

Onto the first grid you will enter all the relevant details for your **current budget** covering the past twelve months. These figures will be based on last year's income and expenditure. Of course, your expenses may differ from those in the example overleaf. It saves time if you work in pencil, as plenty of corrections might be needed as you go along. Add up all the separate months' totals to arrive at the full year's budget. On inspecting this, if you identify an overspend or find you are not making the amount of monthly savings you would like, you can then use the second grid to enter in revised figures for what will now become your **target budget** for the coming twelve months. On the target budget, you can set yourself lower totals for some expenses, so that your overall spending stays well within your expected income. The third grid starts out empty. It will become your **working budget**; entries will be made onto it from now on, at the end of every month. Then these figures of what you have actually spent can be compared with your target spending figures set out earlier on the target budget for the corresponding month on the second grid.

Preparing your budget grids for six months

ITEM	Jan	Feb	March	April	May	June	*totals*
income £							
salary							
interest							
bonus							
Totals							
expenses £							
food							
mortgage							
house							
extras							
insurance							
credit cards							
travel							
TV							
tax							
savings							
Totals							

More belt-tightening may be needed if you are overspending, but tracking where all the money is going every month is one of the most methodical ways of keeping within your spending targets. Running budgets like this is how many major companies monitor their expenditure. Seeing it rising at an unacceptable level almost as soon as it has happened is the only way to ensure you can curb the overspend as early as possible. Using this system, during the following month you can focus on the overspend by trying to correct the excesses, to get yourself back more quickly onto the target budget.

A sensible budget is an ideal tool to control debt

Today, there are simple, relatively cheap computer programmes to help people run their household budgets. I was quite happy running my budget manually in my personal organiser. But if you prefer, take advantage of the simplicity provided by the computer approach. However, here, to show you how simple it is to operate a budget without worrying about being incompetent with computers, we can look at how it works in practice.

The Budget In Action

The first task is to calculate reasonable estimates of what you are currently earning this year and split it up according to the way you are paid. You can then enter the monthly totals on your first grid, which will represent your current situation, similar to the one shown in the budget on page 113. Then, using as many of your own

Pay-yourself-first money

is the most important

item on your budget

recent household and other bills and invoices as you have to hand, make estimates of how much you are spending at present on all the major items. Initially, you should work out roughly how much you spend every week on the basic essentials, like food, household expenses, travel, car and house insurance, your mortgage, credit cards, extras, etc. This will probably only be a rough guide. To enter the figures on the first grid, multiply the weekly spending by four, or a little more than 4, to allow for months containing thirty-one days. This will give you figures for what the monthly totals will be.

Having calculated one month's current budget, you can now proceed to repeat the calculations to cover one complete year, filling in each month's total on your first grid. This procedure will allow you to add in any items of income, such as bonuses, or outgoings, like annual subscriptions to clubs or magazines, holidays, TV licence and car insurance that only occur once or twice a year. The budget below sets out an imaginary budget for just six months, to show how it should be arranged.

A typical 'high spender' budget for six months

ITEM	Jan	Feb	March	April	May	June	*totals*
income £							
salary	1420	1420	1420	1420	1420	1420	8520
interest	25			25			50
bonus						350	350
Totals	*1445*	*1420*	*1420*	*1445*	(C) *1420*	*1770*	*8920*
expenses £							
food	350	350	350	350	350	350	(A) 2100
mortgage	200	200	200	200	200	200	1200
house	200	280	200	280	250	200	1410
extras	200	250	250	180	250	200	1330
insurance			300				300
credit cards	120	120	100	120	120	100	680
travel	455	25	25	25	25	25	580
TV	100						100
tax	280	280	280	280	280	280	1680
savings	——	——	——	——	——	——	——
Totals	*1905*	*1505*	*1705*	*1435*	(B) *1475*	*1355*	*9380*

By summing all the figures along the same horizontal line of your yearly grid, you arrive at how much you are spending on each item, for example, food (point A) in one year. Each vertical column of the grid covers one month, so by summing all the figures down one vertical line, you can see how large your expenses (point B) are in relation to your monthly income (point C) say, for May.

Set out in grid fashion, your current budget can be very revealing. For the six-month budget shown above, you can quickly see from the entries several interesting points about running a budget. At first glance, perhaps, the most obvious feature on this budget is that it definitely contains no pay-yourself-first money. All the saving boxes are empty. Worse still, even if they were not, the budget is constantly in overspend territory because the income received in January, February and March is lower than the level of expenses during those three months. The owner of this budget therefore, will be heading for increasing financial difficulties if he simply allows it to carry on along its current course. Not only does it contain no money saved, but its owner could be faced with mounting debt if the budget just continues to drift.

We must now look at this budget in detail, as that would be the next natural step for you to take when analysing your current budget situation. What this analysis will reveal is where all the money in your budget is coming from and going to. The analysis is designed to help you to create a target budget if your current position is unsatisfactory. This will be your blueprint, a target for you to aim for. It will have a positive balance and will also include some money to save.

Having made all the revisions you think necessary, this revised or target budget can then be written out onto your second grid. It now includes some maximum target spending figures for the coming year's budget. At the very least,

A cash flow table

shows you where

your cash is flowing

the aim must be to bring the accounts back into balance, but you should also aim to provide an identifiable sum of money earmarked for saving. On our example, this will be a new entry on the second grid filling the horizontal line allocated for savings. In this case, there will clearly need to be some vigorous reworking of the current spending to allow the savings boxes on the second grid to be filled every month. Everyone who wants to knock their spending into better shape will probably have to write up a target budget on the second grid, because even if you discover you are not overspending, hopefully, most people reading *The Money Maze* will want to find some extra money to create a realistic pay-yourself-first fund.

If we examine the overspend situation on the table from the figures in the right-hand 'totals' column, we see that at the end of six months the running expenses are higher than the salary plus bonuses that are expected to be received. The difference (£8,920 – £9380) only amounts to -£460. This appears to be a modest overspend, but if the anticipated December bonus turns out to be lower than the June bonus, at the end of the first year of budgeting the deficit of expenses over income will be more than the expected £920 (£460 x 2). This is not a very satisfactory situation, especially as there is no cushion of saved money to fall back on. While the annual income on this budget is modest at around £17,840, I would consider this is a 'high spender' budget, as the expenses are higher than is prudent for the amount of income being received.

The owner of this budget is a high spender. He is relying on his bonuses to keep his deficit within manageable proportions. This may be unwise, as we saw what happened to Paula when she relied too heavily on uncertain sources of dividend income. The deficit on this budget can only be contained at this low level if certain key expense items stay within the estimated figures. If spending on food, for example, amounts to more than £350 in any or all of the six months, the deficit will be bigger. This adverse result will also occur if any of the other **variable expenses**, that is, expenses which tend to vary from one month to the next, like extras, credit card spending, or travel, exceed the allotted estimates.

« *Annual income twenty pounds, annual expenditure nineteen nineteen and six, result happiness.*
Annual income twenty pounds, annual expenditure twenty pounds ought and six, result misery. »

David Copperfield, Charles Dickens

At-A-Glance Budgeting

Setting out the budget in this format provides you with a useful 'at-a-glance' grid. All the way down the far right-hand columns you can see quick totals for all the different categories of income and expenses in this budget over the whole six-month period. The figures along the lowest horizontal row of the grid provide a running monthly total to see quickly which are the heavy months as far as the outgoings are concerned. Clearly, January has heavy expenses and so does March, but there is a long wait until June to put the half-yearly bonus into the budget and get the overspend down to a smaller figure again. If this situation were to apply to you, knowing about the delays in advance would be very useful. Being forewarned can allow you to plan ahead for the higher overspend in the January to March period. Perhaps there is some spare cash on deposit that could be paid into the account to keep the budget in credit from January to March. However, as this budget will always be in debit as it currently stands, the lowest horizontal row of the grid (the 'totals' row), is invaluable for sorting out the cash flow, to which we will soon return.

Another instant use of the grid is to allow you to easily sort out those spending areas where expenses are **fixed**, that is, unlikely to change, at least over a six-month period. These items might include the mortgage, TV licence, house and car insurance and the income tax and national insurance deductions. To bring this budget into line with the income, the owner will have to focus on those variable items where he could exercise more spending restraint without driving himself crazy in the attempt. He might choose to concentrate for example, on extras or travel.

Locate Your Budget's 'Black Holes'

Focusing on one or two high-spending items is a realistic way forward. I call these the 'black holes' in the budget. Most people probably have one or two 'black holes' in their spending habits. If you are not very careful, a considerable amount of your hard earned cash can simply disappear down one of these spending 'black holes'.

In our 'high spender' budget example there are at least two 'black hole' areas where a more focused approach could yield good savings: extras and travel. Reducing the six months of spending on extras from £1,330 to £900 will bring the total expenses down to £8,950, which still leaves a small deficit of £30. However, in addition, if travel expenses could be cut from £580 to £450 for the six months, there would be a surplus of £100 over that period, to give a monthly savings amount of around £16 every month.

Focus on the 'black holes'

ITEM	current spend £	target spend £	total saving £
extras	1,330	900	430
travel	580	450	130
Totals	1,910	1,350	560

Budgeting Bonuses

To benefit from budgeting, you will need to be fairly diligent for at least the first year or two. You may even be able to give it up completely at the end of that time, if your saving efforts meet your targets. But while you are budgeting, you should make careful notes of all your daily, weekly and monthly spending. For

Find just one black hole

to fill and you may have

found some pay-

yourself-first cash

the daily running of the budget, use a small notebook or a specially prepared budget grid in your organiser, to enter up all your daily outgoings and basic spending items. These can then be added up on a weekly basis to prepare the monthly totals.

To monitor the budget on a monthly basis, you will use the third grid which now becomes your working budget for the twelve months ahead. At the outset of running this coming year's budget, all the columns and rows will be empty on this third grid. They will be filled in down the second vertical column at the close of the first month, and so on, until the whole six month or yearly budget has been worked through.

Budgeting really gets to work on your overspending when you begin to compare the spending for each completed month with what you had budgeted for on the target budget on the second grid. If, for example, spending on extras is well over your allowance in March, you can go on a savings drive to cut it back more energetically in April. To see how this might operate, we can recap again on the three great advantages in running your budget along these lines.

Shrink The Deficits

First, you can begin to think positively about reducing the existing deficit by searching for the 'black holes'. These are the areas where you think you are spending far more than you should be spending if you are to live within your current income. As we saw in our 'high spender' example, some obvious areas to consider as 'black holes' will be the monthly spending on extras and travel, but other possibilities include store and credit card spending and perhaps even food.

We saw how a saving of £560 could be made by targeting two big items, extras and travel expenses. After deducting the overspend in the budget, this adjustment brought the non-existent pay-yourself first fund up to £100 over the six months. Two more areas could also be addressed. For example, by reducing the food expenditure to £330 per month we could add another £20 per month or £120 over six months, to the savings total. A further £20 each month reduction on the credit card would bring in another £120 over the six months. These additional reductions produce an overall total saved of £340 (£100 + £240 = £340), to raise the monthly saving total to a more respectable level, at £56.

Finding the 'black holes' is the first step to shrinking the deficit. If you decide to target food, you could shop more in your local market, watch closely for cut price items in the supermarket, buy fewer packaged goods by cooking some uncomplicated meals, like baked potatoes in their jackets, homemade pizzas or pasta dishes with grated cheese. If you prefer to cut down on extras, set yourself a strict target for a weekly extras allowance. Allocate a special page in your weekly notebook or personal organiser, and when you have spent a whole week's allocation, try to defer more spending until the start of the following week.

The Budget Challenge

It sounds tedious, but I found it became much more interesting if I treated it as a challenge. Who's in control anyway, I wanted to know, me or my spending whims? However, there is more to budgeting than simply beating the challenge. If you don't persist, you may never build up a cash fund. How will you cope then if you suddenly hit a spell of hard times? That could be a very discouraging experience, as you will remember that you did not succeed in budgeting even when your finances were in better condition.

Uncontrolled overspending will stop being fun on the day of reckoning

Having identified two or three 'black holes' to target, the next step is to concentrate over the coming six months on just those few areas where you hope you can cut back on your spending. Be very strict with budgeting to reduce spending on your 'black hole' areas and you will soon find your budget is responding. And once you get into the swing of it, you are well on the way to achieving the second great advantage of budgeting; to find some pay-yourself-first cash.

Finally, the third great advantage you can get from this system of budgeting is to watch your cash flow. This is the way your incoming money matches, or doesn't match, your outgoings. If there are delays in receiving bonuses, while some months have heavier outgoings than others, you can soon run up to short-term debts. When this happens, you may incur an added expense in interest charges, either to the bank or by not paying off your credit or store card account within the interest-free period. Keeping a budget will quickly identify these irregular incomings and outgoings, and show you how your cash flow is working out on a month-by-month basis.

Our 'high spender's' budget clearly highlights this problem. The deficit develops in January and rises to continue for every month until it falls down again to -£460 when the June bonus is received. The table below shows how the cash flow figures can easily be calculated so that you can cover the shortfall from savings, to prevent the extra cost of interest arising on the overdrawn amounts each month. The trick is to carry down either the deficit or the positive balance at the end of each month, by deducting the total expenses from the total income. You then carry forward that figure to the start of the next month. If there is a deficit, it represents an overspend from the last month. You must then add it in when you come to work out the carry down figure for the second month.

Obviously, a deficit gets worse if there is another deficit at the end of the second month, because if there is insufficient income, the two deficits will have to be added in to that month's expenses. And if the third month opens with this mounting deficit, will it get worse or better? Scanning the budget gives the answer ahead of the event. In the example shown below, the deficit in month 3, March, will get worse. Putting figures on the 'high spender' example, January's overspend was -£460. This will be carried forward to the beginning of February. By the end of that month the overspend will have risen to -£545. If this deficit is in turn added to the start of March, it grows to -£830 by the end of March.

Although the table below shows just the rows and columns necessary for calculating the cash flow, by modifying your initial budget grids, you can easily add the necessary rows so you can follow your cash flow information every month on your working budget grid. This adjustment has been made to the budget given in the Action Plan section of chapter 9.

Calculating the cash flow

ITEM	Jan	Feb	Mar	April	May	Jun
carried for'd £		−460	−545	−830	−820	−875
income £	1445	1420	1420	1445	1420	1770
expenses £	1905	1505	1705	1435	1475	1355
difference £	−460	−545	−830	−820	−875	−460
carry down £	−460	−545	−830	−820	−875	−460

Benefits Start Building

For the 'high spender' budget, you can see that the deficits will rise for three months starting in January. They don't begin to fall by any reasonable amount until May. Even after the payment of the June bonus, the deficit is still -£460. If you face a similar situation, knowing all this in good time, you can really start to make an inroad into your overspend. Don't just try to get back to balance but aim to find at least £25 pounds every month to start building your pay-yourself-first fund. But beware of setting yourself impossible targets. It's a bit like dieting. You will get much better results if you try to make steady progress over the first one or two years. It will be totally counterproductive if you tackle it with a fanatical zeal that finally runs out of momentum long before you have achieved your budget targets. If your salary exceeds our example figure of £17,840 by, say, £3,000 or more, you should make a determined effort to find at least £40 or £50 to save every month. Obviously, the more cash you can save, the better.

The first pleasure of financial security is to dump the budget

I certainly became a bit manic about budgeting in 1990 when I started in earnest to tackle our huge debt problem, but I stuck to it until my obsession finally petered out after four years. By 1994, I suddenly realised that we had virtually rebuilt our capital. Once I knew there was enough money to live on, I asked myself, "Why am I bothering with this?" I completely stopped worrying about my budget. What a pleasure it was to just give it up, there and then.

Stay With Budgeting

I still try to save for a retirement that I hope will extend for very many years ahead. But now I simply keep a broad overview of where the money is coming from each month and where it is going every week. That, in a nut shell, is what budgeting is all about.

One useful idea that I discovered purely by chance has proved invaluable. At the local branch of the bank where we keep our current and savings accounts, the manager was quite happy to provide weekly statements free of charge, instead of the usual monthly statements. This enables me to keep a very close watch on all the bank transactions in the week immediately after they occur, making it far easier to spot errors and omissions on a weekly rather than a monthly basis. Not all banks offer a free service on additional statements, unfortunately, but you could try this one on your bank manager! The reason my bank gave for this helpful aid was that they were keen to see people running their accounts better. Exactly so. I have found weekly statements are a great help for both keeping control and staying in credit. If, however, you cannot obtain free weekly statements a weekly computer printout of your current account from your branch is a close alternative and is free at most banks.

The Yearly Wealth Check

Once you have come to grips with the detail of your annual budget you are only a small step away from doing a wealth check. I talked about the value of a yearly wealth check in *The Armchair Investor*. It is the quickest route to discovering the size of your assets, or possessions and the amounts of your debts, or liabilities. Working out your initial wealth check is the first step to discovering whether on your current course, you will ever be able to acquire a nest egg.

« *There is only one long-range financial plan you need, and that is the intention to get rich.* »

Max Gunther

To prepare a wealth check for yourself, you need to make two lists side by side on a clean sheet of paper. The first list will contain all your valuable assets, including your house, car, jewellery, antiques and any other possessions that have an inbuilt monetary value. Then you set out the second list, which comprises all your current debts. These will include your mortgage, loans on your car or furniture, credit card debts which you are not planning to repay within the immediate interest-free period and any other debts you may owe. By adding up the items in each list you can deduct your total debts from your total assets to see what the balance of your wealth currently stands at. This balancing figure is often called your **net worth**. An example is shown below.

A yearly wealth check

ITEMS	current value £	outstand'g debts	current value £
house	75,000	mortgage	−65,000
car	7,000	5-yr loan	−6,750
building society		credit cards	−4,500
deposits	3,500	store cards	−1,000
life assurance	50,000	hi-fi system	−1,200
Totals	*135,500*	*Totals*	*−78,450*

Net worth: £57,050 (£135,500 − £78,450)

Do not be too alarmed if your total liabilities greatly exceed your assets. The idea of doing a wealth check which you can monitor on a once-yearly basis is purely to identify how far away you currently are from building up secure financial assets. Once you have seen the deficits, if any, you are in a better position to begin to put that situation right. Even if you discover you are poorly placed and are well up on the investment staircase, nearing retirement at steps 5 or 6, do not take fright. There is still time to knock your finances into much better shape.

In chapter 9 we shall cover the details of how to organise a constructive plan to start this process in earnest.

If you are still on steps 2, 3 and 4, perhaps with a young and growing family, you will probably have many large commitments and outgoings to meet. However, once you have clearly laid out your true financial position, it can act as a strong stimulus to set you thinking about how you can improve it. There is, hopefully, plenty of time for you to rectify the situation and begin building up your assets for the future.

Set Your Money Targets

With your wealth check laid out before you, now is the time to set targets for building up a capital sum. It is easier to plan for this if you have some specific goal in mind. Do you need to save a cash deposit to move to a larger house? Will you want to build an extension on your present home? Whatever your goal, now is the time to decide where this cash saving will be coming from, which is why doing the wealth check follows on so naturally from your budgeting exercise. If you have allowed yourself four to six years in which to build up your target lump sum, you can monitor your progress by reworking your wealth check once every year. Clearly, the capital you will want to accumulate will include the main building blocks of your financial pyramid, so let us now turn to chapter 6, to look at all these blocks in detail.

« *The only limit to our realization of tomorrow will be our doubts of today.* »

Franklin D. Roosevelt, 1945

Key Points To Remember

1 Find a pay-yourself-first fund.

2 Live like a Lord on unearned income.

3 Income is regular money from a reliable source to spend on daily expenses.

4 Protect your capital; it is your passport to wealth.

5 Vanishing capital means vanishing income.

6 Budgeting puts you in control.

7 Budget to find your pay-yourself-first fund.

8 Find the 'black holes' in your spending.

9 Follow the cash flow to keep ahead of the deficits.

10 Do a yearly wealth check.

CHAPTER 6

Build

YOUR *financial*

PYRAMID

'History shows that over the medium to long term, only asset backed investments have the ability to deliver growth in both capital and income above the rate of inflation. This is vital because as people live longer so their investments have to last longer and achieve more.'

An Introduction to Investments, *Legal & General*

You cannot begin to build your financial pyramid until you start to focus on a pay-yourself-first fund. This is the fund that takes money from your income and turns it into future capital. You will obtain many great bonuses by carefully planning and then building your own pyramid. But by far the greatest is the point we made earlier: the best route to big financial rewards comes from plenty of careful preparation according to a blueprint plan. The use of a financial pyramid provides exactly this. Clearly, the best time to build the biggest pyramid is to start, if possible, well before you are launched on the forty years that form your whole working life. It's a nice thought to recall that the great pharaohs of ancient Egypt actually built their pyramids during their lifetimes; they built to provide an eternal monument for their final resting place. We should be building to create our own financial security.

A start as early as step 1 on the investment staircase would be ideal to really get the full benefits of money doubling. Parents or grandparents can begin gifting money to children with that purpose directly in mind. If you are further up, at steps 3, 4 or 5, do not be depressed. But you will have to work smarter at building your pyramid, to catch up for those lost years. As we saw in chapter 1, your financial pyramid is an excellent way of steadily constructing the building blocks to wealth. It is relevant to everyone as they mount the investments stairs, no matter whether you are in your twenties, thirties, forties, fifties, or even in your sixties. And even at sixty, if your retirement is going to last for hopefully another twenty to thirty years, you should still be trying to increase the size of your financial pyramid just in case you run into an unexpected setback during that long period. Remember, for example, that the death of a husband who had the lion's share of a personal pension scheme, can eliminate a major source of replacement income for the bereaved widow.

« *I am convinced that every dollar a young man saves, properly invested, will return him twenty over the course of his life.* »
Investment Biker, Jim Rogers

Savings and Investment Needs

To guide you in your thinking we will look first at the general savings and investment needs most people should plan for because, as you mount the investment staircase, your financial priorities change. However, everyone of working age, from twenty to sixty-five needs to save and invest both for retirement and for future major events. All working people should also consider protecting their income in case they become seriously ill.

For people of working age but with no family ties, including children and the twenty-plus and thirty-plus age groups, the top priority is to save and invest for the future. The earlier this begins, the larger the eventual capital saved will be.

For the thirty-plus age group who have young dependents, in addition to saving and investing for retirement and major events, there is the added need for protection on three separate fronts at least. They should consider taking out a policy to protect income in case of serious illness. They should also protect all their debts, including the mortgage, in case they die before these are repaid, together with life assurance to provide a reasonably sized income for a surviving widow or widower.

If you die and leave a young family, the state will not provide enough replacement income for them to live on. Buying adequate life assurance when you are young is good value for money to ensure your family is left well provided for in the event of your untimely death. For young, healthy adults, life cover is cheap. If you begin to build your financial pyramid along the lines we are exploring here, you will have amassed a tidy lump sum as some of your life cover expires and ceases to operate. It will have been replaced by the savings you are building.

Moving up the staircase, for the forty-plus and fifty-plus age groups, saving and investing for retirement becomes a larger priority. This will include both pensions planning and using stock market-related investments, initially through unit or investment trusts. Later, and for the more experienced investor, buying and holding publicly quoted companies is an additional route for investing. If you have set your heart on early retirement, which is becoming an increasingly popular option for those in work, an extra-concentrated effort to build your funds through directly held equities can make a huge impact on the size of your freely available funds. This happened in my family when my husband retired two years earlier than scheduled, although we had originally hoped the early retirement would have been for five years rather than two. Protection for income to cover debts and life assurance may still be needed, especially for parents helping youngsters through college. Many parents today also try to help their youngsters with house deposits or setting up in business. All these items can become future claims on the savings pot. For those already in retirement, financial security may seem an elusive goal. We will look later at some options for the over-sixties who are already on the topmost stair.

This summary may seem complicated, but remember, we have whizzed up the whole investment staircase in a few condensed paragraphs. Hopefully, you have a lifetime to turn your financial dreams into reality. When you are making your plans, it will literally take years just to move up each stair, giving you lots of time to improve your financial expertise as you go without the planning becoming too much of an obsessive effort. So now we will turn to consider the three major blocks of financial pyramid building.

A Home To Own

Although it looked at first sight that our high spender in the example budget in chapter 5 was not making any headway with his pyramid plans, he did have a mortgage, so he was actually building what I consider to be the first major block in the financial pyramid. Around 68 per cent of people in Britain own their own homes, which is a higher figure than is found in many other countries across Europe. The wide prevalence of owning a home in the UK means that most young people in their twenties want to follow this well established tradition. They will usually hope to buy their own flat or house at an early date, as soon as they have found a reliable job to fund it from.

Currently, buying a house is one of the largest investments most people make during their adult lives. It is also probably the single largest transaction that they ever make, amounting to many tens of thousands of pounds. However, owning a home is only one of three vitally important blocks in building your financial pyramid. It is equally important to think at an early stage about building up the other two blocks. This means planning to build your pension to a substantial size if possible, and having some insurance-based savings. These types of saving schemes are less volatile than owning stocks and shares directly. They are, therefore, ideal foundations on which to add some more volatile investments which, hopefully, have the potential to provide the largest capital growth.

Unfortunately, in Britain, although most people do want to own their own homes, that seems to be as far as many get constructively in building their financial pyramids. But you cannot eat the bricks and mortar of your home. Nor can you earn an income from it unless you rent out rooms to paying guests or lodgers. The three-pronged basis of a financial pyramid therefore offers more security and flexibility. All three are equally pivotal and are essential elements for achieving wealth creation. Nevertheless, owning your own home is a crucial starting point for most people wanting to build up assets.

I like to think of buying a house as a form of compulsory saving. But it can be your passport to much more, if you understand how to exploit the huge opportunities it offers. Yet, even without knowing the real inside story on how a mortgage can make you richer than you would otherwise have been, it still is one of the cheapest routes for borrowing money you can find. Mortgage rates are invariably much lower than rates for personal loans from banks, primarily because the lender has the full value of your property to fall back on if you **default** on your repayments. This security allows the bank or building society to offer you money at a highly attractive rate.

Your home may not be a castle but it can be a big money box

Of course, many commentators point out that when you borrow £50,000 from a lender to buy a house, you will probably have to repay a sum of money in the order of well over two times more than you borrowed, say around £120,000. However, this cost will be spread over about twenty or twenty-five years. Hopefully, during this long time you will not be idle, but will be beavering away at building the other blocks in your growing pyramid. Then, when your mortgage is finally repaid, your house will not be your only major financial asset. This is the happy situation all long-term planning should be aiming to provide.

On the matter of the large amount the borrowing will cost, now we understand how money works, these repayment figures should not surprise us. As we saw in chapter 2, money magic really gets to work the longer it is allowed to run. The secret for getting the most out of this tremendously cheap loan is to understand right at the outset that it is just one block of three to pave the way for financial security. If you use your mortgage facility actively, you should make full use of the low interest rates you pay by starting to save separately, alongside this oh-so-cheap mortgage as soon as you can. In this way, you will gain far more than just owning your home outright, although I think that achievement alone is a wonderful financial boon. Clearly, when your mortgage is fully repaid, you can live on a much lower income, as the rent element of your expenses (in the form of your mortgage repayments) has been totally eliminated from your budget. Even if your house never increased in value over the whole of your lifetime, once you own it, eliminating the rent element from your living expenses is a very valuable financial advantage.

During the research for the second television series of *Mrs Cohen's Money*, I discovered that many mortgage contracts can be weighted most heavily in favour of the lenders, which means you must be extra vigilant when choosing a mortgage, especially as far as the small print clauses are concerned. In spite of this cautionary warning, I think mortgages to fund the purchase of your own home are very good news for everyone. However, not all financial advisers see mortgages in the positive way that I do. But I would like to tell you about three major benefits which I think stem directly from taking out a mortgage to buy your own home; they cover the impact of inflation, the effect of **gearing** (which concerns the size of your initial debt relative to the value of the house) and third, your ability to make supplementary savings. So we will look more closely at these three advantages in turn, starting with the boost mortgage holders get from inflation.

« *Everything they had was borrowed; they had nothing of their own at all.* »

The Borrowers, Mary Norton

Big Borrowers Love Inflation

We have already seen that for savers inflation is very bad news because it eats into the real value of their capital, leaving them poorer than they would be in a non-inflationary world. But people who borrow the money that savers save gain an unexpected benefit if there is inflation. The sums to explain this hidden gain are simple but because people think in terms of ordinary numbers, the boon of inflation to borrowers often goes unrecognised. Once you begin to think, not in round numbers but in terms of what your money will buy, that is, its **purchasing power**, you will be taking inflation into account and the borrowing story can become entirely transformed.

Suppose your annual mortgage interest rate is 8 per cent and inflation is currently a meagre 3 per cent a year. In real terms, after taking the inflation into account, your interest rate has dropped to the difference between the two. That is a miserly 5 per cent (8 – 3 = 5). When you borrow to buy a home in a period of inflation, you get a double benefit whammy. First, your real interest rate is smaller than the nominal (viewed in money terms) rate; and second, real assets, like stocks and shares, antiques and property, tend to rise during a period of inflation. The value of your new home should therefore be rising while you are paying off your oh-so-cheap mortgage.

If you are getting the benefit of inflation, does this mean the building society has got a bad deal? The building society acts purely as an intermediary, a middle-

Mary was a

marvellous

housekeeper. She

was divorced three

times and every

time she kept the

house!

man institution. The movement was first set up during the eighteenth century to put savers and borrowers into contact. People with money could earn a return by lending it indirectly to people who wanted to buy their own homes.

It is the savers who pay the price for inflation. When they understand how it robs them, they try to counteract inflation by moving their funds into areas which will at least keep pace with the rising cost of living. But for far too many people in Britain during the inflation-prone 1970s and 1980s, their fear of losing money in stock market-related investments kept them tied to their bank or building society accounts. Sadly, these were adversely affected by the high levels of inflation that prevailed during that long period. Often the savings rate, after deducting out the prevailing inflation, was negative. If the rate of inflation was 10 per cent (as we saw, it went as high as 27 per cent during the 1970s) and the rate of interest on deposits was 8 per cent, the saver was actually 2 per cent out of pocket on his interest for that year, without taking into account the loss in purchasing power of his capital.

« *People perceive equity investments as risky. But the performance statistics prove that deposit accounts are the real gamble.* »

Anne McMeehan, director of communications at Autif
(Association of Unit Trusts and Investment Funds)

Wasting Assets Don't Grow

To understand how you gain added value during periodic bouts of inflation over the twenty years of your mortgage, you can compare it with the situation that arises if you buy a series of cars using bank loans. Suppose the year you buy your house you also buy a new car costing £10,000, using a bank loan over five years. At the end of that time, you exchange your car for another new one, and if we suppose you get £2,500 in part-exchange but now buy a car costing £12,500, you will again borrow £10,000 over five years. If you repeat this exercise twice more, you will have bought four new cars over the twenty years you are repaying your mortgage. The overall outlay for the cars will be £40,000 plus all the interest you paid on the loans. If you use an **unsecured** bank loan, the bank will not demand that you lodge other assets with them to protect their loan. An unsecured bank loan of £10,000 for five years would cost around £3,625 in interest at an annual percentage rate (called the APR) of 13.9. For the purpose of keeping this comparison simple, we will assume that the interest rates stay fairly stable, although this is a big assumption which would almost certainly never apply in practice! If we multiply the interest figure of £3,625 by 4, we arrive at a total of £14,500 as the cost of interest on all four cars. The total cost of the cars over twenty years will therefore be £40,000 plus £14,500, that is, £54,500. At the end of that time, we will assume the fourth car has a value of around £2,500 to £3,000.

Although owning a car provides many big benefits, making money is not one of them. You have lost around £51,000 to £52,000 for this privilege.

Buying four cars over twenty years

years	cost of cars (less cash back) £	interest paid over five years £
1–5	10,000	3,625
6–10	10,000	3,625
11–15	10,000	3,625
16–20	10,000	3,625
Totals	40,000	14,500

overall total £54,500

value of 4th car at end of year 20 = £3,000

overall loss from buying 4 cars – £51,500

These figures illustrate the vast differences that arise when money is spent on real assets which hold or increase their value over time and a wasting asset, like a car, that wears out over time and loses most of the value it started out with when new.

« *Inflation is like sin:*
every government denounces it and every government practises it.»

Sir Frederick Leith-Ross

But suppose that ten years after you first set up your mortgage, you want to borrow a sum of money over a five year period to buy that car. As we have seen, the rate of interest you will have to pay on a personal loan will be much higher than your mortgage. It could be around 14 to 20 per cent. So to take the best advantage of your mortgage, if you borrow as large an amount as you can at the outset, you should make supplementary savings plans as you go along. Then you may have saved some money to pay at least part of the cost of your new car when you come to want it in ten years time. Later in the chapter we will discuss how to organise this additional saving.

Gearing Up

Gearing is the second big bonus from buying your own home on a mortgage. It is yet another example of money magic. It is the relationship between *loan* money and *owner* money. High gearing means high loans with large total interest repayments; low gearing means small loans with smaller total interest repayments. Intuitively, you would suspect that high gearing is more risky than low gearing.

And, of course, that is right. But, as long as you keep a tight control over your budget to ensure you meet your loan repayments on time, high gearing is a wonderful aid to wealth creation. Public companies use it constantly. So how does it apply when buying a house?

« *The secret of many fortunes made in real estate is a simple one: OPM, which stands for other people's money.* »

Richard H. Goldberg

Supposing the house you buy cost £50,000 on which you can afford to make a down payment of £5,000 and you arrange a 20-year mortgage to pay off the balance. At the outset, you will only own 10 per cent of your property (£5,000 ÷ £50,000 × 100 = 10), while the building society will be the major investor because your loan amounts to 90 per cent (£45,000 ÷ £50,000 × 100 = 90). Say, for the sake of our illustration, that your house had ten areas, (a kitchen, bathroom, downstairs toilet, lounge and dining room, three bedrooms, a garden and a garage). If you own 10 per cent, you will only own one area while the building society has the giant's share of nine areas. This is very high gearing indeed. It looks as if the building society has got a bargain, but in fact, you will be the winner, hands down. The first house diagram (A) shows how things stand at the outset, when you move in and start paying off the mortgage. Only one-tenth of your property is yours, nine-tenths is controlled by the building society. But the gearing effect will usually begin to work in your favour right away.

Diagram (A) Your house when the mortgage begins; your share is 10 per cent; the building society's share is 90 per cent

Suppose the value of the house rises by 3.5 per cent every year for the whole twenty years of the mortgage. In practice, this is highly unlikely. What has usually happened in the past is that house prices may be static or even decline over a few years. Then they might rise at a rate of around 3 per cent or possibly more, for a few years. Of course, it is essential to realise that what has happened in the past may not be repeated in the future, but it gives us a rough guide to work with. As a house is a real asset, values tend to rise more noticeably during periodic bouts of high inflation. A house is a valuable real asset because there is always only a limited supply of suitable land for building on, especially in the most desirable parts of the country and in towns. For this reason alone, given enough time, houses do generally rise in value, although the timing could be erratic or it may take many decades for the rise to occur.

As we saw in chapter 2, if we divide the growth rate into 70 we shall find how many years it will take for this house to double in value, from £50,000 to £100,000. In this case, the answer is conveniently 20 years (70 ÷ 3.5 = 20). After 20 years the ownership of the house will have completely reversed: you will own it all at a value of £100,000 while the building society will no longer have any interest in the property and the mortgage will have been totally repaid. This is the situation shown in diagram (B) below.

100%

Diagram (B) You own 100 per cent of the house: the building society now owns nothing.

Still using approximate figures, after twenty years, and using interest rates of around 8–9 per cent each year with an interest only loan, you will have paid about £75,000 in interest on your loan, plus £45,000 to repay the loan and the £5,000 as your initial deposit. You will have spent a total of around £125,000. But if your house is now worth £100,000 the cost to you has been £125,000 to gain an asset worth £100,000. Therefore, the real cost over the twenty years it took you to buy it, has been £25,000. On a first impression, this sounds a bit suspicious. Although you did indeed pay out £120,000 in hard cash, the rising value of the house, due to the impact of inflation on real assets, has locked in added value to the property.

But the building society's share of your property consisted solely of a loan, fixed at £45,000, at the date when you first took out your mortgage, twenty years earlier. All the added value in the property therefore, has come directly to you; none of it went to your lender.

> A mortgage allows you to turn a huge debt into a real asset

This is the power of gearing during periods of inflation; it is working to make your money work. It sounds like magic, but the secret is simply that the building society always has a fixed interest in your property which will never exceed £45,000, unless you increase the size of the loan at some future date. As the value of the house rises, all the growth that occurs belongs to you alone; none of it goes to the building society. Indeed, with the rise in the value, the building society's share will gradually fall from the 90 per cent it was at the outset to a figure of zero, as you repay the debt. Meanwhile, because your house is increasing in value over the twenty years, the outright total of the debt at £45,000 becomes a relatively smaller percentage of your asset, even if you do not pay off any capital during the term of the loan. This arrangement will apply if you have chosen an **interest only** loan where, in addition to the interest due, you pay premiums into an endowment policy throughout the twenty years. The policy will hopefully increase in value to mature and repay the total loan of £45,000 at the end of the term.

Money doubling is surely the eighth wonder of the world

Before you rush out to buy yourself a home on a mortgage to take advantage of the benefits of gearing, you should be aware that high gearing will work in reverse when there is **deflation**, (falling prices) rather than inflation. This is the situation that occurred during the early 1990s when interest rates rose very steeply. Many people with large mortgages suddenly discovered that high gearing had wiped out all their value in a property as prices declined. As in all financial planning, therefore, it is essential never to over-extend yourself when you borrow.

We can illustrate the benefits of gearing with an example based on a **repayment mortgage.** Here, instead of paying interest only throughout the term of the loan, you repay both interest and capital as you go along. In the early years, most of the payment is in interest. Therefore, after say, the first seven years on a repayment mortgage, very little of the capital will have been repaid. The value of the house, however, might have risen 15 per cent, to £57,500. As you will still owe the building society only £45,000, their percentage share of the house has fallen to 78.26 per cent (£45,000 ÷ £57,500 × 100 = 78.26) and your share has risen to £12,500 (£57,500 − £45,000 = £12,500). This is 21.74 per cent of the rising value (£12,500 ÷ £57,500 × 100 = 21.74). At the outset, you only owned £5,000, or 10 per cent, in your home. So on this modest 15 per cent rate of house price rise, in just seven years, you have more than doubled your share of its value.

As the years pass, with the building society share still fixed at £45,000 your share in the rising value of the house will go on increasing. The gearing works in your favour because you are the long-term saver and the building society's share in your home is fixed right at the outset. They will give you a splendid low rate of interest at around 7 to 9 per cent, on the security of your home, far lower than any other short-term lender will provide. Although the rate of interest is frequently variable, meaning it will rise and fall as interest rates in the wider economy rise or fall, it still competes favourably with any other loan rates to be found on the high street.

Own Your Home

Although things changed very drastically for the worse during the early 1990s, the sums for house ownership have been favourable to home buyers over the past fifty or sixty years. If you enter into home-ownership with a mortgage as part of your long-term investment plan, buying a property on a mortgage is a form of compulsory saving. To illustrate the point, suppose instead you had chosen to save this £100,000 outright before buying your house. To save this amount and assuming a 5 per cent annual interest rate throughout, you would have needed to save £4,000 every year for fifteen years, to keep the pot growing. However, this takes no account of tax that has to be paid on interest earned. After seven years the tax payable on your growing fund would have been over £1,620 per year, rising to £4,730 by year fifteen. Taking taxation into consideration, therefore, means it might take a full twenty years to save that £100,000.

Moreover, while you are saving up this wonderful fund, you will have to live somewhere and, presumably, pay rent. Assuming you chose to rent a small house similar to the one you might have bought for £50,000, the rent could be around say, £500 each month. This would add at least another £6,000 in expenses every year. By the time you had spent twenty years saving the £100,000 to buy your home, the rent alone would have cost you about £120,000 assuming, doubtfully, that the rent did not rise to keep pace with inflation during that long saving period.

« *The house was more covered with mortgages than with paint.* »

George Ade

Put like this you can begin to see what a superb investment it is to buy your own house as the first block in your financial pyramid. Even if you are Mr and Mrs Average, moving house about every seven years, the arguments still apply, because most people need a long-term loan to build up enough cash to pay for an expensive item like a home over around twenty to twenty-five years.

What is more, a homeowner can still be a gainer if there is no inflation. The no-inflation sums work out like this: to build a sum of £50,000 by saving £4,000 a year at 5 per cent annual interest, you will need to rent a place to live over the twelve and a half years it will take to accumulate £50,000. If the rent is £500 every month, this will cost another £75,000 in rent alone. So the full cost of saving up £50,000 to buy your home outright will be £125,000. And if you never own your home, you will have to continue paying rent right throughout your adult life, or around sixty years. For a frugal place to live in, this could amount to £360,000 in the unlikely event that your rent stayed fixed at £500 per month throughout that whole period.

It is because you will finally achieve this excellent rent-free period when your mortgage is fully repaid that I consider home ownership to be the most important first block in building your financial pyramid. If you buy a house when aged thirty and repay your mortgage twenty-five years later, just about the time you may be saving for retirement as sixty-five, you will never need to pay the equivalent of rent, right through the whole period of your retirement. And this will still be the case if you have moved two or three times during the duration of your loan. When you begin to live rent-free, you realise what a wonderful method of compulsory saving home ownership really is.

The Savings Boost

However, saving steadily to repay your mortgage is not the only available route to strengthening your financial pyramid. The supplementary saving idea is the third major boost that you get from buying your property at an early age on a long–term mortgage. It relies on another of my father's helpful money tips. He said

« *Why use your own money to buy a house when you can use someone else's?* »

If we now think about the long twenty years you will be paying off your mortgage of £45,000, the amount will be spread so that, ignoring any big rises in interest rates, the interest costs will be around £3,600 every year. But hopefully, as you mount the investment staircase, by the time you reach your thirties you should be able to put some money away into savings even if you now have expensive children to provide for. Then, instead of taking out loans which will cost far more than the 7 to 9 per cent or so you are paying on your mortgage, you can build up your savings because your mortgage is fixed at around the same level it was, say, ten years earlier, when your salary was much lower. As a sensible route to financial security, I think supplementary saving is a far better use of your resources than trying to repay your mortgage in a shorter period, of say fifteen years. However, if you do not make any additional savings plans, then you have not taken full advantage of the cheap loan the building society provides over such a long period.

Which Mortgage?

As we noted earlier, you can buy your house on two different schemes. The first, with a straight repayment arrangement, means you will be paying off both the capital and the outstanding interest on it, throughout the term of the mortgage. The second route is with an interest only loan, usually linked to an endowment policy. Here, you continue right through the loan period to pay interest on the full loan, but you take out a savings policy to run in tandem with the mortgage, hoping that over the lifetime of the loan, this plan will make sufficient profits to repay your total mortgage at the end of the term. How should you decide between these two types of mortgage?

Comparing interest only and repayment mortgages

features	interest only mortgage	repayment mortgage
protection of debt	life cover included	separate life cover required
reduction of debt	holds at full level through-out the term	reduces with every year, although not greatly until year 7
frequent house moves	take your endowment policy with you	must start again from scratch
extra savings	only if the endowment performs well	only if additional saving is taken out separately
problems with high interest rates	debt level stays at maximum throughout the term, therefore high interest rates can be a serious drawback	debt level falls throughout the term, therefore high interest rates become less important as the term reduces
simple to understand	interest only can be more difficult to understand	repayment mortgage is simpler to understand
security of savings	you may think you are saving but you are only paying off your debt	you know you are not saving unless you make separate arrangements

I personally prefer a repayment mortgage, for several reasons. First, is the simplicity it offers. As you go along, you know you are repaying your debt, although this does not really begin in earnest until around the seventh year of paying off the loan. Second, with the mortgage taken care of, that allows you to concentrate on building up savings for other events. Third, interest rates may suddenly rise, say after fifteen years. But the capital element owing in your loan will have begun to fall quite steeply at around that time, if you have a repayment plan. So even if interest rates rise, you will be paying interest on a smaller amount of outstanding capital. However, a repayment mortgage makes no provision for repaying the debt in the event of an untimely death. The responsibility to take out a **term assurance** life policy to cover the loan in the event of death rests, therefore, with you, the borrower.

Investing with hindsight is a mug's game

By contrast, when you fund an endowment plan to pay off your mortgage loan, you might be tempted to think you are saving for the future. You may feel more secure than is warranted because you know that you are slowly building up a pot of capital. However, companies who offer these products now stress that in a period of low inflation, returns on them may not be enough to repay all the debt. This is especially relevant to **low-start** mortgage schemes, which are offered to first time buyers. Here the premiums start at a low level and slowly build up to the maximum amount over five years. With these schemes, your savings pot may be inadequate to meet the full debt in due course, but even if it does pay off the entire mortgage, there may not be a large surplus to fund anything else. Moreover, if you hit a spell of high or rising interest rates after fifteen years into your term, you will have to pay interest at this high level on the total loan, as it is all still outstanding. However the endowment policy does include life cover for the whole debt and is transferable to a new mortage if you move.

Instinct and

common sense are

important

investment tools

that should be in

constant use

If you are young and healthy, buying life cover is not an expensive outlay, but it does have to be set up separately if you choose a repayment mortgage. This can in fact, be an advantage, if it sets you thinking about taking out other supplementary savings plans at an early stage. These therefore, should form the third block in building your financial pyramid, but before we look at them in detail, we must consider your next major financial goal, which involves building up your pension plan to replace your regular income when you retire.

Your Pension Pot

Although at present, people who do not earn an income cannot build up a pension, the Labour government, elected in 1997, may change these rules. They want to persuade people to take more control of their own retirement needs. Even if you are someone who cannot at present fund a pension, do not be unduly concerned. Although we are looking at all the building blocks for an *ideal* financial pyramid, there is, fortunately, more than one way to build it. Each individual will use only those building blocks that suit his personal situation. I was not in a position to fund a realistic pension during my adult life, but that did not stop me using the stock market to build a sizeable nest egg for retirement. As a married couple, my husband and I use his pension for our living expenses and the dividends from our portfolio of shares now act as a growing supplement.

« *Better to have fine clothes and a grand salon, and eat dry bread in secret.* »

Letizia Bonaparte, mother to the Emperor, Napoleon Bonaparte

For people with jobs, throughout your working life, part of your compulsory National Insurance (NI) contribution goes towards building up your entitlement to a state pension. This consists of two parts: the basic pension and the additional state earnings related pension (Serps), which is linked to your earnings and is added on to the basic pension. Serps was introduced in 1978 to supplement employee pensions for those without a company scheme, estimated at about half the working population, but the self-employed are not eligible. The size of your state pension will ultimately depend on your lifetime's NI contributions, as both the basic pension and Serps are funded by NI contributions. However, in money terms, as we saw, the state pension has shrunk over the past eighteen years, to only around 16 per cent of average earnings. This is clearly an inadequate sum for any-one to live on and it is forecast to fall by around half this figure over the next two decades. The maximum pension is only paid to men who have worked full-time for forty-four years and to women who worked for thirty-nine years.

When we look at what happens to the NI contributions you make, we discover the major flaw in the system which ensures massive changes will have to be made. Your NI contributions are not invested into a fund to build up your pension in the way they would be if you were paying premiums into a personal or company pension scheme; they are paid out directly as pensions to today's pensioners. Obviously, this system will not be sustainable in the future if there are fewer workers to support rising numbers of pensioners. It is to address this problem that recent governments are looking at ways to persuade, or even force, the working population to take on more of their pension planning directly for themselves.

Around seven million people contribute to personal pensions, which will provide an income on top of the basic state pension. However, no one can pay money into a personal pension and be a member of a company scheme unless that is funded from different income sources. Some or all of the cash going into your personal pension plan may come from the state rather than directly from you, if you have opted out of the Serps system. On top of your invested NI contributions (up to 4.8 per cent of salary between set limits) you can also make regular contributions of your own. These are termed **voluntary contributions**. Of the five million who opted out of Serps in favour of personal pensions after 1988, over three million do not make extra contributions on top of the state rebate and therefore will receive inadequate pensions.

« *We continue to overlook the fact that work has become a leisure activity.* »

Mark Abrams

On the present system, very few workers overall build up the full pension that the tax regime allows, although public sector professional workers do have an excellent, well funded system provided entirely by the state. Many directors of large public companies also have ample pension arrangements organised by the company that employs them. But unless you have a marvellous job with fantastic prospects and bonuses, it will probably take you your whole working life to build up a pension 'pot' which has grown large enough to buy you a pension (or **annuity,** which is an income guaranteed for life) that is about 70 per cent of your gross income in your last year of work. This pension pot will then be needed to provide a replacement income during your retirement. The entire fund will be used to buy you a pensions annuity (although personal pensions allow you to take 25 per cent as a tax-free lump sum if you prefer). The annuity provides a guaranteed income – usually for life – in return for the lump sum investment you have been accumulating while you were working.

In practice, you will buy an annuity only if you have built your own pension fund through a **'money purchase'** scheme, also known as a **defined contribution**. The millions covered by this type of plan include all the self-employed and, increasingly, many employees. The money purchase scheme arises when you have either invested in a personal pension plan on your own or through a scheme which involves contributions from your employer. A 'money purchase' arrangement is becoming more popular not because it is a better scheme, but because it depends on the investment performance of the funds being saved. This puts the onus for pensions provision on the employee, rather than the employer.

It differs from **'final salary'** company pension schemes, also called **defined benefits,** which are organised by your employer for the duration of the time you are working in that employment. This will provide you with a pre-agreed level of pension during retirement. The final salary option is usually based on providing two-thirds of your salary in the form of a pension. However, this is more expensive for employers as it commits them to pay benefits related to your final salary even if the investment fund is not large enough to provide that level of pension. Recent changes in pensions law, especially in 1997, made pension planning more expensive. Therefore, more employers might, in future, decide against a final salary scheme. Moreover, although such pensions are ideal for highly paid long-serving employees, including company directors, they are hopelessly inadequate for employees who change jobs frequently. Frozen contributions in many funds are a serious handicap for them. The Office of Fair Trading produced a report on pensions, highlighting such defects for women who take career breaks to have a family and those who make many job moves. The report said a worker who changed jobs several times could find his or her pension was up to 30 per cent lower than someone who stayed in one scheme throughout.

If a situation looks bad,

the safest course is to

assume that it is

Pension Snags

Whichever route you take, the pension you achieve on retirement needs to be of a suitable size to be treated as your replacement income. It should be your main source of income to be used for daily living expenses.

Unfortunately, there are at least five important snags associated with funding a pension, and it may be that more could crop up in the future. First, although it may be **index-linked** to keep pace with inflation as measured by the Retail Prices Index, (the cost of living index), it will rarely grow by leaps and bounds in the same substantial way that your income did. Keeping pace with rises in the cost of living is certainly no substitute for the regular pay rises that most people can expect to obtain as they progress through their working careers. While you were working, if your periodic pay rises or bonuses proved to be unsatisfactory or failed to materialise, you could hopefully move on to another job paying a higher salary. This is a natural progression for most people in work. If your pension is your only source of replacement income, therefore, you may find it difficult, if not impossible, to cope with major emergency events, or even to pay for annual holidays or changing your car.

« *If you resolve to give up smoking, drinking and loving, you don't actually live longer; it just seems longer.* »

Clement Freud

Inflexible Pensions

Unfortunately, on present planning, most people only get one pension and it will not grow very much, if at all, in real terms to account for these additional items. More sensible planning is therefore needed. One way to get round this problem is to arrange a pensions staircase by contributing to several separate personal pensions which you can convert into annuities at different ages, say sixty, sixty-five and seventy. This means that when you buy the later annuities, you will get a higher rate as the conversions improve for older lives. Moreover, the later annuities will act as an injection of extra spending income as you progress further into your retirement years. Any measures you can use to improve the flexibility of your pensions savings will prove their worth later on.

Saving in several different schemes sounds an attractive solution until you consider that the second major pension snag is the fact that they are not transferable, even to a surviving spouse. Suppose you retire at sixty-five with an accumulated lump sum of £100,000. According to Stephen Phillips of National Mutual Insurance Company, as a rough rule of thumb for retirement at age sixty-five in 1997, a fund of around £100,000 would buy a pension of about £10,000. That pension, however, would be prior to paying tax, but with no indexation (so the pension will not rise in line with retail prices during your lifetime), and no provision after your death for your surviving spouse. If you die at seventy, this pension dies with you, and it will only have paid out a total of about £50,000 to you (£10,000 × 5 = £50,000). This is a very poor return for the lifetime fund of £100,000 that you built up. Buying an annuity is yet another illustration of the lottery principle that can apply to so much of our financial planning. On the figures we are using, you will need to live to at least seventy-five to approximately break even with the fund you had accumulated at age sixty-five.

138

inancial

lanning puts

ou in the

riving seat

Right at the outset, when you buy your annuity, you can choose between several options to give more flexibility. These are covered in the Action Plan in chapter 9. You may decide you want your pension to be guaranteed to be paid for a minimum of five years or arrange for it to pay a reduced pension after your death for your surviving spouse. You may even decide to have it index-linked so it will rise in line with inflation. All these options have a cost: they reduce the size of the initial annual pension. Moreover, you cannot change any of the conditions once the pension has been set up: you cannot even change the payments arrangements of the pension from one annual amount to twelve monthly payments. So when deciding on purchasing an annuity, considerable thought and planning is needed, especially if it comprises a large segment of your future retirement funds.

Bites From Your Pension

The third major problem with pensions is that they usually have tax deducted at source, so you always have to live on the tax-paid balance. For most people, their pension could be far less than two-thirds of their working salary. Living on this amount will probably leave very little extra money for luxury items and big spending plans. Linked to this problem is the fourth serious snag, which like the tax, can greatly affect the final size of your pension. It concerns the very high charges many companies take on regular pension contributions. Charges can be as much as around 30 per cent of total contributions over the lifetime of the policy, in the worst examples. High charges make a terrible dent in the performance of your investment. The commissions are based on the size of the premiums and the length the contract will run, but they vary considerably between companies. If you are well informed, there are several ways to mitigate the high charges.

Intense competition in the industry means you may be able to negotiate a rebate directly with the salesman. You could opt to deal with an adviser who takes a fee and returns all the commission to you. For example, a typical regular premium pension from a company such as Allied Dunbar might have costs of around £580 in commission to an independent financial adviser (IFA). This would be paid at the outset of establishing your pension plan. Qualified fee-based advisers charge from around £50 to £150 per hour. If an IFA charged you £150 per hour for three hours to sort out your pension, you would save £130 (£580 – £450 = £130) Although advisers should be honest, charging fees could serve as a big temptation for extended advice sessions. To avoid this, you should plan to be as fully informed as possible at the start.

This precaution would also apply if you buy your pension direct, by telephoning one of the several companies who now offer this service. By relying on the use of

press advertisements and existing client recommendations instead of expensiv
salesmen to sell their products, direct pension providers have managed to reduc
both costs and charges as they do not pay commission and by using telephon
services they have reduced administration overheads. But you need to be extremel
well informed so you can make your own pensions decisions.

Different pension options to reduce high charges

pensions options	advantages
negotiate a deal on commissions with the salesman	reduces the charges on your plan
use a fee-paid adviser	he will refund you all the commissions he receives when you take out your plan
use one of several direct pensions providers via the telephone	big reductions in charges and commissions as there are fewer expensive overheads
use single premium payments instead of regular premiums which carry much higher costs	big reductions in costs and much more flexibility in pensions planning

Finally, you can make single premium payments to your pension. Here, charge
are much lower than for regular plans as each contribution is classed as a 'on
off'. The commission deductions for a regular pension plan can amount to as muc
as 90 per cent of your first year's premium, although adverse publicity on the que
tion of high set-up charges is forcing many companies to spread the charge
throughout the plan's lifetime. By contrast, the commission on a single pensio
contribution is usually only 5 to 6 per cent overall, allowing a far higher propo
tion of your premium to be invested. There are other attractive addition
advantages in using single pension contributions. One useful idea is to spread the
each year among two or three different companies, instead of building one larg
fund as would be the case with a regular contributions plan. By building sever
smaller pension funds with single contributions, you gain the flexibility of bein
able to take each fund at a different age, to help your rising income needs durin
retirement. You will also ensure that a wider spread of investment managers is ha
dling your funds, in case the one you choose for the regular premium plan turn
out to have a poor long-term performance. There are advantages in paying regul
premiums, however, to add to the convenience of knowing your monthly premiu
is always paid on time. These vary with different companies, but may include th
ability to make flexible contributions so you can change the amounts you pay i
within one plan, and payment holidays in case you lose your job or are off si

for a long period. But the charges problem is such a major issue we will expand on it in more detail as the dilemma of high charges must be squarely faced.

« *Money interferes with the basic needs of life, but we have to deal with it.* »

Anita Roddick

The Charges Problem

As we noted earlier, charges tend to be very high with some personal pension plans. So high, indeed, that the amount of your money that is withdrawn in the early stages of the plan as management charges and commission is almost certain to adversely affect the long-term performance of the funds invested. On forecast growth rates it may take ten years of saving in some of the worst personal pensions products before the money you have paid in begins to show a positive return. High charges invariably mean low performance. This is yet another money seesaw.

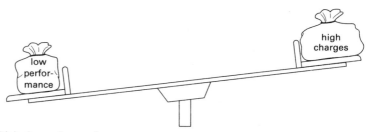

The high charges/low performance seesaw

This is such an important issue that you should be certain you have asked and been told in writing, the full extent of charges that will be taken from the plan right through to maturity. When this information is given to you in writing, you should be sure you have understood the details fully. It can make a considerable adverse impact on the level of your final accumulated fund. The charges are high if the forecast transfer value of your fund will be lower than the total premiums you will have paid in over three years.

As noted already, one important option to consider is the use of **single premium pensions** (where you only make one large single premium) instead of plans where you pay monthly or annual premiums over a long span of years. Single premium pension contributions have a very much smaller commission charge than pensions set up to run for several years. This can have a major impact on your investment returns, but you will have the bother of remembering to make regular annual single contributions to ensure your pension stays fully funded. The simplicity of the long-running plan once it is set up has to be weighed against the steep rise in the amount of charges levied on your premiums over several years. One aid to memory on the dates for making new single premium pension payments would be to have them coincide with the date you do your yearly wealth check, say, in the month of March, before the end of the tax year.

Never Lose Any Money

However, even if you have neglected to examine the impact of charges on the forecast performance of the fund, there is the so-called 'cooling off' period of ten days in which you may change your mind and back out of the contract. This is a safety feature in case you have second thoughts and consider you should not have bought the plan the salesman was selling. This 'cooling off' period now applies to all pension and insurance policies. It should be clearly obvious in the

When in doubt, stay out

paperwork. It allows you to cancel the policy and have any premiums repaid, but only within that short period. If you have omitted to ask any questions during the interview, before this deadline passes, it is advisable to ask the salesman or the helpline directly to inform you of any flexible options linked to your plan and to explain all the small print clauses in it which may adversely affect your flexibility of options during the lifetime of the plan and before it reaches maturity. All these small print clauses should appear in the 'key features' document that the company is obliged by law to send you as part of the offer document.

If you feel doubtful about the answers to any of the three vitally important aspects of your future pension – performance, charges and small print clauses – you should think very carefully about proceeding. If you have any doubts, remember Warren Buffett's timely warning. 'Never lose any money.' This is not an idle warning. Remember, over 25 per cent of insurance policies are surrendered within the first two years and around 30 per cent of personal pensions are either lapsed or transferred to another company within three years. To ensure your money stays safe, don't forget the first rule we discussed in chapter 4: start very slowly.

The Targets Keep Moving

And finally, just when you thought you might have reached the end of all the nasty pension snags, there is the dilemma that it invariably takes a whole working lifetime to build up your pension fund but in the money-go-round world of personal finance, conditions are forever changing. Unfortunately, too many of the changes seem to be detrimental to the interests of the savers, so that they have to save even more money, simply to stand still in the pensions accumulation stakes. To see what is involved, we will look at three key factors: the cost of living longer, the growing army of pensioners and constant financial tinkering by the government of the day.

As we noted in the introduction, people are now living much longer. How can that excellent news affect your pension planning, you may wonder? Actuaries, the professionals who calculate **annuity rates**, have to factor this increasing longevity into their calculations, because future pensions will need to be paid over a longer retirement period. That means annuity rates will have to fall and in the future, people with a money-purchase pension scheme will have to save much more to buy a reasonable pension.

Money itself isn't wealth. Real wealth is represented by the things that money will buy

The imminent arrival of the post-war 'baby-boomer' generation at the gates of retirement poses yet more problems for the actuaries. As they are now approaching fifty-plus, over the course of the next twenty years, the demand for annuities, and therefore all fixed interest investments on which they are based, will rise. Higher demand will tend to drive up the prices of gilt-edge stock and the other fixed interest products, which are used to fund annuities. The knock-on effect of these rising prices will be that the **yields** (the amount of interest paid out) on these products will fall. The price of the gilt and its yield are yet another money seesaw example. As prices rise, the yields fall and vice versa with falling prices and rising yields. As yields fall when the baby-boomers begin to retire, it will cost much more for everyone who wants to buy an annuity.

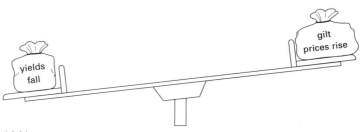

The gilts/yield seesaw

Government Changes

Another aspect of the bad news on annuity rates is the fact that they had fallen steadily from a high of 15.6 per cent in the third quarter of 1990 to around 10 per cent in the summer of 1997. Then, during the autumn, rumours spread that Britain will join the European single currency earlier than was expected. With a sudden rush, gilt-edged stock began to rise and the yields fell, as convergence of interest rates between Britain and the rest of Europe began to be anticipated by the markets. This activity had an adverse knock-on effect on falling annuity rates.

If you have to buy your annuity when rates are low, you will be locked into a low income right through the rest of your life. This disadvantage was made worse by 1997 budget changes, so we will move on to consider the impact of recent government changes on pensions.

The abrupt abolition of advance corporation tax dividend credits for pension funds in Gordon Brown's first Labour budget in July 1997 was a shocking development. At a stroke, pension savers of all ages right throughout the country lost a valuable part of their dividend income. From that date, this would be paid net (after tax) instead of gross. As we saw earlier, the BZW Survey calculated that a major element for building long-term capital growth was by regular reinvestment of the annual dividends. Any measure that reduces the amount of dividends received is therefore bound to have a detrimental effect on the growing size of your pension fund.

Overall, there was an instant drop in the value of most company pension schemes where benefits are guaranteed. The change had a huge cost for companies with internal pension schemes. Calculations suggested BT would need to make an additional contribution of £166 million a year, to restore the fund to its previous levels. Other companies faced equally large extra contributions: £92 million for British Gas, £62 million for ICI and between £100 and £50 million for British Aerospace, Unilever, BP, Barclays, Lloyds TSB and NatWest banks, among many more. The extra funds will have to come from profits. So there is a growing threat that companies will scrap expensive final salary schemes in favour of cheaper and less valuable money purchase schemes. Such action will transfer the cost of extra contributions directly to employees. Mobile telephone group, Orange, switched to a money purchase scheme in 1997 and Legal & General acted promptly after the budget to close its final salary scheme to new entrants.

However, abolishing this tax credit was a serious blow to all savers for two notable reasons. First, there is the concern that although this measure will adversely affect the size of the savings being built up for all future pensioners for years ahead, because it only appeared to be of concern to the stock market, its arrival created very little adverse reaction among the general public. As with the idea of 'money illusion', people seem to have great difficulty realising that professional fund managers who work for the major insurance and pensions companies are investing millions of pounds, not for themselves, but for the entire working population of Britain. We could call this fallacy, 'stock market illusion'. Lane, Clark and Peacock, a firm of actuaries, carried out a survey on the effect of the abolition of dividend tax credits on pension costs for major UK companies. They concluded it will cost the UK's 100 largest companies between an extra £1 and £2 billion a year. Bob Scott, a partner in the firm, summed up the root cause of the dilemma all pensioners now face for decades into the future:

« *Pension funds were a 'soft target' for politicians as they had lots of money in them and nobody understands how they work.* »

All this company reaction implied more employees may themselves have to make extra contributions to plug a £2 billion shortfall in pension funds caused by the loss of the dividend tax credit. Overall, according to the National Association of Pensions Funds (NAPF) this change could cost a total of £75 billion, although others claim it will force company pension schemes to use different valuation bases or change their investment strategies.

But, second, and possibly far more seriously, this measure was imposed with immediate effect on the day the budget was announced. It had been 'leaked' in the financial press a couple of weeks before the budget, which in principle I think, is a very dubious method of broadcasting major changes in tax policy. Moreover, there was no consultation with industry on the long-term adverse effects of this sweeping change. The notion of changing key aspects of long-term saving schemes in this peremptory manner, without proper and wide-ranging consultation, bodes very ill for the future. Rapid changes of this nature are totally inappropriate for millions of ordinary people who are making long-term financial plans.

There is the added danger that once one disadvantageous element is railroaded through a Parliamentary Finance Act, others may follow, and possibly be introduced in the same cavalier fashion. If so, it is even more essential that people should begin to learn about pensions funding, as the conditions surrounding it are almost bound to be changed, perhaps detrimentally, within the next few years.

More Saving To Stand Still

Financial advisers calculate that as a result of the abolition of these tax credits, pension fund annual returns would fall by around 0.5 to 1 per cent. Although this change does not affect final-salary schemes, where the employer must, by law, top up a fund, if required, so it can pay the promised benefits, this safeguard does not apply for people taking a transfer value from a final salary scheme, from one employer to another when they change jobs. Moreover, for all investors with money-purchase plans that budget change also had serious consequences. If the saver took no action, depending on the length of time to retirement, the pension could be up to 13 or 15 per cent lower than expected. Millions of people of all ages with money-purchase pensions were therefore adversely affected, including those with personal pension or executive plans, retirement annuities, voluntary contributions, small self-administered schemes and all other group money-purchase arrangements. The problem is compounded because the government did not increase the maximum pay-in levels to compensate for the tax credit shortfall. Savers in a money-purchase company scheme will run up against the unchanged limits of 15 per cent of income per year, to an upper ceiling of £84,000, although the employer's contribution is not constrained. While personal pension plan holders are limited by set contribution percentages that rise with age.

Furthermore, some pensions advisers were suggesting that around 90 per cent of the 5.6 million people who left the state earnings related scheme (Serps) to top up their own personal pension, risk losing thousands of pounds in retirement income. They calculated that those on average incomes could be up to £360 a year worse off, in 1997 money terms, when they retire. Leading insurers thought these people should opt to rejoin Serps before the end of the 1997-98 tax year, on April 5 1998. For higher earners, the loss could be much higher. It is a sobering thought to wonder how many of these five million people will have the right information to hand to make this crucial pensions decision on time.

Brian Wilson, head of Benefits Research at consulting actuaries Bacon & Woodrow spelt out the stark facts for millions of savers who had earlier opted out of Serps:

> « The terms of the contract have been unilaterally changed by the government. I would definitely want to revisit the contracting-out decision if I were in that situation, and my advice to anyone else is to revisit it. People have made a decision on a set of assumptions that are no longer valid. »

Pensions Are Not A Panacea

All these gathering problems indicate quite clearly that pensions alone are rarely the best route to a secure financial future. They also suggest that people facing a long future retirement will have to set much more of their current incomes aside, first to counteract these adverse measures and second, in order to ensure they are building a fund that will be large enough to provide for a reasonable retirement. Every failure to respond to changes in pensions savings means less money in retirement.

It is difficult to judge which of these shock-horror effects will do the most damage to future pensioners. The instant plunder of pensions funds by the newly elected Labour government will no doubt have serious repercussions for decades to come. However, of all these major imperfections, the loss of the accumulated fund on death seems the most harsh outcome to me. It seems especially sad that money you have accumulated throughout your working life cannot be passed on to those whom you would like to benefit; family, friends, colleagues or favoured charities.

Every failure to respond to changes in pensions savings means less money in retirement

Annuity Options

And there is yet one more key issue surrounding pensions that needs to be seriously addressed. Although for many people, a pension annuity will be one of their major sources of income for the rest of their lives, very few pay adequate attention to this important aspect of financial planning. The need to be well briefed is doubly important. First, investing in any form of annuity is an irreversible decision. There is absolutely no facility for a change of mind or even transferring to another provider. Second, the conversion rates vary enormously, so it is vital to obtain the best possible rate as it can make a huge impact on the size of your annual income. Pension annuities are taxed as earned income, so any improvement you can achieve in the rate at which you buy it might make a big difference to your available income.

Despite these important considerations, sadly, many investors appear to be totally unaware that they can buy their pensions annuity with an **open market option**, that is, buying it from any company, not simply the one with whom they have built up the accumulated pension fund. You can choose from a wide range of possible providers, all offering different terms. Even with identical annuity products, the variation between best and worst rates is a typical 9 per cent but can be as much as 25 per cent. There are firms who specialise in finding annuities to suit investors' needs (two are listed in the fact sheet at the end of the book). Yet Annuity Bureau, one of the firms involved, stated that under 15 per cent of buyers trouble to find out where they can obtain the best deal. I think this is certainly a case where some expert advice can be of enormous benefit.

As a general rule, everyone should seriously consider taking the maximum allowable tax-free lump sum from the accumulated fund; this is now a standard 25 per cent. Although taking the lump sum reduces the fund to 75 per cent of the total proceeds, it introduces greater flexibility. At retirement, the lump sum may be used for a variety of purposes: to repay a debt, invest directly in stock market equities to achieve a higher long-term return or it can be used to buy a **purchase life annuity**. This latter can be purchased by anyone with disposable money. It can be particularly attractive to elderly income-seekers as it will often provide a higher overall income than can be obtained if the entire accumulated fund was used to buy a pension annuity. Taking the lump sum also ensures that at least 25 per cent of your accumulated fund can be passed on to other people on death, especially if you place it in stock market-related investments for added growth.

« *People struggling to understand how to save for retirement must look enviously at the simplicity of products such as PEPs.* »

Peter Davis, chief executive of Prudential Corporation
(The man from the Pru)

In addition to the use of an open market option, there are various other options that can be considered, so many indeed, that seeking professional advice to find your way through the choices seems a sensible route to take. The selection on offer includes the use of **with-profits** or **unit-linked** annuities. Then there are schemes that allow **income drawdown**. Introduced in 1995, income drawdowns are a flexible alternative to locking into an annuity when you retire. They offer a phased retirement income for those who do not need to draw the maximum annuity immediately. However, as with every step on the route to securing your replacement income in retirement, there are advantages and disadvantages in this scheme, depending on your particular circumstances, so turning to a specialist for advice would certainly pay dividends here. Finally, some people will be termed 'impaired lives' because they have heart disease, diabetes or high blood pressure, or are heavy smokers. They should shop around for a special annuity rather than opting for the standard variety. There are now annuity providers who offer impaired life annuities, and this can make a difference to the amount of available income in retirement.

Money Observer had an excellent article on annuity options in the September 1997 issue. Back copies are often available directly from the magazine. However, with such a vast choice, so many confusing complications and no opportunity to change your mind and have second thoughts once you have made a decision, seeking independent advice seems the most sensible course to take before finally sealing yourself into a pensions annuity. There is a special section on working your way through the annuity maze in the action plan in chapter 9.

Supplementary Savings

It is precisely because pension planning is so hedged around with limitations and complications that it is important to realise as early as possible that pension provision is only ONE plank of your financial planning. No one should consider that their pension is the ultimate panacea for all their family investment needs. Everyone should prepare for the time when they are living on a pension by building up their capital as a useful extra nest egg sum, to complement that pension and pay for those spicy additional items that help to make life comfortable.

This brings us back to the supplementary savings idea that we mentioned when discussing mortgages, earlier in the chapter. For young people setting out in married life, buying a house and beginning to fund a pension for retirement are clearly both most desirable elements for laying sound foundations when building a tailor-made financial pyramid. But putting some money into supplementary savings plans from an early date is equally important. Insurance-based plans with a package of savings and life insurance is one route that was popular for young couples with growing families during the 1970s and early 1980s. But since the advent of

PEPs and TESSAs, together with a larger range of unit and investment trusts, people have had to sort through a greater, and often bewildering, choice.

With-profits endowment policies became unpopular in the 1980s when insurance companies were required by law to reveal how much they took in charges, particularly during the first few years of the plan. Because of these high charges, if the policy had to be surrendered long before maturity, the values were very poor. Many of the most respectable major companies now spread their charges over the full length of the contract, so you can get more of your money back if for any reason you have to cash in the policy early. In addition, over the past decade, the second-hand endowment market has grown substantially and selling your policy to another investor through a reputable broker rather than surrendering it back to the insurance company, can increase the size of your expected return by around one third if you have to sell before the policy matures. However, as with all other financial decisions, you should think long and hard before you make a commitment to any one plan, as changing your mind prematurely can prove to be an expensive waste of your valuable savings cash. Yet, many financial advisers still consider insurance-based savings plans are inefficient.

Invest in haste, regret at leisure

« *Where you put your savings has a lot to do with who you are, what you've got, and what you want.* »

Richard H. Goldberg

They do not like the fact that tax is deducted from the investments within the plan. Nor do they like the idea that they are 'packages', providing both savings and life assurance, which may not be the most cost-effective route for young families. However, tax efficiency, while important, is not the only factor that needs to be taken into consideration. When you save through a joint with-profits endowment policy, the life cover and other options apply to both partners. This can be an attractive solution if one partner is less fit or older than the other. The current clutch of with-profits endowment policies are far more flexible than earlier products. They now contain waiver of premium and critical illness options which give you added security by ensuring the premiums are paid should you fall sick or lose your job.

If you start planning early enough for a big outlay, like helping a child through university, making an investment through a with-profits endowment policy should provide a lump sum by the time your child enrols at college. This type of plan is useful as it is designed to smooth out the volatile performance of the stock market, including all the peaks and troughs. So that even if it matures during a bad year, the returns will not be as severely affected as more direct stock market-related investments would be.

You can build up your plan in monthly instalments or by a lump sum investment at the start. The insurer uses these premiums to invest in a wide spread of assets on your behalf. Each year you receive a **bonus** on the plan, the size of which depends on the general investment returns that your chosen company has achieved. However, these returns vary widely. Once the annual bonus is paid, it cannot be taken away, so the value of your fund never falls. You will also get a final **(terminal)** bonus when the policy matures. Annual and terminal bonuses reflect the smoothing process on endowments; in a good year, the company will pay a smaller annual bonus than it could so that it can continue to pay bonuses in bad years. On a ten-year plan, the terminal bonus may amount to around one sixth of the final payout, while it can be as much as half of a twenty-five-year contract. For this reason alone, it can be a tragedy to surrender one of these with-profits policies before it matures. And the juicy terminal bonus is the attraction that has expanded the size of the second-hand market in these policies.

« *Betting on today is chancy enough. Betting on a day twenty or thirty years in the future is absolutely crazy.* »

Max Gunther

The way these policies are structured, therefore, make them an ideal investment vehicle for young families who want to take a cautious approach, with a high degree of reliability for savings which are intended to pay for specific expensive items. Taking all these factors into account, with-profits policies can fulfil your supplementary savings plans. They are a useful addition to a financial pyramid if they are begun by young parents on step 3 or 4 of the investment staircase.

Protect That Life

Life assurance is invaluable rainy day money. It is money in the bank when someone dies. Some of the major insurance companies provide life cover at very reasonable costs. Nowadays, you can also buy cheap life cover from companies other than those which are purely insurance based; your local supermarket might now be selling life cover along with the brussel sprouts. For a young father of thirty to thirty-five, buying **term assurance** (which lasts for only a specific number of years) can be extremely cheap. It will, however, run out at the end of the term you have chosen, say in twenty years' time. But then, perhaps unexpectedly, more protection might be needed, to cover a situation that was unforeseen at an earlier date; a second marriage with a second young family is one example. Buying life assurance at forty-five or fifty is very much more expensive. But if your health has unfortunately deteriorated along the way, you may be totally uninsurable at fifty.

When you are young, **whole of life** plans will also be very cheap. These are self-explanatory, lasting throughout your life, but you will have to continue paying the premiums until you die or make the policy **paid up**, which means it will be frozen at the level of benefits at which you have ceased to pay any more premiums. Alternatively, you can allow the life cover to decline in real values, after inflation, as your rising savings have made continued high cover unnecessary. But you will have eliminated the guessing factor of how much life cover to buy on a fixed term, which may prove later on to be too short a period to solve your money worries.

A pessimist is someone who sees a cloud in every silver lining

Life assurance is especially important if you leave dependents before your nest egg has grown large enough to support them until they have become fully independent. In general, young people with families need life assurance because they have not had time to build up a big cash cushion to fall back on if trouble strikes. As you progress up the investment staircase, your savings portfolio will expand and grow so that as your life assurance declines, its place in your financial planning will be taken by your growing investments.

Well planned life assurance is another money seesaw: when you have only very low levels of savings but several dependents, you need high insurance protection. But when you have built up a high level of savings you need less insurance protection. As you build your investments, it will be far less important that the total amount of your insurance is declining.

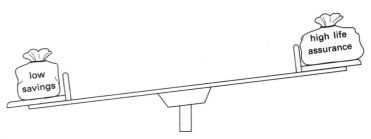

The life assurance seesaw

Based on this reasoning, you can immediately see that when you take on a huge financial commitment, like buying a house or funding a business, you should also ensure you have enough life cover to fully cancel out the debts if you die before you have turned those debts into assets. Then, instead of leaving your family in a financial quagmire to add to their grief at your loss, the life assurance will clear the debts and give them time to rebuild their shattered lives.

Buying life cover or a refrigerator have this in common: once you have it, you realise that a bigger size would have been more useful. If this applies to a refrigerator, it can be an inconvenience; but if it applies to life assurance it might mean a financial disaster. It costs relatively little to buy this protection when you are young, fit and healthy, so take on a little more than the absolute basic amount, to give you some flexibility in your planning. So how can you calculate what is the right amount of life cover in your situation?

To fund a replacement income for a widow which will provide her with around 70 per cent of the breadwinner's lost income, you must think of a capital sum that, when placed on deposit, will release this 70 per cent figure from a 4 or 5 per cent annual return. If you earn £22,000, your widow would need at least £15,400 as a replacement for your income. She would need to have a lump sum of around £400,000 to leave on deposit, to provide about £16,000 at a 4 per cent annual return. This amount of life cover would of course, need to be revised as either your income rose or your family expanded, meaning more dependents if something happened to you.

To see what this might mean suppose after ten years, you are earning £45,000 and have acquired some more debts along with a more comfortable life style. On the same calculations, your widow would now need a lump sum of around £787,500 to give her a replacement income of around 70 per cent, that is, £31,500. Unless you get a benefits package with your job, provided by your employer, you will need to almost double your existing life cover from the £400,000 you still have. But now that you are ten years older, the additional £387,500 cover will be more expensive in monthly or annual premiums.

However, it is not only working fathers who need to consider these facts and figures. A working mum should also take an interest in what fate might befall her family if either she or her husband were to die prematurely. And mothers who provide all the housekeeping services for a young family are a doubly precious possession. The death of such a valuable mother can wreak havoc with a father's life if his wife dies prematurely. Insuring yourself against adversity is a fundamental principle of good financial planning.

Will You Leave A Tidy Estate?

At the same time as you are considering buying life assurance to protect your family, don't forget to write a will! Everyone who has accumulated any valuable possessions should write a will, as it is better to bequeath your possessions as you would wish to see them bequeathed than to leave this to the arbitrary decision of the public trustee. His job is to sort out the estates of people, currently over two thirds of those who die, who did not make a will during their lifetimes. It is a shocking statistic that such a high proportion of adults omit to take care of this basic but necessary piece of financial tidiness, to ensure their possessions end up in the hands of those whom they would like to be their beneficiaries. If you have many assets it is very important to consult an expert to avoid heavy inheritance tax liabilities.

« *Whenever I prepare for a journey I prepare as though for death. Should I never return, all is in order.* »

Katherine Mansfield

Building The Three Core Blocks

When you embark on taking out a mortgage, a pension or an insurance plan, there are a few useful pointers for sifting through the huge available choices when deciding on which companies you should use. Many building societies and banks have been established for well over a century, while most of the major insurance companies have been in business for over one hundred and fifty years. A few have been offering their products to clients for more than two centuries. In general, you should look for a company with a sound reputation that will still be around in the future to provide the benefits you want to achieve.

In Japan, the escalating costs of house purchase produced the 100-year mortgage, covering three generations of buyer within one family

On the mortgage front, many companies now produce a whole set of booklets covering all aspects of buying a house. These are easy-to-read guides which may answer many questions relating to your mortgage. As they currently stand, these leaflets will probably answer some of your most basic questions. If they do not, ask at the local branch about any items you do not fully understand or points that may be bothering you. Always read the full terms and conditions of your mortgage; it is an important legal document. Be sure you have fully grasped the meanings of all the crucial points that are stated in the offer document. Go through these with the help of an adviser in the branch of the mortgage lender you are planning to use before you sign any long-standing agreement. If you have used a mortgage broker, the same precautions apply. Make sure you have run through with him all the key items presented in both the offer document and the terms and conditions. Unfortunately, at present, all the obligations seem to lie with you, the borrower, while almost all the rights appear to be weighted in favour of the lender. Moreover, some of the small print clauses may easily be inadvertently overlooked, even though they will work against you, especially in the event that you run into arrears with your mortgage repayments.

Think very carefully about over-committing yourself with a large mortgage debt. Many insurance companies now offer products which will continue to pay the mortgage payments for you if you are ill or unemployed. These are often expensive and complex policies with a variety of small clauses which hedge the payments around through specific limitations. If you decide not to use these products, it is even more important to keep the level of your debts to manageable sizes.

Security In Retirement

Hopefully, with enough time and financial foresight, when people reach their sixties and are on the sixth stair, the three core blocks of their financial pyramids should all be securely in place. But suppose you are already there and feel somewhat insecure about your personal financial situation? You may find that most of your savings are in a building society or National Savings Certificates, and perhaps you are living in a large home on which your mortgage is fully paid, but you do not have a sufficiently large income to live on. In these circumstances, a full financial review may be of help. Even if you decide to use an independent financial adviser to consider your options, it is still wise to do some preliminary reading to ensure you are well prepared to make choices from the alternatives he might suggest.

The reward for taking on risk can be measured by the excess return

To boost your income, you might decide to convert some of your savings certificates into government Income Bonds which provide a regular monthly sum. If you have large building society deposits, perhaps you could consider purchasing a life annuity, which is an option open to everyone and is not tied to an accumulated pension fund. Another route to increasing your annual income is to unlock some of the equity stored in your home, through an income plan. Various insurance companies offer this option, but all the products are slightly different so, again, using a financial adviser will help you sort through to find the one best suited to your circumstances. Income plans are ideal for people who do not have close family members to leave their possessions to.

If your financial situation is not too desperate on the income front, you might consider adding some toppings to your financial pyramid with the intention of maintaining the value of your savings during retirement. If that is your next move, you can consider the various pyramid toppings that we will be discussing in chapter 7.

More Pyramid Building

For everyone who is ascending the investment staircase, including those who have arrived at retirement, as you progress along the different stairs, with the main foundations of your financial pyramid gradually set in place, you will want to begin looking at other savings areas, so you can have money available to cope with various major events that you expect may crop up. Whatever your age, as both your expertise and investment funds increase, the overall size of your pyramid will also be growing, so now is the time to consider the next steps and what they involve. We will look at these investment ideas in the next chapter.

« We must all be long-termists now »

Gordon Brown, November 1997

Key Points To Remember

1 Everyone should focus on building the three core blocks of their financial pyramid.

2 Buying your house with a mortgage is a form of compulsory saving.

3 Gearing is an added advantage that comes with your mortgage in times of inflation.

4 Buying your home with a mortgage allows you to make supplementary saving plans.

5 Protect all your debts and your family dependents with life assurance.

6 Your pension should serve as a replacement income throughout your retirement.

7 Pensions have several snags, so other forms of saving are equally important.

8 Every failure to respond to changes in pensions savings means less money in retirement.

9 Supplementary saving is an excellent method of planning to pay for expensive future events.

10 Make a will to leave your possessions to those you choose, not those the public trustee will choose.

CHAPTER 7

topping

THE PYRAMID

'Historically, the share of equities in households' portfolios has risen as the proportion of over thirty-fives in the workforce has risen, as it is this group which buys equities to prepare for retirement.' Investors Chronicle

For most people reading this book, the first major issue to focus on will be to address any weaknesses in the three essential building blocks of your growing financial pyramid: buying a house, a pension and insurance-based savings. These are the big priority areas of wealth creation, the core foundation of your future financial security.

Tax-exempt equity-based schemes are the icing on the cake of your financial pyramid!

Everyone should concentrate on these three areas right from the outset to try to ensure they are satisfactory to your expected long-term needs. To stay on track, you should review your plans regularly, together with your current financial position, at least twice every year. But with your key blocks in place, you can then feel more relaxed about turning your attention to the upper segments on the pyramid. These are either equity-based or tax-exempt, or both. As we now know, they have the greatest prospect of outpacing inflation and creating wealth. Mixing metaphors a little, I like to call them the icing on the cake.

If you are already an investor and have gained some previous experience in collective fund investments, you may like to start immediately implementing some of the ideas we will shortly be discussing. But for most novice investors, looking at too many different ideas at once can be confusing and counterproductive. Far better to focus on one step at a time.

Cautious first steps

For ultra-cautious investors, or those near to or actually in retirement, some savings with tax advantages should feature in their plans. One group of such products which is not being covered in *The Money Maze* is government bonds, or gilt-edged stock. As the BZW annual surveys have repeatedly shown, these have been very poor long-term investments. Although there are obviously times when interest rate movements allow gilt holders to make good capital gains, it needs some expertise to get the timing right or you must put your faith in an expert to do that for you. I personally do not think these bonds have a natural place in the financial plans of most people looking for a secure financial future, especially as we are, in general, living much longer nowadays. However, even by excluding government bonds, there is still a wide range of savings products that are well suited to a cautious approach.

They include **National Savings** and TESSAs. Although these are certainly safety-first assets, they can play a role in everyone's family of investments. People arriving at the forties and fifties stage will want to start saving more deliberately to build up a sizeable nest egg in retirement by buying stock market-related investments, mainly unit or investment trusts. Within set limits, these can currently be sheltered in a tax-free Pep, but after 1999, only the new Isas might be available. We shall look at all these various investment ideas shortly. Whatever your age, as both your expertise and investment funds increase, you might want to consider progressing on to run your own portfolio of directly held company shares. Although this course requires more time and dedication to ensure you get a successful outcome, I would strongly recommend it to everyone who wants to see their money increase many times over. I believe anyone can make a success of investing in the stock market directly, as long as they are willing to learn how this can be achieved. However, this vast topic will not be discussed in *The Money Maze* as it is extensively covered in *The Armchair Investor*.

Finally, for cautious investors seeking a higher than average income, **guaranteed income bonds (Gibs)** can be considered. As the name implies these bonds give a guaranteed income but they do not give investors any capital growth.

Moving On

Before you can begin to think about increasing the size of your capital nest egg, you should first aim to build up a safety fund. *Emergency funds* are there to solve short-term crises or pay for unexpected expenses. Your cash fund will help to prevent you falling into unplanned debt. Ideally, you should aim to keep a sum of money readily available which is at least equal to between three to six months of your annual salary. If you earn £18,000, this emergency fund should never be less than £4,500. For added safety, or when circumstances look more uncertain than usual, the fund should rise to be around £9,000. Hold this money on short-term deposit, even if the rates of interest are minuscule. You are not hoping to make a big return on this money; it is there to be available on short-term notice, in case it is suddenly required.

Building up this sensible emergency fund should rank as one of your first priorities so you can cope with any unexpected outlays without running into debt. You will then be ready to turn your attention to the exciting task of real wealth-creation.

You do not need to make a super-human effort to improve your financial situation quite considerably if you know what you are doing and make a careful study of the risks. But naturally, a certain degree of skill and application is required to ensure you achieve good results when you are investigating equity-related investments, such as collective funds, with a view to making a purchase.

Selectivity is one of the keys to financial success

As we saw, all the essential elements which comprise this skill and what you need to know in order to master them, were covered in chapter 4. Fortunately, however, all the same basic principles apply to tackling any type of investment so this knowledge will be useful whether you decide to stick only to the three main building blocks or progress on to invest in equity-based schemes. But from the start, you should adopt a routine assessment approach which will be applicable to each and every investment you are considering adding to your pyramid, whether it is a mortgage, a pension, an endowment policy or a unit trust. The first essential at the outset, is to cover the various types of plan that you might now want to consider, to put yourself in the picture of what in general is available, what each scheme is designed to achieve and how it would operate if you build it into your pyramid.

Sifting Through Choices

When you start searching for ways to build the top layers of your financial pyramid you will immediately be confronted by an unbelievably huge welter of possible choices. How will you decide which particular investment schemes will be best suited to you? And assuming you can work out which schemes are suitable, how will you know which among hundreds within any particular section will be the right choice for you? Essentially, these questions also apply to around 4,000 possible mortgage offers available in 1997 and over one hundred different personal pension plans. It is precisely because there is always such a volume of competing choices for all financial products that you should explore them at a leisurely pace, to be sure you do not make any hasty and unnecessary mistakes.

PEP It Or Add A TESSA?

At the time of writing *The Money Maze*, the government was in the process of revising the current tax-exempt schemes, both TESSAs and PEPs, that have served savers and investors very well over the last few years. By autumn 1997, about 10 million PEPs had been sold, but this total includes many plans owned by repeat buyers. There were also around 4.5 million TESSA savers. About £35 billion was invested in PEPs and over £26 billion in TESSAs. Tax relief on both schemes was collectively costing the Exchequer around £1.3 billion every year. If you had invested the maximum allowable amount in PEPs, around £82,500 per person, your tax-free funds could have reached between £200,000 and £300,000 over the ten years in which they were available. It was rumoured that one lucky couple had sheltered £600,000 in PEPs.

« *Customers are fed up with companies which try to make a fool out of them by cleverly designed charges which disguise the true level of product costs.* »

M & G Fund Manager

PEPs were launched in 1987, although there were several alterations during the following decade. By mid-1997 they had become so popular that half the mortgages taken out with the Halifax were linked to PEPs. TESSAs were first introduced in 1991 and proved to be very popular with savers. In his July 1997 Budget, the new Labour Chancellor of the Exchequer, Gordon Brown, was not forthcoming on the detail of key changes he was planning. How both schemes might change or whether they would be discontinued after 1999 remained uncertain, although by the time *The Money Maze* is published early in 1998, more information should have been made public.

In April 1999, a new savings vehicle is likely to be introduced which may supersede both PEPs and TESSAs: this is the proposed tax-efficient Isas, Individual Savings Accounts. Yet again, how these will operate is currently unclear although the Chancellor said that Pep holders would be able to transfer their funds into the Isas. The government hopes to persuade more people, including those on low incomes who did not take out either TESSAs or PEPs, to become long-term savers and investors. The new tax-free plans therefore are likely to discourage early withdrawals, perhaps by removing the tax-free breaks for early encashments. By the end of 1997 a consultative document was due to be produced. The government plans to publish detailed proposals by mid-1998. Until then, this leaves over 7 million savers and investors in PEPs and TESSAs unclear as to what their future actions should be.

Constant government tinkering with people's long-term savings plans is simply an inescapable fact of financial life

If, as you read *The Money Maze*, you are gradually coming around to the view that you will now have to take a more active interest in your future financial well being, simply to keep one step ahead of the politicians, this will not be a problem for you. It is simply another vivid illustration of continuous government tinkering with long–term savings plans. Because such constant changes are a fact of financial life, it is absolutely imperative that you should familiarise yourself with what is going on, so you can continue to stay in control of your money affairs, no matter when or even what changes are introduced. For the unwary, however, the launch of this new Isa product could lead to a re-enactment of the pensions mis-selling scandal of the last decade. It was a change in the law on pensions in 1986 that encouraged unscrupulous salesmen to exploit widespread public ignorance about company and personal pension provision.

Tax-Free Tempters

The essential point about tax-exempt schemes is that they are there to encourage us to save. But governments are perennially strapped for cash and cannot therefore afford to be too generous. So when the government offers us a tax-free scheme, we should always examine it very carefully, hoping we can take advantage of it if we possibly can. The main problem with government tinkering is that bits and pieces either get knocked off or stuck onto an existing scheme. This makes every one an untidy jumble of rules and limitations which, invariably over time, add several layers of unnecessary complications.

Although I personally have found some of the Pep rules to be infuriatingly narrow, hedged around with endless restrictions and conditions, I am glad to know I am not alone in this opinion. In 1997, a Gartmore fund manager was quoted in the *Financial Times* in an article on questions surrounding the Isas; "PEPs have made their mark, despite constant changes in their product structure, demanding administration requirements and impossibly complex product rules."

« *I am convinced that the extra return conferred by tax concessions always ends up in the hands of product providers and salesmen.* »
Haydn Green, The PEP Shop, specialising in discounting PEP charges

However, as legal tax-free schemes are few and far between, you should examine them closely to see how or whether they can help you in your financial planning. I have taken advantage of the PEPs since 1990, although not the TESSAs, as saving in banks does not fit in with my ideas about the best way to make my money grow. As with all investment decisions, the tax considerations are secondary. They should never be the prime reason for using a scheme, however attractive the tax concessions appear to be.

One big factor on the plus side is that by the time the new Isas are finally introduced, you should have learned a lot about how to handle your financial affairs to improve your situation. You will also have had more experience of reading the financial press. So you will be in a good position to evaluate any new schemes to decide their suitability to your circumstances. You will hopefully feel more confident about being your own financial adviser by then. Therefore, when the time comes, you will know how to sort through all the information to find the important details on what is being offered, what the professional advisers think and what you will have to do, to make an investment. You will then be ready to make your own careful assessment of how the new tax-exempt schemes will help you with your own personal pyramid building.

Safety First

Tax-exempt savings accounts include both National Savings and TESSAs. These schemes are very popular forms of saving in Britain, because people are exceedingly nervous about holding equity-based investments. Essentially, British people have a building society mentality to saving. However, at both ends of the investment staircase, for children and people in retirement, tax-free accounts with a guaranteed rate of interest paid gross throughout the term are very good news. Grandparents, parents or friends and relatives can buy National Savings Children's bonds which give a higher than usual interest rate. They are only available up to a stated ceiling and are fixed for five years, which is not a problem for youngsters who are building up funds for the future. Further investments can be made every time a new issue is launched and the funds can be cashed in on a twenty-first birthday.

In retirement, some steady investment schemes give a sense of greater security and reliability. They can be used to balance buying investments in more risky schemes, such as those focused on equity-based unit trusts. There is a wide choice; savings certificates offering fixed interest or index-linking, income or capital bonds for lump sum savings, premium bonds for a flutter and First (Fixed Interest Rate Savings Tax-paid) Option bonds. Here, your cash, from £1,000 up to £250,000 receives a guaranteed rate of interest that is fixed for twelve months, giving you more flexibility than you would get by tying up your money for a full five-year term.

There is plenty of certainty in tax-exempt savings accounts, including the certainty that they will not make you rich

People over sixty can buy pensioner bonds which provide a regular monthly income at a fixed rate of interest which is guaranteed for five years at a time. As with most National Savings products, the income is paid gross, without deduction of tax. Some National Savings products are totally tax-free, but with others, tax-payers do have to declare this interest on their tax returns. The full current range of National Savings products is listed on page 163. The leaflet describing the pensioner bonds savings plan is somewhat misleading because it tells you that your capital is 100 per cent secure. This claim, as we now know, is an example of 'money illusion'. Your capital is only secure in nominal terms, but it will be losing its purchasing power if inflation continues over the five year term at around the current level of 3.7 per cent. The leaflet writers for National Savings products emphasise this idea on the cover of the booklet describing Index-linked Savings Certificates. Here, a couple appear to be checking some facts, while the message reads, "We know our savings will keep their spending power."

Then there are the TESSAs, which allow you to save up to certain fixed amounts each year for five years. There is a facility to roll the lump sum over after five years, but not the interest it has earned, which denies the saver the magic of compound growth where interest would be earning interest throughout the second term of the rolled-over TESSA. There is a wide range of TESSA plans to choose from, available through banks, building societies and those large societies which are recent converts to bank status, such as the Halifax, Alliance and Leicester, Woolwich and Northern Rock.

Although at the outset, TESSAs were intended to be simple tax-efficient saving plans, in practice most of them have become bogged down in complex charges and small print penalties and restrictions. Yet despite the plethora of different terms and conditions, you should attempt to understand them fully before you start a TESSA as most of the serious penalties apply if you move from one TESSA provider to another during the five-year term. TESSA savings are relatively safe and steady, but the first five-year figures compared unfavourably with returns obtained from the average unit trust fund.

The smart investor plans for the long haul

Finally, a late addition to the PEP stable of investment schemes, the corporate bond PEP, acts as a half-way house between equity-based PEPs and TESSAs. By purchasing a mix of bonds issued by major UK companies often with a proportion of government gilt-edged stock, it aims to produce a higher than average income. Because they rely on a spread of relatively low-risk good quality bonds issued by some of the UK's leading companies, including the utility groups, like BT, Powergen and National Power, the income might be considered more solidly safe and reliable than comparative investments in equities directly. By 1997 there was a choice of 48 to 50 different corporate bond PEPs on offer and a product that had initially set out in 1995 to be a simple half-way house between bonds and equities had become a complicated hybrid savings package full of bewildering choices.

The actual rate of return you will earn on your corporate bond PEP investment depends on several factors: the date on which you make your purchase, (this affects the price at which you will buy your units), the movements in unit prices (which tend to fluctuate) and the length of time it takes for the PEP manager to reclaim the tax credits on the bonds from the Inland Revenue. Again, the long-term future of corporate bond PEPs is uncertain after 1999.

National Savings products

(NB Interest on some National Savings products is paid gross, without deduction of tax, but if you are a tax-payer you will have to declare the interest on your tax return. National Savings Schemes that are completely tax-free for everyone are marked in the Table with *.)

plan	no. of years	risk level	age groups
fixed interest savings certificates *	5	low	all ages
capital bonds	5	low	7+
premium bonds *	indefinitely	low	16 + direct; below 16 through parents, grand-parents or guardians
first option bonds (the tax is pre-paid)	1	low	16 +
pensioner bonds	5	low	60s +
income bonds	indefinitely	low	all ages
index-linked certificates *	5 but retain their tax-free index-linked interest, even if cashed in earlier	low	all ages
children's bonds *	5	low	all ages up to 21

Tax exempt schemes currently available (in 1997–98)

(NB Although these plans are due to be replaced [or phased out] in 1999, there will almost certainly be some successor products which should be considered by all long-term savers and investors. There should be a place in everyone's family of investments for tax-exempt schemes.)

plan	no. of years	risk Level	age Groups
TESSAs	5 + roll-over	low	40s–60s +
single company PEPs	unspecified	high	30s +
general PEPs	unspecified	high	20s–60s +
corporate bond PEPs	unspecified	medium to high	50s–60s +

The Starting Point

There is clearly a place for safety first savings schemes in your financial plans. You might think they are a top priority for your investment plans, especially if you are currently a cautious saver. But I like the idea of using unit trusts

If at first you as a starting-off point for novice investors who want to invest but are anxious to control the risks. In fact, buying unit trusts can actually

don't succeed, enter into everyone's pyramid-building. They are a wonderful beginner's tool for people of all or any age who want to start creating a pay-yourself-

don't worry as first fund. And this will apply whether the saver is seven or seventy because regular small additions put into your fund over years,

you're just like if not decades, can build up into very sizeable sums by gaining all the geometric growth advantages of investing long-term in real

the rest financial assets.

However, if you know you are a person who has been hopeless with

of us money for years, think very carefully before you decide to tackle more than one idea at a time. I believe it is better to concentrate first on getting your budget into good shape, laying out your full wealth check and financial targets, and correcting any omissions in the core foundations of your financial pyramid before moving on to consider unit trusts.

The Investment Trust Route

First we must distinguish between investment and unit trusts. The main difference between the two is that an investment trust is a public company of a fixed size. It is not actually a trust but can buy shares in other public companies and is quoted on the stock market. This means that the price of its shares can reflect whether the company itself is attractive to investors or out of favour with them. At times, this may not have a close bearing on the value of the underlying assets.

« *As with so many other aspects of investing, the devil is in the detail.* »

David Schwartz

The share price therefore depends mainly on the levels of supply and demand for the shares that apply at any time. When demand for an investment trust's shares is high, they might sell at a **premium** (at prices above the value of the shares held in the trust). Conversely, and particularly when they are out of favour, as was the case during 1997, the shares might trade at quite a **discount** (at prices below the total value of the shares held in the portfolio). If you know what you are doing, you can make money by buying when prices are at a discount, but when they are at a premium, they may be overpriced and therefore not offering good value for money.

I think variations in prices that depend on supply and demand introduce an additional element of uncertainty into managing investment trusts. This is why I believe they are perhaps better avoided by beginners, although for some savings to hold over the ultra-long term, they are a very good route to consider, especially since the charging structure is lower than with unit trusts.

There are two important uses for investment trusts in a well diversified portfolio for novices. First, you can use a monthly savings plan to invest in one of the major international funds, such as Foreign and Colonial. Using monthly savings is a useful way of avoiding buying all your holdings of investment trusts when they are trading at a premium when the shares are therefore expensive to buy. With monthly savings you are bound to buy at least some shares at lower prices as these will continually fluctuate. Second, concentrate only on the main investment trusts which issue ordinary shares. I would caution novices against buying new issues which involve warrants. Try also to avoid split funds where there are several different types of available shares. Understanding the intricacies of the various different types of shares that can be issued, as well as warrants, is a special skill that some investors might like to progress on to after they have acquired a broader level of investment expertise. The investment trust industry produce a monthly newsletter (listed in the fact sheet at the end of the book) which may help prospective investors to familiarise themselves with the products on offer. A monthly newsletter highlighting attractive investment opportunities has recently been launched. It is called *Investment Trust Newsletter*.

The Unit Trust Route

By contrast, a unit trust is not quoted on the stock market. It is a true trust, having trust status, and must accordingly appoint trustees. It is managed by a professional company that prices the units in the trust and then buys shares quoted on the stock market with money paid in by investors to the unit trust itself. Money can be sent in either directly by investors or through a financial adviser, acting as an intermediary. As more people invest, the trust can grow larger. Conversely, the overall size of the trust will get smaller if a large number of investors collectively want to sell their units back to the managers at the same time. This is because unit trusts are open-ended funds, unlike the fixed investment trusts which are closed. Unit trust managers can create more units if the fund proves to be very popular and there is a large demand for units. However, you should not confuse the size of the fund with how well it is performing, although very small funds sometimes show big rises as a small investment in a company that rises strongly might make a big impact on the overall performance of the trust. Small-sized funds usually focus their resources on a small number of companies. This is one way of improving the returns, but it can be more risky.

Pricing the units in a unit trust is a simple exercise. It depends directly on the underlying value of the assets, that is on the entire number of all the units the managers have sold to the investors and the total value of all the shares held in the trust. For this reason, it is far more straightforward for novice investors to know exactly what their money is buying when they are allocated units in a unit trust fund. Twice a year, the manager of your fund will send you a brief report on the progress it has made during the past six months.

« *You do better to make a few large bets and sit back and wait. ....*
There are huge mathematical advantages to doing nothing.»
Charles Munger, Warren Buffett's business partner

Converting To OEICs

However, even here big changes are afoot. The corporate structure of unit trusts will gradually be changed to comply with fund structures widely used in Europe and America, the **OEIC**, Open Ended Investment Companies. These have considerable advantages for fund management groups and some advantages for private investors. For the managers, the conversion of existing unit trust funds into OEICs offers more flexibility and a chance to rationalise any range of funds that is outdated. The flexibility derives from the ability of OEICs to be set up as umbrella funds, with several sub-funds. This should allow the managers to respond more rapidly to changing investor demands by launching new funds. However, I would caution all but the most sophisticated unit trust investors against the lure of fashionable new funds, as fashions can be notoriously fickle.

The big advantage for investors is on the difference in pricing. There is only a single price for the OEIC or sub-funds within an umbrella OEIC. It reflects the value of the assets in the fund so that all additional buying and selling costs should be totally transparent. For example, Allied Dunbar and Eagle Star were reorganised during the second half of 1997 into an OEIC umbrella fund with a 3.75 per cent **initial charge,** against a **front-end load** of 5.5 or 6 per cent in charges taken at the outset on its unit trusts. The reorganisation affected 140,000 unit-holders and 38 unit trust funds with £4.7 billion of money invested. After it was completed these were consolidated into 17 sub-funds together with 6 new funds within one umbrella OEIC, called Threadneedle. Over the next few years more fund management groups should take this route, converting their unit trust portfolios into OEICs.

Choices On Choices

I recall a visit to have breakfast in a Denny's restaurant in California with my family many years ago. We wanted a cooked breakfast but we soon discovered that ordering eggs in American restaurants involves numerous choices. Did we want one egg or two? Did we want them scrambled, poached or fried or any other way? For those who chose fried eggs, the next choice was sunny-side up or over-easy? This is a delightful American expression for frying the eggs either on one side only or on both sides. And that was just to sort out the eggs. Then there were countless choices for other items to accompany the eggs – hash browns, pancakes, burgers, different sauces – and so it went on. You could develop quite an appetite just working your way through the order procedure. It might seem a bit like ordering a breakfast at Denny's when you start deciding on how to choose your collective trust investments.

For, having decided that you will start with a unit rather than an investment trust, you are then faced with a huge range of available choices. How will you decide on only one from over 1,640 UK-registered unit trusts, investing in different sectors in Britain, or in different countries right around the world? Do you want a **growth** or an **income** fund? Will you choose a UK or European fund? Would South-East Asia be a good place for your funds or perhaps, Japan? Would Latin America be better? Should you worry about foreign currencies? What about gilt or cash funds?

« *An investment is simply a gamble in which you have managed to tilt the odds in your favour.* »

One Up On Wall Street, Peter Lynch

Although sorting through the choices seems a daunting and complex task for novice investors, thankfully, there is a good escape route. By adopting a highly focused approach, you can eliminate a vast amount of time and trouble spent on sifting through all the available funds. The key priority for every beginner who wants to start building up capital, is to ignore all the complexities at the outset. Concentrate on just three or four pivotal ideas first.

These are easily identified, so we will list them before we consider what they each cover; first the **tracker fund** and second, the international growth funds with very good long-term performance records. These I consider as 'musts' or core holdings for every portfolio. Then there are two add-ons, or optional extras; a UK fund, either for growth or income, and a 'fun' fund for the really ultra-long term.

Keep Tracking

Investing for growth is like shooting at a moving target; the choices are forever changing. Fashions come and go, but some are certainly much more useful than others. When I set out in 1990 to build up some capital, I had never heard of a tracker fund, although doubtless there were a few around, used primarily, I believe, by professional fund managers.

The idea of the tracker is extremely simple, and fortunately for us, highly effective. A tracker fund just tracks. This means it aims to match as closely as possible the behaviour of one particular stock market index, which acts as a benchmark for investment performance. The index might be the FTSE 100 of one hundred leading UK companies, or the more broadly based FTSE All-Share index which covers around 900 publicly quoted companies. Today there are also trackers for European indices and for smaller companies indices.

A FTSE All-Share tracker covers at least 900 shares, reducing the risk that a huge drop in any one company can adversely affect your investment

The fund manager achieves the tracking by designing his portfolio to replicate the return he would obtain if he had shares in all the companies in that index. He cannot get an exact match because he has to pay commissions to buy and sell shares. But as a counter-balance, he will receive the dividends on the shares he holds, although these are ignored in most of the index figures. Trackers are usually said to be 'passive' funds, lacking active management. However, David Rough, group director of Legal & General's investment funds, told me this is not an appropriate description. There are real managers who must cope with daily price changes and regular changes in the index constituents as some companies enter while others leave. This means continuous monitoring is necessary to stay on track. With the aid of computers, the manager does not need to buy all the 100 shares in the FTSE 100 index, if that is the index he is tracking. Instead, he buys only a representative selection, a sample, duly weighted, to match the complete index itself. It is because different fund managers use different selection procedures that some small differences arise in the performance of different tracker funds. Trackers are certainly passive in the sense that the share selection has been done for the managers, by the compulsion of using only the shares listed in an index. This differs greatly from **active fund managers**, who do undertake their own share selection, according to their particular investment approach.

Trackers Are Not Passive

The recent growing popularity of tracker funds derives from two important effects. First, despite their fat pay packets, over 75 per cent of active fund managers, who select the shares for their own portfolios hoping to outperform the market averages, do not in fact even manage to keep up with the key indices that act as benchmarks for their relative performance. Even fewer, about 10 per cent in total, actually manage to beat the relevant index. As these statistics have become more widely known, investors have naturally become more hesitant about placing money with actively managed funds that fail to beat the benchmarks. An article in the *Financial Times* on trackers pointed out a fact I had not considered: since the index is effectively an average of all its constituents, about 50 per cent of them are almost bound to underperform the index to which they belong. However, professional managers, it seems, are not much better than amateurs at avoiding the laggard stocks.

« *Experience shows that you are more likely to buy an active fund that proves to be a dud than a star. But a tracker fund should lag behind the index by just a little, year after year.*»

Financial Times

Trackers do not have this problem. The share selection already exists and achieving the proper weightings completely eliminates the problem of underperformance. As we have seen, for long periods in the past, the stock market has spent more time rising than falling, so if you keep your money in the market long term, and your fund is closely tracking it, your money will enjoy virtually all of that rise every time the market begins another upwards spurt. This pattern eliminates a large part of the uncertainty associated with actively managed funds and explains why trackers have become much more popular with small investors. A major attraction of tracker funds is the elimination of additional risk. You know in advance that whatever the performance of the index, your fund will closely match it. Certainty in investing is very rare indeed: it is a very effective way of reducing risk, for both amateurs and professionals alike. So let us look at how it works in practice.

Just Keep Riding The Tracker

In a tracker, then, you are sure to enjoy all the profitable benefits of a rising market. Although buying units in your tracker and just leaving them to grow, year after year after year may seem boring, it may be one of the soundest routes to achieving long-term wealth. It took me years to realize that selling to lock in profits was not a sound recipe for long-term investors. Invariably, if a share fell, confirming my selling strategy, I was not alert enough to buy it back when a new buying opportunity re-presented itself. Buying good blue chip shares and holding them for years will pay great dividends if you are prepared to be patient, a point we will shortly return to.

So this takes care of the gains in a rising market, but suppose prices take a sudden plunge? The tracker funds will fall to reflect that. Although this sounds scary, it has a positive side. If the market fell rapidly by around 20 per cent, which would be an exceptionally heavy drop, the trackers would fall by approximately that amount. This might be much less than an actively managed fund would fall, since the manager will have chosen shares he hopes will outperform the market. This involves taking an aggressive approach to risk because, in general, the higher the risk, the better the prospects of higher returns. His fund will contain shares in several small companies that have a higher than average chance of growing strongly.

But in a sudden downturn, some of these could fall very much further than the corresponding index as anxious investors rush to sell but the market makers cut their prices savagely to discourage this. The greater slide in smaller companies would probably make a far bigger dent than 20 per cent in the performance of the active fund manager's portfolio.

Some huge drops of 40 or 50 per cent did occur in unit trusts during the panic of the October 1987 crash although the FTSE 100 index itself dropped by almost 22 per cent from Friday October 16 (2302) to 4.30pm on Monday October 19 (1802), a drop of 500 points in two working days. The low point of the crash was reached a month later, on November 19 1987, when the FTSE 100 hit a 12-month low of 1565. With tracker funds, you know that a fall in line with the index will be the full extent of the drop your fund will experience. And the sudden fall sometimes presents a good buying opportunity.

Historically, the stock market spends more time rising than falling

The second factor is equally central to the better consistency in performance that trackers provide. Instead of employing the services of highly trained professional fund managers, plus their equally expensive colleagues, the analysts and researchers, who help them select companies they hope will outperform the market, the tracker manager relies mainly on statistical selection of shares chosen essentially by computer analysis. Employing fewer expensive staff makes the tracker far cheaper to run, so the charges to the investor are correspondingly smaller. As we noted in chapter 6, any measure that reduces the charges for the investor can improve the performance of his investment because more of his money is invested instead of paying the higher costs.

Even major institutions, such as pension funds and insurers, utilise tracker funds in their broad portfolios, alongside direct stakes in companies, property and fixed interest assets like gilts. If professional fund managers want to get a quick exposure to a rising stock market, tracker funds are a good short-cut for them. Buying a stake in a tracker means they can rapidly short-circuit the lengthy process of having to select and then build up large separate holdings in a huge number of different companies. For fund managers, this is the equivalent of grabbing a ready-cooked meal off the supermarket shelf, instead of laboriously buying all the separate ingredients to make the whole meal at home for themselves.

« *The argument for trackers is pretty strong.*
Over the long term, it is pretty hard to beat them.»
Phillip Warland, Chief Executive, Autif, (Association of Unit Trusts and Investment Funds)

The success of the trackers has resulted in a massive inflow of funds. Virgin Direct alone had £750 million of client money tracking the FTSE All-Share index in 1997. UK tracker funds now account for more than 15 per cent of share purchases and could be on their way to emulating American trackers which account for almost 40 per cent of the market. By October 1997, the unit trusts tracking the FTSE 100 index had outperformed the average **UK growth unit trust** fund (where the unit trusts are looking primarily for capital growth rather than income in the fund) by a mind-blowing 12 per cent over one year.

Ride The Dips Long Term

As we now know, if you decide to be a long-term investor, you can ride out the dips secure in the knowledge that the long-term trend for the markets over many decades has been upwards. We saw evidence for this in chapter 1, but it can also be clearly seen in a detailed study of the UK stock market carried out by analysts at Barclays de Zoete Wedd (BZW). They looked at the record from January 1945 to December 1996, using a rolling system of separate periods to cover the whole 51-year span.

since Jan 1945 there have been	you'd have made a profit in	you'd have made made a loss in	your percentage of winning investments would have been
51 1-yr periods	36 periods	15 periods	71
49 3-yr periods	44 periods	5 periods	90
47 5-yr periods	46 periods	1 periods	98
42 10-yr periods	42 periods	0 periods	100

Source: Upfront Newsletter by Virgin – all figures based on gross income reinvested up to December 31 each year. Charges have been ignored

Although clearly, the future may be very different from the past, statistically, the probability is that the markets will continue to perform long term as they have over the last eighty years. In October 1987, the global stock markets suffered some of their greatest and certainly their most rapid major falls in prices since the crash that occurred in October 1929. For investors at the time, this was a truly harrowing experience. Yet over the course of the following ten years, markets around the world not only recovered from that serious crisis, but they went on to reach even higher levels, except in Japan, which had specific problems of its own.

« *Nervous investors may want to take their profits now while the market is at record highs and come back in again after any correction. But if you are brave enough to sit it out, statistics show that you will reap the rewards.* »

Ian Millward of Chase de Vere, August 1997

When you look at the FTSE 100 chart spanning the thirteen years from 1984 to 1997, shown on page 16, the crash of October 1987, a monumental disaster at the time, seems little more than a minor hiccup on the long-term upward progress of the market.

Buying tracker funds eliminates one of the major problems small investors face when they have to decide which particular unit trust they should put their money into; the dilemma of selecting a unit trust which will do consistently well and make money for them. If you broadly follow events occurring in the stock market, as I have been suggesting you should do, you will roughly know through your reading if the smart commentators are beginning to think the gloomy times have been overstressed and might be coming to an end. When this happens, you can expect the market might start rising again soon. Then if the rise duly arrives, your tracker will match it. You might even be tempted to invest more money as the next upward surge arrives. By selecting a tracker, you have avoided the need to find a successful fund manager whose fund will perform well over the long term. Instead, you are really relying on the UK economy to continue steadily growing. So a tracker should form one of the core investments in your total portfolio. It is less risky than most actively managed funds and all your money will be invested in the largest and mostly successful UK companies.

Trackers Do Vary

Although you might think that all tracker funds should move closely in line with the index they track, in practice, performances do vary. There are two key points to notice.

First, even among the many trackers following one index, say, the FTSE 100 trackers, performances tend to vary a lot. This is due to the way the different trackers sample the companies in the index and weight them in their own funds. For example, during 1997, when stock markets around the world were booming, index-tracker funds produced impressive results.

The longer you are prepared to leave your investments to grow, the better your chances of making money

Between July 1 1996 and July 1 1997, the FTSE 100 index itself rose by 26.9 per cent but several FTSE 100 trackers left the index way behind. Fidelity Moneybuilder showed the greatest rise, at 29.35 per cent, while the Legal & General UK Stockmarket Fund rose 27.65 per cent and Barclays Unicorn FTSE 100 rose 27.60 per cent over the same period. (All figures were **bid** to bid and net of income). A month earlier the figures were equally interesting. From June 3 1996 to June 3 1997, the FTSE 100 index rose by 23.3 per cent but some of the trackers beat that handsomely, producing an annual gain exceeding 26 per cent. The Equitable UK Index Tracking Fund made 26.7 per cent, Direct Line FTSE 100 Tracker and Fidelity MoneyBuilder Tracker both returned 26.6 per cent while Lloyds Bank FTSE 100 made 26.5 per cent. However, Legal & General's UK Index Fund only grew by 19.9 per cent and Foreign & Colonial's Target Index (Investment Trust) Fund grew by a modest 15.8 per cent.

Some of the performance figures over three years from June 3 1994 to June 3 1997 were even more impressive, with the FTSE 100 index growing by 55.6 per cent while Barclays Unicorn FTSE 100 grew an astonishing 88.4 per cent and HSBC the Footsie Fund rose 71.5 per cent. If you keep watching the financial press you can follow the progress of these tracker performance tables at regular intervals. Then you can see whether these groups continue to maintain these performance variations.

The second point to note is which index the fund is tracking. While the FTSE 100 grew by 23.3 per cent from June 3 1996 to June 3 1997, the more broadly-based FTSE All-Share index lagged behind at 20.6 per cent. Here, the FTSE All-Share trackers did not make such large gains over the index, with Royal Life UK Index Tracker and Lloyds Bank UK Equity Index both making 21% and HSBC UK Index making only 20.4 per cent. However, if you know you are an ultra-cautious person when it comes to investing, you should be quite content to use a fund that tracks the FTSE All-Share index. As such funds track over 900 shares, they should be even less risky than one tracking the FTSE 100 with only 100 companies to follow.

Your future financial security rests on your own hands

To avoid the problem of buying your units when the market has already enjoyed a strong rise and is therefore offering poor value, you can drip feed your money into the unit trust of your choice by using a monthly savings plan. This method should also suit your new budgeting routine, allowing you to build a respectable pay-yourself-first fund on a monthly basis, hopefully for years to come, as you feed money regularly into your chosen tracker.

Growth Versus Income

The second sensible choice for a unit trust fund for novices is to select one of the many large, international funds that invest globally. Most of the main investment fund management groups, like Fidelity, Perpetual, Mercury Asset Management, Jupiter and Gartmore, among others, run big international unit trusts focused on achieving high growth rather than income.

This is an important distinction between various types of fund, so we will pause for a short diversion to explain the difference. Among the large range of companies listed on the stock market, many will be enjoying a growth phase. This may arise from one of several reasons: they may have new products, new markets or new managers, or may simply be undergoing an expansionary phase. Companies that are actively growing like to reinvest most of their profits to help finance extra growth. They therefore pay out small dividends, but investors do not mind as they are hoping exciting earnings in future years will more than compensate for the smaller present dividends. High growth companies often command high prices on the stock market precisely because investors are looking forward to these bigger future returns. However, slow-coach companies, or those experiencing problems, operating in mature markets, or with a steady rather than exceptional growth potential do not usually command the same high prices on the stock market as growth companies. This means the yield, or return obtained from their dividends will be higher because the yield is calculated by the gross annual dividend paid on a share divided by its current market price. If you buy when the market price is relatively depressed, these types of company shares will be more attractive to investors relying on high and regular dividends.

When you choose a growth unit trust fund, you are hoping your choice will help you create long-term capital growth. You will not be unduly worried if your fund is invested in companies that pay out small, sometimes insignificant, dividends, rather than giving you the large dividends which come from investing in **income unit trust** funds. With these latter funds, you get the option of leaving in the dividends, to add extra growth over the years, or you could decide to withdraw some of the dividends which will be paid out to investors as regular distributions from the fund.

Income funds select companies that are specifically offering large dividends, often because they are currently in unfashionable sectors of the market. They may be in stable mature industries, like the privatised utility companies, or are experiencing problems in their products or markets, perhaps because the pound sterling is high relative to other currencies. Such companies tend to pay out dividends that are large relative to the price their shares are trading at. However, in the past, there have been occasions when some of these shares got **re-rated** by the market. This means they experienced a large rise in their value over several months, either because the sector they operate in comes back into favour, the companies become bid prospects, or they solve their problems and start making big profits. When a major re-rating happens, the income funds enjoy the double whammy of having the growth in their capital plus the high income. In the past, many income funds have been among the top performing funds when this additional capital growth has occurred.

The Global Reach

If income funds have such a good record, you might wonder why I am suggesting you should choose an international growth fund as your second core unit trust. As a result of jet travel and satellite communications, we now live in a global village, where many different areas of the world are experiencing growth which is

Don't buy or sell stock market investments based on short-term predictions

either higher or more consistent than in Britain. Today, we all buy a range of foreign imported goods that we have become familiar with; be it exotic South African fruit, a Sony Walkman or Miele dishwasher. In addition, many of us buy foreign cars, computer games or software, personal computers, even mobile telephones. A great many of these consumer goods are made by foreign companies which are listed on foreign stock markets overseas. As another method of controlling risk, everyone should try to diversify the investments they make so that they do not focus exclusively on British companies.

When you buy units in an international growth fund, you are relying on the expertise of the professional manager to decide which areas of the world show the greatest promise of growth. He will move the funds around, as he thinks fit, depending on the conditions that prevail in different regions of the global economy. You will reap the benefits of his global stock selection techniques without having to worry about fluctuations in foreign currencies, or which areas are due for a fall and which show the most promise of a new rise. Again, here you can avoid the worrying problem of timing your purchases by using a monthly savings plan.

« *People have nothing to fear from the stock market. Put it this way, you won't find many building society managers who invest their pension fund in a deposit account.* »

Anne McMeehan, Autif (Association of Unit Trusts and Investment Funds)

One tracker and one international growth fund are the essentials for creating your first balanced core unit trust portfolio. But if you have more money ready to invest and want another type of fund in addition to these two, you could select one of the many UK-growth or UK-income unit trusts, based on whether you are looking for long-term growth or a rising income stream. Here, the factors that apply are those we have already mentioned, on the difference between growth- and income-producing companies. Many of the largest fund management groups, with long performance records, run UK-based funds catering specifically for either growth or income. You can cut the coupons in the weekend financial press to discover more about these funds.

Are You Backing Britain?

A big plus factor favouring the use of these two types of UK-based unit trusts, either income or growth, comes from the Geneva-based World Economic Forum. In a 1997 report, 'Global Competitiveness Report', it ranked fifty-three countries by their medium-term growth potential. This was based on a variety of factors, including openness, government, finance, technology, and the quality of management and labour. The growth potential is then multiplied by the country's share of the global GDP (Gross Domestic Product). The resultant figures generate a ranking for each nation's contribution to the total predicted growth of the global economy. Surprisingly, the results indicate a mix of developed and developing nations leading the rankings. At the top was America, followed by China, India, Japan, Indonesia, the UK, Brazil and Mexico.

« Risk comes from not knowing what you are doing. »

Warren Buffett

The UK's high ranking is terrific news for British investors. We are very fortunate to live in a country which has the third largest stock market in the world. We should be exploiting the home-based wealth creation it offers us. We can choose from a wide and varied selection of major profitable companies who trade internationally. Furthermore, evidence shows that over the long term, many of the UK's biggest companies have outperformed their European rivals. According to research by Professor Youssef Cassis, big British companies have been consistently more profitable than their German or French counterparts. And, of greater importance, they have a far better track record for survival. Between 1910 and 1990, twenty-four big companies in his British sample remained large and independent, compared with nine in France and ten in Germany. Now could be the right time to start thinking seriously about plugging into this excellent crop of UK high performers.

Emerging Market Rollercoasters

Finally, if you have the inclination, why not consider a small part of your investment cash for an investment in a 'fun' fund. This will be one of the numerous available choices that now specialise in the emerging market areas of the world. A fun fund will create plenty of excitement. It will probably give you a hectic switchback ride. It may rise steeply for several months when the areas it invests in are fashionable and everything looks positive. Then it may fall with a rapid plunge if there is a sudden crisis. These markets cover young countries which are emerging rapidly from an agricultural base to become modern, industrial nations, trading their products on the global economy. Among their number would be included many countries in eastern and southern Europe, such as Russia, Poland, Turkey, Greece and Spain. Other emerging areas include Latin America, India, China and parts of South-East Asia.

Many of these markets contain lists of relatively few publicly quoted companies, which tend to be young and therefore fairly small in absolute size. This combination will make these markets somewhat illiquid. This means prices will be volatile, fluctuating upwards wildly if everyone wants to buy at the same time; or worse, they will plunge abruptly when everyone is clamouring to sell. The illiquidity is due to the fact that the markets are very small in overall size and there are usually only a small number of companies listed on these stock markets. Investments in emerging markets are particularly prone to volatility: prices may rise steeply when foreigners pile in, according to the latest fashion, but can fall just as swiftly, if there is an economic crisis, a war, currency turmoil, or any other problem. Then, dramatically, the foreigners rush to get their money out again and prices can drop with a shocking rapidity.

However, all these regions are relatively young developing areas, likely to produce much higher economic growth rates than will occur in the mature economies of western Europe, Japan, America, Canada or Australia. They may grow at rates over 5 to 8 per cent for decades, while in mature economies the growth rate is usually around 2.5 to 4 per cent. You will therefore not be surprised to realise that emerging market unit trusts are growth-oriented, rather than income funds.

Over the long term such areas have the potential to achieve exceptional growth. The secret of making money there is simply to ride out all the short-term volatility. To take advantage of these special conditions, you should be willing to leave your money in the fund for several years and ignore the plunges when these economies hit a temporary bad patch. In fact, such occasions could offer another buying opportunity, when prices and sentiment are very depressed. Buying at bargain basement prices will not be a problem if you are firmly convinced, as I am, that an investment in emerging markets should be held for at least seven to ten years, if not longer, because the performance may vary tremendously over shorter periods. You should be prepared to lock this money away for a reasonable time to derive the greatest benefits from the potential growth.

Every extra year you leave your money invested moves the odds of a bigger profit outcome more in your favour

As with any other unit trust, if you diversify your money between several different countries you will experience less volatility, as some will be rising while others are falling. Bob Akester, senior portfolio manager of Delaware International, part of Lincoln International, the pension fund manager which launched an emerging market fund in the UK during 1997, explained how such a diversification strategy can work. "While Asia has been destabilising, Latin America has been stabilising. It's a star region and valuations are cheap." The riskiest route is to select only one country, say China, as all the risk is concentrated in the performance of this one location. Conversely, if your chosen area does extremely well, your fund should derive all the growth from that situation and you will see a healthy gain.

John Templeton, aged over eighty, and still, in 1997, at the helm of the highly successful international fund management group which bears his name, has a lifetime's rich expertise in picking undervalued areas of the world to make fortunes in as their bargain values later become fully recognised. When you read his inspiring story, you certainly feel the excitement that can come from investing in

For patient long-term investors extreme volatility creates a buying opportunity

emerging markets. He was investing in these newly developing markets over forty years ago, but the fun is far from over. There are still new zones that come into the category of emerging. Finding a young developing area of the world where you can invest your money, and make a positive contribution to the expansion of that area is a win-win situation. We can all benefit from allocating a little of our pay-yourself-first money to emerging markets because they are perfect places to invest for the ultra-long term, where the magic of money doubling can turn small sums into superb nest eggs. However, two key rules on emerging market investment must be observed: first, only invest between 5 and 10 per cent of your wealth in these markets, as they are so volatile. And second, leave it there through all the rollercoaster bumps for at least seven years and preferably over ten.

« *If you buy the same securities as other analysts, you will have the same performance results.* »

John Templeton in *Global Investing: the Templeton Way*

Why Choose Only Three Or Four?

Having sifted through the huge selection of available unit trusts on offer, to focus on three or four particular types that are ideally suited to novice investors, we can now summarise why these above all others offer the best choice. As noted earlier, a tracker is a must for all portfolios; even the professional fund managers use them. Its prime importance rests on the fact that tracking has proved to be less risky than actively managed funds as far as performance is concerned. Trackers are cheaper on charges and concentrate exclusively on UK shares, providing an investment in a wide range of Britain's largest companies. Tracker funds are hugely popular in America, so you could buy a US tracker fund if you want to invest there. But you have to consider that there would be a currency risk if sterling grew stronger against the US dollar while you were in the US tracker fund. You make a double profit if you are in a good foreign-based fund which is rising in value at the same time as sterling is falling against the relevant foreign currencies. The international growth

« *The figures confirm our belief that the stock market is the best place for long-term savings.* »

Ian Millward, Chase de Vere

gives you a global coverage, to exploit the strengths of the fund management group you choose. It will take advantage of areas of the world which are currently likely to show strong growth. Money invested into an international growth fund can sit there for years, even decades, building up real wealth. If you have more available cash, a UK-based growth or income fund will provide another option to your growing savings pot, although you might prefer to choose two different trackers instead, a FTSE 100 tracker and a FTSE All-Share index fund, for example. Finally, the emerging market fund is really an ultra-long term adventure, backing some of the smallest, most exciting emerging countries of the world. Over a prolonged period, a modest investment in this type of fund should prove highly rewarding.

Performance Matters

All the financial advertisements caution on the truism that past performance is no guide to future performance. However, you can learn a lot about the future prospects for any company by looking at the past performance of the funds underpinning the plan you are proposing to invest in. Although a successful fund manager may leave the company without you learning of this fact, you will want to find a fund management group who can demonstrate a consistent performance stretching back over several years. They will not necessarily be the top performing group, as few groups achieve this accolade every year on a long-term basis. You will want to choose a group that consistently has its funds featured in the top quartile, (top quarter) of the league tables in the investment area you are considering.

« *Investing without research is like playing stud poker and never looking at the cards.* »

Peter Lynch

You can obtain plenty of information on performance from companies you think might be suitable. There is now so much competition for your business, most companies have a free-phone number for you to telephone to ask for this performance information to be sent to you. You can take advantage of this facility to telephone the company and ask them to send you brochures on the products that mainly interest you. Alternatively, simply cut out coupons in their advertisements in the money section of the weekend press and send away for the advertising material relating to a particular product. Now, you might even be able to track it down by surfing the Internet.

High Charges – Low Returns

When it comes to the charging structure of financial products, we confront yet another money seesaw; high charges invariably mean low returns. Conversely low charges can bring higher returns. We met this idea in chapter 6, in connection with the poor value some personal pensions offer because they have very high charges. As we have seen, low charges with the possibility of higher returns are the major selling point in favour of the tracker unit trust funds instead of selecting funds that hope to outperform the market. The high charges and low returns seesaw applies to all the unit and investment trust products you are likely to buy. So it is most

Almost invariably, high

charges are bad news;

they mean a poorer

performance for your

investment

important to find out the full level of relevant charges as they vary quite a lot across the whole range of unit trusts on offer. The advertising material or annual reports that unit trust managers produce should provide this information on charges.

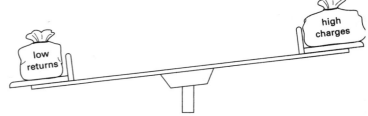

The high charges/low returns seesaw

How to Allocate Your Funds

Deciding how much money to invest in any one unit trust fund is another aspect of building the topping to your financial pyramid. If you have no pay-yourself-first fund at present, then clearly using monthly savings plans to begin accumulating a nest egg is a very straightforward solution. You can open a monthly account with as little as £20 for some unit trusts. But suppose you have idle money in the building society in excess of the cash you need for an emergency fund? Suppose, when you have done your first full wealth check, you decide there is £10,000 to invest in unit trusts. You could aim to invest around 45 per cent in each of your main two funds, the tracker and the international growth fund, with around 5 per cent in the emerging market fund. This allocation would leave you 5 per cent in cash to give some flexibility to your future plans. This would mean investing £4,500 in both the tracker and international growth fund, with £500 to put into an emerging market fund and £500 as a cash reserve. If you have £15,000 you can use the same sort of proportional split. You would then be putting £6,750 in the tracker and into the international growth fund, £750 in the emerging market fund and £750 as cash. The table shows how this would work in practice.

Allocation of funds in unit trusts

unit trust choice	amount to invest as a percentage	£10,000 portfolio
tracker fund	45	4,500
international growth fund	45	4,500
emerging market fund	5	500
cash	5	500
Total allocation	*100*	*10,000*

Do nothing hastily. Send for and read all the relevant information from the companies you are interested in investing in. Check their performance records in a magazine with plenty of coverage, such as *Money Observer*, and then, if you are able, check the present mood of the market. Is it at an all time high, or has it fallen back from the highest peaks? If you still feel somewhat hesitant, especially about your timing because of the current state of the market, you can invest this money slowly, rather than all in one lump sum. You could put £500 into your chosen fund at one-monthly intervals, for example until you have allocated the full £4,500 to the two main funds of your choice. This spreads the investment input over nine months.

What The Records Show

Statistics produced in 1997 by Autif, the Association of Unit Trusts and Investment Funds, tell the story. If you had invested £50 a month in the average UK growth unit trust over ten years, you would have had a fund worth £10,646 by mid-1997. This same amount saved in the average instant-access building society, would have produced £7,657. This is a large difference but it gets even more marked over longer periods, through the magic of geometric growth. If you had invested £50 a month over fifteen years, by mid-1997 the building society account would have grown to £14,216 compared with the unit trust fund total of £25,984 – making it 83 per cent ahead of the savings account. Looking at how a one-off lump sum would have fared, £1,000 invested in the average UK growth fund over ten years produced £2,048, a sum of £345 more than the deposit, but within an international growth fund it would have grown to £2,213. Bearing in mind that these ten- and fifteen-year periods include the 1987 October crash, we can see that in the longer term, short-term fluctuations do not impair the performance.

« *We like to buy businesses. We don't like to sell and we expect the relationship to last a lifetime.* »

Warren Buffett

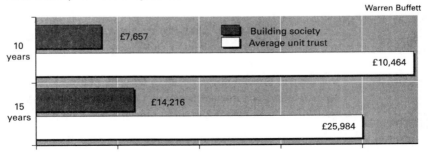

Investment of £50 over 10 years and 15 years in the average building society instant-access account and in the average UK growth unit trust

Finally, bigger savings invested over a longer period have certainly paid off in the past, illustrating the power of really long-term investing. A sum of £100 saved every month for twenty years from August 31 1977 to August 31 1997 would have given you a savings pot of £24,000. But on figures supplied by Autif, invested in an average unit trust fund, with the dividends reinvested, it would have grown to £138,967. This same investment in an average international growth fund would have achieved a nest egg of £173,499. In 1997, looking back over twenty-one years, to the great collapse in share prices that occurred in 1973 and 1974, a notional investment of £1,000 in the FTSE All-Share index since January 1975, with dividends reinvested would have grown almost 120-fold to approaching £120,000. Even without the dividends reinvested, the growth would have been 36-fold, although this turbulent twenty-one year period was flawed by high levels of inflation. These figures illustrate what a FTSE All-Share Index tracker fund might produce over twenty-one years.

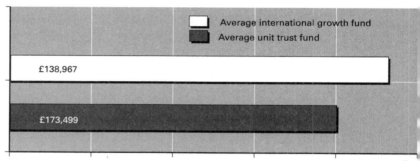

Growth of £100 over 20 years in the average unit trust and in the average international growth fund with dividends reinvested

The record for some of the international growth funds is therefore quite impressive. On a personal note, I selected the M&G pension international fund when in 1990, I transferred my minute pension pot to obtain a regular annuity income by pur-

When you buy investment products, it is far better to be safe than sorry

chasing a **unit-linked pensions annuity**. I bought units in M&G's international pension fund so my future pension is linked to the performance of that fund. In the first year, 1990, the gross annual payment was a tiny £60. This had grown by 150 per cent to £150 by 1997. Admittedly, this is in a tax-efficient pension fund, but when you have your cash invested in a global growth fund, you should be able to simply leave it there to grow as one decade follows the next. When I interviewed Martyn Arbib, chairman of Perpetual Fund Management Group, he told me he had had a lot of his own money invested in Perpetual's International Growth Fund since 1974. By 1996 this investment had grown 60-fold.

The ideal way to view an investment in an international growth fund is, therefore, to buy it, add more cash to it as often as you can and leave it to grow. The longer you stay with it, the bigger your returns should be.

For emerging markets, if you are seriously planning to leave your money in for the really long haul, you could consider an investment trust holding, as some of these have traditionally produced very high returns. You can read about the spread of countries a fund is invested in from the manager's annual report. Templeton's US-based Emerging Markets Fund is the best-performing listed investment trust fund over ten years, with an astonishing growth of 717 per cent. The records over five years are more mixed, with City of London Emerging Markets unit trust topping the chart with a return of 221 per cent against Templeton's Emerging Markets Investment Trust Fund's 186 per cent return and Foreign and Colonial Investment Trust Emerging Markets 139 per cent.

« *International capital flows are notorious for their boom-bust pattern and I cannot believe the present boom will not be followed by bust until history has proved me wrong.* »

George Soros, speaking at the International Monetary Fund
annual conference in Hong Kong, September 1997

Summary of different types of investment schemes

unit trust route			
plan	no. of years	risk level	age groups
unit trusts			
trackers FTSE All-Share	3–5	medium to high	10s–60s +
trackers FTSE 100	3–5	medium to high	10s–60s +
international growth	5–10	high	10s–60s +
uk-based growth	3–5	high	40s–60s +
uk-based income	3–5	high	40s–60s +
emerging markets	7–10	high	10s–60s +
investment trust route			
investment trusts			
international growth – monthly savings plan	5–10	high	10s–60s +
emerging market – monthly savings plan	7–10	high	10s–60s +

Therefore, investing in unit trusts, according to the choices we have outlined; trackers, international growth funds, UK-based growth or income funds and an emerging market unit trust, should prove to be ideal for novices hoping to build a large pay-yourself-first fund. If you organise to pay your contributions through monthly savings schemes in all three or four types of fund, you should certainly achieve a good return over a period of between seven to ten years. Money invested in a reputable international unit trust and emerging market fund stands a strong chance of achieving 15 to 20 per cent yearly growth over long-term periods. Take time to choose your funds and then be patient, and stay in the funds of your choice to gain the benefits of geometric growth over several years.

Where Next?

However, a few years on, when you have made some headway with building your financial pyramid and have put your investment plan, covered in chapter 9, into action, you might feel confident enough to branch out further with the toppings for your pyramid. You might then decide to look more closely at the investment trust scene, including warrants and split capital trusts, or check out commercial property or alternative investments, like stamp collections or antiques.

Or you might feel fired up and ready to embark upon an entirely new full time career, investing in the stock market directly. When I did this in 1990 it was my lifeline to escaping from huge debts. How I solved our family debt problem may help you if you find yourself mired in debt, so now we will turn to chapter 8 to tackle this ever-present problem – coping with debts.

« *They found themselves in a society that offered expensive pleasures – horses, gambling, clubs, fine clothes and furniture, drink and drugs – and the temptations of easy credit. Debt was the condition of the age.* »

Mrs Jordan's Profession, Claire Tomalin
(This description refers to 1807–1810, during the Regency period in England, but sadly, it still seems applicable now in the 1990s)

Key Points To Remember

1 Build up an emergency cash fund worth between three and six months of your annual income.

2 Novices should concentrate on taking one investment step at a time.

3 Collect a portfolio of tax-exempt and equity-based schemes for the topping on your financial pyramid.

4 National Savings and TESSAs are safety-first assets, but can play a part in everyone's family of investments.

5 Familiarise yourself with government changes to personal finance legislation to stay ahead in your planning.

6 Consider gifts of National Savings Children's bonds for your children and grandchildren.

7 Investment trusts are ideal for ultra-long term investing if you focus on the major international funds and use monthly savings plans.

8 Select three or four unit trusts for your investment family: a tracker, an international growth fund, a UK-based income or growth fund. A small investment in an emerging market trust is a fun investment for the ultra-long term.

9 Use monthly savings plans to drip feed your money into your chosen funds.

10 Graduate on to investing directly into publicity quoted company shares to make a huge impact on the rate at which your money grows.

CHAPTER 8

coping with

DEBTS AND TAXES

'For decades she had earned more than she had ever hoped or expected to; she had spent as she needed, given generously, and saved for her three eldest daughters. In her letters she mentions debts, tax problems and the setting aside of money for the children; she often sent cash to her sons. ... Since she was almost always paid in cash, and gave large sums to the Duke, (of Clarence – later William IV) estimating her tax must have been a nightmare.'

Mrs Jordan's Profession, *Claire Tomalin*

One important lesson to learn at an early stage with matters of personal finance is that no rules can ever be set in concrete. Events and circumstances are constantly changing. You should therefore be ready to stay flexible at all times in your attitudes towards managing your money, so you can adjust quickly to all the changes as they come along. In this context, I believe coping with debts and taxes are both special situations. They need a slightly different and certainly more focused approach from other aspects of handling your money matters. Therefore, while it is still important that you yourself do know clearly what is going on in these two areas, and how you should respond to any complications and difficulties that may arise, in both these cases, seeking professional advice can be of enormous help. If you have to spend money on professional advice, in many cases you should find it is money well spent. For people deep in debt, there are now free counselling services, offering money-management programmes to help resolve the problems.

(Details of addresses and telephone numbers are given in the fact sheet at the end of the book.)

The Debt Culture is 'Back-to-Front' Saving

Over the past decade, with the recent explosion of credit cards, shop credit and unsecured bank loans, we have become a nation of debtors. Temptations to borrow more confront us everywhere. It is far too easy to run up huge shopping bills and defer paying off the loans each month, because the credit card companies are often only too willing to increase the total amount of credit you can have. Paying off the minimum amount each month may lull you into believing you are completely in control. In such cases holidays, Christmas and other big spending items are routinely bought on credit and the debt habit becomes firmly ingrained.

« *I couldn't help it. I can resist everything except temptation.* »

Lady Windermere's Fan, Oscar Wilde

So let us consider first the true situation that applies when you use a credit card to buy some major item or indeed, many small purchases. If you pay off the total amount owing before the end of the free period, your credit card is certainly a useful budgeting tool. It allows you to pay off several purchases at once, with only one transaction. It also gives you a short period of interest-free credit. This period is shrinking rapidly, as credit card companies constantly try to maximise on the amount of interest they can extract from us, their customers. But if you roll over the total due to the following month, minus the small compulsory down-payment you must make to honour your agreement with the card company, you are actually indulging in what I call 'back-to-front' saving.

Short-term borrowing, on shop and credit cards that is not repaid at the end of the interest free period are all examples of this. So how does 'back-to-front' saving work in practice? After you borrow on your cards to pay for holidays or big ticket items, at some future date, you will be obliged to save the money you owe by paying it off in instalments, or arranging some form of compulsory repayment. This may begin immediately after your spending spree, or a few months later. But whenever you decide to begin paying off your debt, your payments, either as one lump sum or as regular instalments, are an obligatory undertaking to cancel out the debt on the credit card that you have previously run up. Repaying your debt is a form of compulsory saving imposed upon you after you have spent your money, instead of before. The sting in the tail is that now it costs more than your purchases alone, because you must add on the interest you will have to pay on the money you owe to the amount you have previously spent.

Most people are credit-worthy customers, who will ultimately repay all these purchase-based, short-term debts. The major retailers and credit card companies are cashing in on this reliability. They offer you higher borrowing limits when you become a big spender, because they can make excellent profits from this type of business. Your interest payments on short-term borrowings to shops and credit card companies keep their profits ticking higher.

Unless you have made a deliberate budgeting decision, and know exactly how and when you will pay off your shop or credit card debt, the moment you defer repaying it by rolling it over to be added into the next month's statement, you have virtually lost control of your account.

The credit card company is now in charge. They will monitor your spending to ensure you do not exceed the total limit they have set. If you do not repay by this belated compulsory saving route, your debts will simply mount until a forcible correction has to be imposed, often by your **creditor** (the company to whom you owe the money).

Repaying debt is 'back-to-front' saving

Debts Can Be Good

Although running up huge, unmanageable debts must be everyone's secret nightmare, we should remember that not all debt is bad. In moderation, debt, when properly managed, can be an excellent tool for building wealth. We have already seen what a wise financial decision buying a home on a mortgage can be. Taking on debt to buy real financial assets in a time of inflation is almost always an excellent method of compulsory saving to generate future wealth.

When you are climbing up the investment staircase, into your thirties with a young and growing family, moving into a larger house invariably means increasing the size of your existing mortgage. All the future benefits of gearing should, ultimately, come to your rescue if you take on this additional debt when inflation is still around, because it will be linked to a larger, more valuable property in which the lender's share is firmly fixed at the outset. This arrangement ensures you enjoy all the growth in the value of your home, while the mortgage becomes a smaller percentage of its increasing value. The additional growth can be considerable over a period of many years, even if inflation is as low as 3 per cent each year.

Your house is not a substitute for your future pension

And this, in essence, is the true secret of maintaining control over your debts. If you take on extra commitments, you must ensure you have some real disposable assets to fall back on if things start to go wrong. You obtain the greatest benefit from the gearing that borrowing entails, if the size of your loan is large in relation to the overall amount you are borrowing. However, even when you buy a larger house and take on a much bigger mortgage, it is most important to keep a proper sense of proportion. Never delude yourself into thinking that because house prices have risen throughout the last fifty years, this situation will always apply. Never regard your large house as a perfect substitute for your future pension. The future is always uncertain. No one can know how events will unfold. This does not mean that it is useless to make financial plans for the future. But it does mean that you must practise all the new money skills we are discussing in *The Money Maze*: acting slowly with extreme caution, reading widely before entering into any major financial commitment, staying flexible, so that you are ready to act promptly if circumstances change and above all, learning enough to feel confident to act on your own advice.

New Debt For Assets

Apart from buying your home with a long-term loan, there are several other important financial events where taking on more debt can be a useful option to consider.

What you are really

doing when you

manage your

money is controlling

the risks.

It can certainly play a helpful role when you are planning to build a new business or expand one that is growing. Remember most British businesses expand by borrowing money. But to be safe, you must be sure you can repay the debts you take on, even if events do suddenly turn sour. Making financial plans is rather like a game of chess: you should always think through the next few moves ahead, to be ready for the unexpected.

Having examined your ability to handle the extra loan, taking out a **second mortgage** or extending your existing one, can allow you to increase the value and comfort you obtain in your home if you want to make major improvements. Many alterations spring to mind which can serve this purpose: adding one or more extra rooms with a home extension or a loft conversion, redesigning your garden, installing central heating, double glazing, a fully fitted kitchen or bedroom or modernising a bathroom. Although your reasons for making these changes may be centred on the pleasure or comfort you will gain from the improved facilities you will be making, there is the added bonus to consider that sensible home improvements which incur additional debts may later be offset by increases to the value of your property.

As we saw in chapter 2, wasting assets, like new motor cars, do not appreciate in value with age. In fact, they **depreciate**, or lose their value with the wear and tear of continuous use. Although this does not negate the use of loans for cars or other similar new items, like carpets or furniture, you must try to keep such borrowing firmly under control. From the calculations involved in borrowing to buy four new cars, one following another at five year intervals, we saw that at the end of every five-year period, the value of the new car had fallen considerably. This loss may be compensated in part, if you are self-employed and therefore able to claim tax relief for a proportion of the use of your car for purposes associated with work. In addition, a similar proportion of the interest on the loan taken out to buy the car may also be classed as a tax-deductible expense. By counting part of the loan as a business expense, you are able to offset part of the outright loss you made by borrowing to purchase the car initially. If you are self-employed or running a small business in partnership, these tax considerations are important aspects of making the same amount of sales revenue stretch further, by reducing the amount of tax you have to pay. We shall look more closely at coping with tax later in the chapter.

Control Those Debts

Although taking on debt can therefore play a useful role in your financial plans, if you have only debts and absolutely no real assets, how will you cope if circumstances take a sudden ugly turn? You may find yourself hopelessly trapped in a situation in which you lose all you possess and may even be hounded by your creditors for years to come.

So buying an expensive new car on credit when you have no emergency cash fund to rely on if a bad situation develops, would be a most incautious move. Similarly, in the late 1980s, this turned out to be the case for thousands of people who bought houses and borrowed over 90, sometimes up to even 100 per cent of the value of those houses. When the recession abruptly arrived in late 1990, interest rates were forced to very high levels, making mortgage repayments extremely expensive. Property prices fell as the recession bit deeper, and many of these people became victims of **negative equity**. This meant the size of their mortgage debt was larger than the overall value of their homes, which was falling. This, as we saw in chapter 6, is the reverse effect of gaining through gearing at a time of inflation when the value of your house will be rising. With the rise in the value of your house, the value of your ownership in it also increases as you repay your mortgage over many years. High gearing when prices fall results in extensive losses, or with houses on mortgage, in negative equity. As the recession deepened, the amount of negative equity increased.

The inevitable outcome of ignoring financial risk is a loss that is measurable in hard cash

The problem first arose during the recession of 1990 to 1993 and was compounded by the fact that house prices were falling steadily throughout the recession; so as house prices fell, the negative equity rose. This was yet another illustration of a money seesaw. It is possible that no one could have clearly foretold how the housing boom years of the 1980s would collapse into such a devastating housing recession during the early 1990s because the housing recession was aggravated by very high interest rate levels due to our membership, at that time, of the European Exchange Rate Mechanism. However, if you had followed the newspaper reports to keep in touch with financial matters, as I suggest you should do, you would have read about the rapid boom taking place in the housing market. Then you might have been forewarned. Statistics showed that during the late 1980s, when the housing boom was reaching its most unstable peak, net new borrowing (after allowing for repayments) topped a staggering £30 billion. Equity withdrawals (which was money borrowed by people with high values locked up in their homes to spend on more consumer goods) raced up to £20 billion. As a consequence of this enormous house-related borrowing binge, hundreds of thousands of new homeowners, including thousands of young first time buyers, became ensnared in all the emotional and financial traumas of negative equity debt.

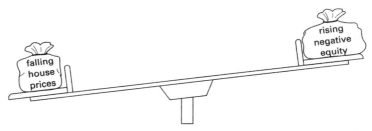

Falling house prices/rising negative equity seesaw

Learning From The Past

The first priority when

coping with a debt crisis

is to face up to the

reality. Then you can

start tackling the

problem at the earliest

possible moment

Was there any way this disaster could have been avoided? Of course, hindsight is a useless companion, but there are lessons to be learned from this bruising experience. As was mentioned earlier, mistakes are only expensive if you do not learn any lessons from them so that you can make better decisions next time around. Naturally, in the future, this same combination of trying conditions may never occur again together. It could be more than a generation before any situation of an even remotely similar kind emerges. However, managing money and controlling debts always require the same set of skills. What you are really doing is controlling your risk, the risk of unforeseen events upsetting your carefully laid financial plans. When this happens, if you have not followed the safe routines of managing your money as skilfully as we have been outlining throughout *The Money Maze*, you will find yourself swamped by unanticipated difficulties. Invariably, the inevitable outcome of ignoring financial risk is a loss that is measurable in hard cash.

For countless victims of negative equity, many of the lessons are those we saw were applicable to Paula when she filled her retirement basket with 20,000 Ford shares and very little else. The whole purpose of becoming your own financial adviser is to ensure you act in a cautious manner over all your investment decisions and think ahead to cover as many of the loss-making risks as you can. Essentially, taking on more debt than is suitable to your current financial situation is almost

Never take on more

debt than you can

safely afford – it is

a recipe for financial

disaster

inevitably risky because it reduces your ability to extricate yourself from a later difficult situation when events have moved against you. It is therefore vital that you never over-extend yourself financially, in the hope that you will make more money by doing so. You may be lucky and events will turn out as you planned, but if they do not, the consequences can be truly harrowing.

So here, in summary, is a list of the mistakes that should have been avoided by those unfortunate homeowners who found themselves in a negative equity situation. First, they should have ensured they did not take on more debt than was prudent. When a debt situation turns really ugly it can be a very traumatic experience. At the outset, their total mortgage should, for safety, never have exceeded more than 75 to 80 per cent of the value of the house they proposed to buy. It is also extremely important when making a huge financial commitment to ensure a complete wealth check has been properly carried out before starting up the mortgage. Then these new home owners would have been more completely in command of all the facts relating to their current financial position.

Mistakes made by victims of negative equity

mistake	how it can be avoided
taking on too much debt	calculate how much debt you can safely manage – not more that 75–80 per cent of the house value as a mortgage
insufficient knowledge about the current financial position	do a proper wealth check prior to taking on a big loan
inadequate budgeting	run a tight budget when you take on large debts
ignoring the cash flow	watch the cash flow closely
no cash cushion	build an emergency fund as early as possible
leaving the problem to fester	talk to the lender as early as possible
ignoring the boom that was developing in the housing market	remember booms often end in crashes – so be prepared

Again, if they had known that as a result of the new mortgage, their running costs would now be high and the money situation tighter than before, they should have tried to run a proper budget. This would have ensured that they knew how they were going to pay out all their important expenses, and especially the mortgage, every month. As we saw in chapter 5, when you run a business-like budget, to find some savings and keep a firm hand on the cash flow, you have put yourself ahead of any impending problems. When the cash flow figures begin to go awry, they will be your wake-up call, alerting you in good time to the dangers that are building. The cash flow figures give due warning that your budget is running into overspend territory, giving you advance notice before disaster strikes.

Moreover, having a cash cushion would have been another very useful aid to anticipate the crisis. When interest rates started climbing and the cash cushion rapidly disappeared, that would have been another early warning signal that it was time to rearrange the finances before they got hopelessly out of control. Immediate action should then have been taken. And if all else failed, discussing the problem with the lender at the earliest possible time might have helped to tackle it constructively as soon as it had emerged.

Booms Usually Lead On To Bust

Finally, there is a really important lesson for everyone to learn from the horror story of negative equity. This term first reared its ugly head in connection with the steep recession that plunged the UK into a severe downward economic spiral in the early 1990s. However, negative equity was the inevitable outcome of the housing boom of the late 1980s which span out of control through a combination of two factors: high interest rates due to our membership of the European Exchange Rate Mechanism and the Conservative government's liberalisation programme for the banking and building society industries. New rules allowed the building societies to compete more aggressively with banks for new customers to whom they could sell their mortgage loans.

It is not only in the stock market that an over-extended boom can end in a crash. Money magic really gets into its stride in a crash. Money you thought you could rely on disappears suddenly, without trace. Everyone who buys financial assets needs to understand the market they are entering so they can plan to make their purchases at a time when they will be buying real value for money. At the very least, you must avoid buying when prices have reached absurd levels. You can often recognise this, because buyers are absolutely crazy to buy. In the housing market boom of the late 1980s, this revealed itself as **gazumping,** when new buyers offered ever higher prices to scupper a previous deal on a house. There are invariably signs when a market is overheating, with imminent danger to your precious capital, but you must be willing to do a little sensible reading.

I think the saddest effect of that housing boom was that it hit hardest on the young and impressionable sector of society. In the years 1987 to 1990, they did not realise they were buying their first properties at grossly inflated prices at what turned out to be the peak of the boom. Like stock market investors or any people who buy real assets at the peak of that market, when prices began to fall back, they were locked rigidly into their losses. To avoid a repetition of any such widespread disaster, I seriously believe that the skills involved in managing money should be a compulsory subject taught at school.

Degrees On Debt

For young people starting a university course, learning to live with debt could now become a cruel fact of life. Unless parents are willing and able to fund the entire bill, most students will have to get used to the idea of building up debts which will have to be repaid from income after graduation. One high street bank, NatWest, has begun a money management programme aimed to cut students' debt and encourage them to confront their money concerns at an early stage. This follows research by the bank which indicated that one in three undergraduates could avoid permanent debt if they had help in managing their money. Over half the sample questioned admitted that they would have benefited from more preparation on the financial demands of student life, again, a sad reflection on our education system. The NatWest programme of money management stresses the role budgeting can play in the life of debt-prone students. For undergraduates facing the prospect of rising debts, budgeting can literally become a financial lifeline, playing a central role in their lives. By keeping detailed records of all grant cheques and part-time wages, together with bills for all living expenses and those connected with their course, like books or travel, students will have a far better grasp of their debt situation. They will also be well placed to watch the cash flow and take remedial action if debts begin to build up at too fast a rate. If the burden of debt becomes too great, students should seek help from parents, university tutors or their bank manager as early as possible.

Keeping debts under control is especially important for students if they are to build up a credit-worthy record, so that they encounter no difficulty in raising a mortgage in their twenties when they want to become home owners. Students from poorer backgrounds will be exempt from paying towards their tuition fees, but for the majority, when contributions to fees begin in September 1998, the level of debt when students leave college after a three-year course is estimated to rise from the average of £2,000 in 1997 to over £10,000 by the year 2000. Debts of this size could easily become unmanageable, if they are not treated with considerable financial skill.

Fortunately, the high street banks recognise that today's students are likely to be tomorrow's academics, professionals and company executives with high and rising salaries to come, far into the foreseeable future. They are offering exciting student packages to cover cheap insurance for personal belongings, a modest free overdraft limit and help with budgeting. In addition, there is the government funded student loan scheme, operated by the Student Loan Company, where a new loan can be taken out for each new year at university. The rate of interest is set by the Education Secretary but it is index-linked to inflation, so that the value of the money repaid is equal to the value of the money borrowed. The repayments are spread over five to seven years, depending on the numbers of loans taken out and they can be deferred if the graduate's annual income is less than 85 per cent of the national average income.

My Brush With Debts

Having looked at the lessons we can learn from cases where people have over-reached themselves with debt, we can look briefly at my experiences to see how I tackled this gut-wrenching situation. During the late 1980s, I decided to publish a set of three books on a research project I had spent years investigating, when the publisher with whom I had a contract reneged on the deal. Over the course of eighteen months I spent all the accumulated savings my husband and I had made, remortgaged our home and ran up large debts with the bank, and all for the sake of this self-publishing venture which meant a great deal to me at the time, and, I have to say, still does. However, when the icy reality of our new situation finally struck home, I was truly appalled.

Facing impossible debts is a time for taking stock

The savings had disappeared, the borrowings were huge, the future looked exceedingly grim. Yet the burning question was really quite simple. How was I going to extricate myself from this horrendous self-created mess?

I have always been a saver and planner by instinct. In retrospect, I can now see that I spent my whole adult life trying to build a sound financial pyramid of real assets as we, and our growing family progressed together up the investment stair-case. However, it has only been in recent years, since I have been sharing my financial experiences with others, that I have realised what a central role financial pyramid building has actually played in my life. But I never thought of it in those terms until I came to write *The Money Maze*. I find it rather sad that I was not able to pass all this financial expertise on to my children when they were young and could have gained the most from it.

Confront your debt problem head on to ensure you can get it back under control

But now, I can see that at the time when my menacing debts were gathering, I never really exceeded the bounds of prudence. Although it was obviously fortunate that we lived in a large house where there was still some equity locked in, even after the large remortgage arrangement had been made, it is clear that I did try to keep the borrowing within containable limits. However, I do sometimes wonder if I would have behaved differently if we had not lived in a house where there was sufficient value there to allow me to remortgage it. Knowing my approach to managing money, I think perhaps, caution has always played a part in how I try to manage our financial affairs.

And for me personally, tackling the problem head on heralded a run of good fortune. This only began to emerge when, at fifty-three years old, I decided to drastically rearrange our remaining assets to repay most of the debts, so I stood a better chance of finding the financial security which has always been close to my heart. Sadly, this meant selling the big house we had lived in for twenty-three years, in which our children had grown up. Selling was a painful wrench, but by moving to a smaller house, I was able to repay most of the debts. I was then left with a little nest egg of free capital. I knew I should have to start investing seriously in the stock market so I could enlarge the modest sum that I had managed to salvage from the wreckage. The key objective now was to rebuild our assets. And focusing on the problems and turning them into a solution proved to be the best way through the maze.

In September 1997, when I was giving an afternoon talk to a group of ladies about managing money, I told them the story of how I had got out of debt. One of them asked me where I had turned for advice. I had to search back in my memory through the course of events before I was able to answer her, because, I must confess I had turned in upon myself when seeking for the right way forward.

Tackling A Debt Crisis

However, when it comes to coping with debt or managing your taxes, these two activities are the rare exceptions which do not obey strict personal finance rules. Some expert advice here can be invaluable. But you must still aim to be well informed, so you can keep control and remain firmly in touch with what is going on. If you leave your financial affairs to others to resolve, you may never derive the full benefits you can reap by becoming your own adviser.

One of the surest ways to discover if your debts have run out of control is to find that you are regularly recycling your debts between your different credit cards. This is by far the easiest and most certain early warning signal that financial trouble is looming. I imagine many people have resorted to this desperate measure over the past decade as we have become more of a nation of debtors. I know it was one of the early warning signals that finally alerted me to the distasteful reality that the time had come to act. I would advocate to anyone similarly deep in debt that you should never resort to recycling your credit card or other debts, if you can possibly avoid it. To any reader now in that parlous situation, I would say, pluck up your courage and wake up to the fact that you must now start to sort out your money problems.

Money doubling applies with the same relentlessness to interest on debts as it does to interest on savings

If you discover you have accumulated too much debt, however distasteful the task, the first priority is to face up to the unpleasant reality of it. There is no way you can bring the situation back into balance until you have confronted the full extent of the problem, no matter how awful it seems. So, what should you do if you find yourself in a similar plight to mine, when debt consumed my every waking thought? If you cannot see a clear way through the dilemmas, do not be afraid to turn to professional advisers. Your most important aim must be to start tackling the problem at the earliest possible moment.

Now you know how money can multiply itself many times over, if it is left to grow unattended, you should be aware that money doubling applies with the same relentlessness to interest on debts, as it does to interest on savings. Try not to panic and make hasty decisions which may only worsen a terrible problem. Begin, therefore, by assembling all the key documents that matter: bank statements, the most recent mortgage account, the credit card accounts, together with any other information which will prove relevant to help in solving the problem. This might include letters from the bank manager, alerting you to charges on spending above your agreed overdraft limits. Compile a dossier of all the most pertinent facts together with these documents. Keep copies of all the letters you write. Go to the Citizen's Advice Bureau or use one of the free debt counselling services, for additional help and guidance on the steps you should take, especially on how to prioritise your debts, so that those with the most onerous penalties for non-payment are tackled first. Expert advice at an early stage may help you to prepare a plan of action, particularly if you do not want to start reorganising your affairs by informing the main lender to whom you are over-indebted.

In fact, I believe it is a far more constructive route to explore all the ramifications of the problem fully *before* you face your main creditor. Usually, the company will be represented by the manager or another senior official at your local branch, whether it is a bank or building society. Even one of your credit cards will usually be linked to the bank you use. Try to talk to someone in authority, so you can begin to resolve the crisis. The official you deal with should be a person with the authority to speak for the company in respect of how they will sort out your debt problem. When you finally do arrange to discuss your money problems with him, you should prepare very carefully for the first interview. Sometimes, it helps to rehearse what you will say to him. You should prepare a list of key points you want to discuss. Remember the secret of winning the argument at an interview is to take control. This will be the last thing your lender will be expecting, which will give you an instant advantage.

Try, in your preparation, to see the situation from his viewpoint. He will be most anxious to avoid having to write off your debt completely as it will affect the profits of the bank or building society he works for. So he might well be far more amenable than you think about any sensible measures that you can offer to keep your account active. If you become a 'bad debtor' everyone loses. The bank has to write off your debts and you lose your good credit rating, which you may need in the future. The official who is going to sort out your problem should therefore be willing to listen to any suggestions you may have on various ways to restructure your repayments.

Temptations to borrow more than is prudent confront us everywhere

If you find yourself facing this nasty situation, it may be some comfort to know that it can happen to anyone; from major trading nations, like Britain in the 1970s, to living millionaires today. Like them, you will be hoping for two important concessions: first, an extended repayments period, and second smaller monthly payments. Together, these two adjustments should allow you, in due course, slowly to bring your overstretched finances into better balance. For now, the real impact of 'back to front saving' takes charge.

Tackle your debt crisis

major issues	what you should do
recognise the problem	Face up to the fact your debt has run out of control.
panicking over the size of the problem	Decide to tackle it step by step starting right away. Important DON'TS include not recycling existing debts and not taking on new debts to repay others before doing a complete assessment of the current situation.
where to start?	Assemble all the key documents together. If possible put the debts in a proper order of priority for repaying them.
a jumble of facts?	Compile a dossier of relevant information and key facts.
insufficient knowledge of the way forward	Seek advice, e.g. the Citizen's Advice Bureau, your partner, accountant, bank manager, a free debt counselling service.
big monthly overdraft building	Start budgeting and watching the cash flow on a daily basis.
how to face the lender	Prepare very thoroughly for the interview. Rehearse what you will say. Write out a list of key points to be raised.
too little money to get the debt account back into balance	Negotiate with your lender to ease the burden of repaying your debt.
anxiety and stress	Share the problem with your partner, a friend, your doctor or your priest.

You may be so overwhelmed by the horror of what has befallen you that you cannot force your mind to address the issues. However, one crumb of comfort to cling to is that many famous people, now successful in business today, have been

coping with DEBTS AND TAXES

If you are hopelessly in
debt, the worst thing
you can do is – nothing!

through the traumas of being extremely over-indebted and have come through the ordeal to enjoy a happier situation once more. This can be achieved if you are able to apply yourself to getting through the difficulties involved.

If you find also that you are suffering a considerable amount of associated stress, do not be afraid to share your headaches with someone else: your partner, a close friend, a business colleague, a grown up son, your doctor or a priest. Such sharing may help you to clarify your thoughts and allow you to take the most necessary actions. The worst thing you can do if you are hopelessly in debt is – nothing.

Preludes To Debt

It is difficult, perhaps impossible, to feel amused when you are trying to extricate yourself from a serious debt crisis. However, one old saying which seems appropriate is, "If I was going to solve this problem, I wouldn't start from here." To avoid ever getting into this money morass, you should set out very early in life to follow the key principles of sound money management we have been discussing in *The Money Maze*.

Among the most urgent in this connection would be two elements in particular. First, is the aim to build a significant cash cushion. This will be emergency money in the bank or a savings account that will help to see you through the really tricky patches if your financial affairs go astray. And second, it is essential that you build the most stable, well diversified financial pyramid that you can, to ensure you and your family are as properly provided for as you can possibly make yourself, so that you can cope well with all eventualities – including managing your debts.

Escape From Debt

As I have indicated, in our education system at present, little attention is paid to learning how to budget to stop the debts spiralling out of control. Yet budgeting can be a powerful friend for helping you to reduce your debts. If ever there was a case for introducing sound budgeting, coping with debt must surely rank as the top illustration of when it can be of the greatest service. So budgeting is an excellent friend at every stage. It will help you control your debts in the first place, avoid the crisis overspend when things go awry, and help you get your spending back into balance when you are trying to escape from debt.

« *Neither a borrower nor a lender be.* »

Hamlet, William Shakespeare

But you must get your priorities right. This means sorting through all the details of your three budgets, the current, target and working budget, as was described in chapter 5. To keep your eye fixed on the main goal, namely tight control over your spending, try to target just a few of your variable expenses where some reductions look possible. Your top priority now is clearly to find the money to repay debt, rather than finding the money to save. But if you can get through this money crisis, you may feel happy to continue setting money aside, on a monthly basis, which will now become your pay-yourself-first fund.

Taxes Can Work For You

Coming through a serious debt crisis can make a lasting impression on your future ability to become financially secure. This was certainly one of the greatest benefits I achieved from my experience with debt. Of equal significance in my case was the knowledge I gained about how to use both the business debts and the existing tax system to the greatest advantage. One of the most exciting aspects of becoming your own financial adviser is to realise that there are plenty of ways you can legally reduce your tax bill, if you are sufficiently interested in learning about how to successfully manage money.

Getting Involved Makes A Difference

So let us look at the various ways in which this has worked in practice for me. I had created a small private partnership with my husband for the self-publishing venture, but it generated monstrous losses. These, however, were not just huge debts with a complete loss of our savings, plus a 'black hole' in our current account. We also had a large amount of trading losses. These were losses in the profit and loss account relating to our business. They had accumulated while I was trying to advertise and sell my books on mail order. I discovered that the trading losses could be offset against my husband's established and regular income, although the major loss of our capital remained irretrievable. In fact, over the course of the following two years, we were able to reclaim almost his entire tax bill.

You will make more progress faster if you take one step at a time

I was fortunate that my business adventure coincided with the peak of Mrs Thatcher's enterprise economy push of the late 1980s, when her government was keen to set up classes for people to learn how to start up in business on their own. I went to classes where I was taught the rudiments of accounting and this later stood me in good stead. Evening classes are still run in many local areas on learning basic accounting skills. I did this not to become an accounting expert, but simply to learn a few of the ways I could benefit from the current tax regime, without doing anything illegal.

When I realised that because we had traded as a partnership, some of our accumulated trading losses could be offset against my husband's income, the rebates on his taxes over the following two years were of considerable help. I submitted the tax returns for the loss-making business under a scheme at that time which allowed business people with very small revenue operations to receive help, as tax-payers, in compiling the total amount of tax due. This help was available from the local tax office. Using this facility saved me laying out even more money on accountant's fees. I struck up a rapport with officials in my tax office and my husband's tax office, to enable me to follow and monitor the entire proceedings, right through to the successful conclusion of reclaiming the over-payments of my husband's taxes.

There are plenty of

ways you can legally

reduce your tax bill

When the tax losses had been established in my tax office, I then had to deal with a second tax office: the one that was handling my husband's affairs. I made a point of discovering the name of the lady responsible for sorting out his tax commitments and contacted both her and the **tax collector** himself on a regular basis until I had finally banked the over-payment cheques due.

By involving myself at every stage, I was able to help our sorely over-stretched cash flow because I managed to get the repayments of tax paid much earlier by my sheer persistence. If you call regularly, to find out what is holding up the over-payment of tax, you will discover it is probably due to the large workload the tax office handles. Persistent but polite, telephone calls do finally ensure your file gets to the top of the pile and the problem will then receive more speedy attention.

Although I found this was a long and protracted task, it was well worth the time involved in terms of improving our cash flow. I have found that if you are courteous to the tax officials handling your affairs, they will respond, you can get the results you want and perhaps this approach helps in settling the outstanding issues more speedily. The new-look Inland Revenue has accepted that it must treat all us tax-payers as its clients. It has made a big effort to become more user-friendly since the days in 1990 when I was trying to sort out this tax problem for myself.

Useful Business Tax Advantages

However, obtaining over-payment of taxes cheques is not the only route you can take to reduce your legal tax obligations. It may not have occurred to you, but you can actually arrange to pay your tax ahead of time if you have money already allocated to deal with that. The Inland Revenue pays interest on early payments. Another area to explore is the possibility that in your family some personal tax allowances are being wasted. Everyone has a personal tax allowance, whatever their age or level of income. If there is only one breadwinner in your family, examine ways of making use of the non-earners' tax allowances. Perhaps you could transfer some income-producing investments to a non-earning wife, or arrange to give some income-producing investments to your children.

If you are a sole trader or in partnership, you could employ your wife on a part-time basis for help she provides in your business. When she has an income, she will then be able to start up a small pension of her own. You might like to consider electing to become **VAT** (value-added tax) **registered**, even if the level of revenue in your business is lower than the current statutory limit. There are instances when being VAT registered offers you a tax advantage. For example, you will have to pay value added tax on the revenues, salaries or commissions you earn, but you can claim back the VAT on the business expenses you make. Obviously, in most businesses, the revenue is greater than the expenses, otherwise there surely would be no purpose in being in business at all. But even if the tax you reclaim on your expenses is not substantial, it reduces the overall tax you have to pay.

If you involve yourself in every stage of sorting out a tax problem you can achieve quicker results

For this financial benefit, you will have to keep very detailed records of all your revenues and expenses and fill in the correct forms to submit figures to the Customs and Excise office on a regular, three-monthly basis. Simple computer programmes are now available to take the drudgery out of this accounting process. But even if you tackle it manually, it is not such a bother if you are running a business, because by keeping all these records, you are well on the way to compiling the income and expenses accounts you will have to make in order to pay your taxes. Again, simply handing all this straightforward record keeping to an accountant has a double cost: first, in the size of the fees he will charge which are based on the time he spends on sorting out your accounts; and second, by delegating this task to an expert, you are once again deferring the time when you can become your own adviser.

We talked earlier about taking advantage of tax relief on the purchase of a car which you use partly for business purposes. How would this work in practice? You must try to calculate how much of your time is spent in your car devoted exclusively to business rather than pleasure. The percentage would be negotiable with the **tax inspector**, who agrees the amount of tax you owe. But suppose you could establish that 25 per cent of your car usage was for business, you would then be able to claim 25 per cent of the purchase price as a fixed asset in your business, which you would be allowed to depreciate over five years. Moreover, 25 per cent of the running costs of the car would also be allowable as taxable expenses, as would 25 per cent of the interest if you bought your car by taking out a three- or five-year loan.

Stay Ahead With Self-Assessment

Now that the new regime of self-assessment is in full swing, there is an added incentive to keep proper records and tackle the tax issues in good time. Delays will result in fines. Failure to meet the end of January deadline, with the amount of tax you owe already calculated, will result in an immediate fine of £100. This could be highly profitable for the Inland Revenue. If just 100,000 are late submitting

Handing your

tax affairs over

to an

accountant

does not

absolve you

from the

responsibility of

his mistakes

their returns, out of the 8.5 million tax-payers eligible for self-assessment, the Revenue will gain £10 million. Inevitably there will always be some late payers. Try to ensure you are not among them. Over 100,000 people missed paying the first half of their 1996-97 tax liability by the end of January 1997. They were charged interest at the rate of 8.5 per cent, on these late payments. So tardiness in sorting out your tax affairs could prove expensive.

The introduction of self-assessment is a perfect opportunity to learn about managing your tax affairs for yourself. If you have begun to keep a budget, the records of your income and tax-allowable expenses will all be together in one place as part of your budgeting routine. The invoices and bills will also be in one tidy collection as will your domestic bills, some of which may be eligible as taxable expenses. Your filing system can be as simple as one envelope for each month of the year to hold all income and expense items together for that month.

When you are calculating your taxable income, if you are eligible for taxable expenses, make the effort to find out all the relevant allowances applicable to your particular business or occupation. You should try to claim all the allowances which are due to you. Naturally, this will reduce the amount of tax you have to pay.

If you know a little about the tax system you may be able to spot the errors. When I submitted my first self-assessment tax form in September 1997, the calculation of the tax due arrived within a fortnight. I had made an error on the form, but the Inland Revenue had adjusted it so they could still calculate the tax due without returning the form to be corrected. However, when I looked at the figures, I thought they had overcharged me. Although I receive a very small state pension, they had added £186 to my tax bill for National Insurance contributions. A quick phone call to the tax office established that I did not need to pay National Insurance. So it is clear: constant checking is well worthwhile.

The Discipline Of Self-Assessment

In the past, paying tax for the self-employed and others who received a tax return could become a rather long, drawn out affair, with letters and appeals passing to and fro while the nitty-gritty details of the tax due was being established. With self-assessment, this relaxed attitude has become totally outdated. Keeping records for a whole year is now a legal requirement, but if you run a business or have income from letting property you must keep records for five years. However, keeping detailed records is a help when filling in the complicated tax return. Incomplete forms will not be acceptable, therefore it is essential not to leave any part of the form blank and if you make an estimate, be sure to tick the box indicating that you have done this. Building up cash in advance to meet the tax liabilities could prove a sensible move as fines will be imposed on those who do not settle on time in addition to interest charges on the outstanding balance. Taxpayers who fail to pay their 1997/98 tax by February 28 1999 will be liable for an automatic 5 per cent surcharge. Moreover, the Revenue will charge interest on taxpayers who get their tax sums wrong and owe more tax than they had calculated.

Over 8 million people received tax return forms in April 1997. This covers all the self-employed, company directors, many higher-rate taxpayers and people with tax affairs that are not straightforward. But around 15 million taxpayers do not need to fill in their own tax return. For those who did receive a tax return, it was accompanied by a step-by-step guide to completing the form and a calculations guide for those who intended to calculate their own tax liability. In addition, there are nine supplementary sections to cover such topics as share schemes, self-employment, partnerships and capital gains. At an early stage, therefore, you must contact the Revenue if you think you should have been sent a tax return that did not arrive or if you have not been sent the appropriate supplementary sections that apply to your income.

Under the new regime, everyone will pay tax in two equal instalments; on January 31 and July 31 of the year in which the tax applies. This is what is

If you are late in sending back your tax return you face an automatic £100 fine and there could be interest to pay on top

meant by paying your tax 'on account', as you will be paying it in the same tax year as you earn the income. For example, on January 31 1998 you would have paid the first payment of tax on account for the year 1997/98. But this is just an estimate based on the previous year's earnings. So in addition, on January 31 1998, you would have paid any shortfall on the tax due for the previous year, 1996/97. The calculation of this actual 1996/97 tax liability will have been done for you if you sent in your completed self-assessment form by September 30 1997. If you have an accountant, he would have calculated this figure for you so it can be paid in full on January 31 1998. If you have overpaid tax for 1996/97, the Revenue will repay it plus interest. However, if you owe tax, you will have to calculate the amount owing pretty swiftly at the end of the financial year, that is, after April 5 1998. You will then have to make the second payment for the year 1997/98 on July 31 1998. By this time, you will be required to pay any shortfall due for the tax year ending April 5 1998, so that your tax payments are completely up to date. To keep up with this compressed timetable, everyone will have to focus on their tax affairs in a much more disciplined way than was necessary before self-assessment was introduced.

It is crucial to know and abide by the timetables for self-assessment so that you avoid the penalties that will kick in automatically if you are late at any stage. The timetable to follow is outlined below.

The Self-Assessment Timetable

September 30: **File your tax return** if you want the Inland Revenue to calculate your tax bill in time to meet the January deadline for paying the bill.

October 5: **Ask for a tax return** if you have not received one but have earnings where the full amount of tax is not deducted at source. The revenue can fine you for missing this deadline.

January 31: **File your previous year's tax return** if you have not already done so. There is an automatic £100 fine if you miss this deadline.

January 31: **Pay the first instalment on account of the current year's tax.** If you miss this deadline you will be charged 8.5 per cent interest on the outstanding tax. If the bill is not paid within one month, there is an automatic 5 per cent surcharge.

July 31: **Pay second payment on account for tax due for the year ended last April 5.** The amount of tax now paid must be the full amount due, not an estimate, so there is only four months in which to calculate the total amount of tax due for the previous tax year.

I hope the new system will prove to be a boon for helping people to become more financially aware. This is still a crucial issue, since even if you use an accountant, the errors he makes do not absolve you from responsibility as far as your tax is concerned. So it is even more important than ever to start learning how to handle your own financial affairs.

Tax Advantages On Savings

We discussed in chapter 7 the various ways that you can consider using tax-exempt schemes to boost your savings. To recap briefly, it is clearly to your advantage to use both PEPs and as long as they are allowable and to investigate the new proposed Isas to see how you can gain from investing in them when they are introduced. Again, money paid into your pension plans is tax-deductible at source, although the pension itself when you receive it, is taxed as earned income. However, the tax-exempt status of the pension premiums is a valuable concession, as it means the cash you are saving is entering your pension fund gross. This should help your money to increase in size more rapidly than if you were saving with funds on which you had already paid your tax.

I believe everyone who saves through a personal pension plan should avail themselves of the opportunity to take the full amount of tax-free cash to provide greater flexibility in their pension planning. Everyone needs to save for a pension as it is the main source of replacement income when you stop working. You need to rely on a pension for everyday expenses and use the nest egg savings of your capital for supplementary spending and to pay for big items. Everyone should recognise the key difference between capital, which is your income–earning cash, and the income itself, which will provide for your routine expenditure.

Many pensioners and children do not earn enough to pay tax, so it is important to fill in the correct forms to ensure bank and building society accounts pay interest gross to these special tax-exempt savers. One of the great advantages of National Savings is the fact that interest is automatically paid gross. This can save these vulnerable members of society from the bother of filling in tax forms to reclaim over-payments, although for those who are tax-payers, gross interest has to be declared in working out the final tax bill. During the filming of the first series of *Mrs Cohen's Money* I discovered that an enormous amount of money due to people who are entitled to get their interest gross, still goes unclaimed every year.

The Tax Calendar

Take full advantage of

the total allocations

allowable for pension

provision to provide a

realistic replacement

income in retirement

Something that never ceases to amaze me is the panic that appears to set in when the end of the tax year approaches. I have found that it is almost impossible to contact the stockbroker I use during March, because people are then frantically busy updating themselves on opening new PEPs or sorting out other aspects of getting their tax affairs in order. Yet the tax calendar is rather like the gardening calendar. The key items that need attention in your garden or for tax planning need to be addressed at the same time every year. This never changes. Planning ahead would ensure these sudden bursts of excess activity in March, before the tax year ends on April 5th, would become outmoded. In particular, the money sections of the broadsheet newspapers, both daily and at the weekend, are good sources of information to update yourself on what you need to do to get your tax affairs straight before the deadline for the tax year-end expires.

The tax-planner's checklist

tax items	date to act by	action needed
annual accounts	5th April	prepare income & expenses schedules
pension contributions	5th April or relate back to earlier years	calculate maximum amount of allowable contribution
tax-exempt savings	5th April	completed application forms plus cash must be submitted prior to 5th April
investments	5th April	take maximum advantage of capital gains allowances
bank or building society interest	during March	obtain evidence of interest earned
bank or building society interest	during March	reclaim tax if interest can be paid gross
newspaper reading		update on the tax calendar

coping with DEBTS AND TAXES

Plan early to avoid the

ritual end-of-year tax

panic

Learning about the tax system can prove to be of benefit to everyone now that the new system of self-assessment puts the main onus on the taxpayer to keep all his financial affairs in order. It could be the vital spark that people need to get them focused on personal finance matters, the first step on the road to becoming more informed about how to manage these issues for themselves.

« *In this world nothing can be said to be certain, except death and taxes.* »

Benjamin Franklin, 1789

Key Points To Remember

1 When coping with debts and taxes, the main principles matter.

2 If necessary, seek proper advice for sorting out your debts or taxes, but become well informed so you stay in control.

3 Borrowing is 'back-to-front' saving.

4 For big investments, some debts can be good.

5 Tackle your debt crisis to escape from debt.

6 Learn about your tax affairs to gain expertise so you can take control of your own affairs.

7 Meet the deadlines to avoid paying fines.

8 Find out if it would pay you to become VAT registered.

9 Claim all the allowances due to you.

10 Use the tax calendar sensibly to keep ahead of the deadlines.

CHAPTER 9

YOUR *personal*

Investment Plan

*'It is Enterprise which builds and improves the world's possessions...
If Enterprise is afoot, Wealth accumulates whatever may be happening to
Thrift.'*

John Maynard Keynes

We have covered a lot of ground in the past eight chapters. Having worked our way through the money maze we are ready now to draw all the various strands together. Fortunately, most of the basic ideas that were introduced during the first five chapters have run, like a recurring theme, throughout the book so that by now, hopefully, you have become familiar with many of them. They are, in essence, the first principles of sound money management that must be grasped in order for you to become more expert at managing your own money. A summary of these key points was included at the end of every chapter. These are the main ideas you need to keep in the forefront of your thinking.

We shall look at the process of setting yourself some achievable money goals and discuss how to prepare a successful wealth-creating plan that is tailor-made for your special needs. This blueprint, your own investment plan, and how to design it, is one of the two main topics to be covered in this last chapter. Finally, we will look at how you should set about putting that plan into action.

There is no doubt that it is far easier to make your money grow when you understand in detail how money works. But there are endless twists and turns within the money maze. You must be able to sift through all the vast clutter of information to focus your attention purely on the core essentials that will always apply when you make important financial decisions. If you cannot slice through the reams of facts and data, you will soon be floundering. You want to grasp just the necessary hard facts, to save on time and effort, to arrive at the successful results you want to reach. All the endless complications are so much distraction. When you can fix the key principles in your mind, the task of handling your money becomes infinitely more manageable.

Your Starting Point

Many people like to leave the best morsels to the end, and as I know this is one of my little quirks, you will not be surprised to find that *The Money Maze* is no exception. For by now you should feel you have been fully briefed on all the vital background information you need. Refer back to the Key Points To Remember sections at the end of each chapter if you need a quick refresher at any time. Absolute novices should never feel shamed by wanting to re-read whole sections, if not the whole book, for more clarification. When I was learning how to invest successfully, I wrote little bullet point notes in my personal organiser on the books I found most useful. I found this was an excellent way to learn. I have passed on to you some of the Warren Buffett and Peter Lynch quotes I learned in the preceding chapters of *The Money Maze*.

The best route to big financial returns comes from plenty of careful preparation according to a blueprint plan

Hopefully, you now feel ready to begin to construct a made-to-measure investment plan that will enable you to meet the broad but realistic financial targets you are going to outline for yourself. Having organised your targets and designed your own personalised investment plan, you will be well on the way to turning your paper goals into real financial assets.

Right at the outset, escaping from the money maze means knowing how to make the most of your existing funds and learning how to increase them without taking undue risks. Above everything else, it certainly means being in control and becoming your own financial adviser. You will know you have arrived when you begin to take your own advice – with confidence.

Ten Top Tips

A useful way to master some of the key ideas is to think about them in the form of the ten most important aspects of getting control over your financial affairs. In this context, the idea of ten top tips works really well. We have discussed them all in earlier chapters, and some of them are core activities to preparing an investment plan. Here they serve only as a focused summary. The first seven are guiding principles on better money management, which have been covered in previous chapters, while tips numbers eight, nine and ten are essential ingredients in designing your plan, so they will be featured again when that is being discussed later in the chapter.

i Start slowly.

ii Safety first.

iii Save and invest.

iv Read about investing.

v Learn about risk.

vi Benefit from your mistakes.

vii Become your own expert.

viii Start budgeting.

ix Do a yearly wealth check.

x Set your money targets.

i Start slowly: This is one of the best ways to avoid making hasty mistakes which can prove to be costly or difficult, if not impossible, to unravel. It is far better to take your time and be certain, before you launch into a scheme that turns out to be less suitable than you first thought it would be. Although it sounds like a contradiction, you will make more progress faster if you just take one step at a time.

For novice investors, tackling too many ideas at once can be confusing and counter-productive

However, even though starting slowly is definitely the best policy for everyone to adopt, in addition it is very important to *start soon.* The longer you have to achieve your financial goals, the longer the time in which your savings can grow. The benefits to you will be immense, since you will have more chance of reaching your financial targets if you give yourself plenty of time. And this applies even if you save very modest amounts, because you will have allowed geometric growth plenty of time to work. But if you are long past that luxury planning stage and already heading towards fifty, just bear in mind that experience is on your side; you will have to work smarter, to catch up for the many lost years. That however, should not be a problem, because you can put a lifetime's rich and varied hard-learned lessons into your efforts.

ii Safety first: The old saying, 'A fool and his money are soon parted' is well applied to hasty investment decisions. Always treat your capital with a healthy respect. If you look after your capital with due care and attention, then it will look after you in your retirement. Increasing your capital is literally your lifeline to a happy and prosperous future. If you lose your capital, you have lost its remarkable income-producing ability. Take as much care of your capital as you would take over any of your other really precious possessions.

At the forefront of your thinking about safety first is the red herring of 'money illusions'. Never forget the vital difference between real values and the loss to your purchasing power that stems from persistent inflation.

iii Save and invest: To recap on this crucially important distinction: saving is a way of building up funds for future use; investing is your route to making those funds grow substantially over time, through growth in both the capital sum and the income it provides. Cultivate the habit of saving and investing regularly, and start at the earliest possible date. The combination of these twin elements will allow your funds to grow consistently through many years. However, initially, a top priority for everyone is to build an emergency fund so you can cope with short-term problems or pay for unexpected items that may crop up.

Your financial pyramid is an excellent way of steadily constructing the building blocks to wealth

With your emergency fund securely in place, all the rest of your free cash can be dedicated to investing in funds which will hopefully offer a higher return. If you are currently sitting on large amounts of accumulated cash in bank or building society deposits, you should now feel ready to turn your back on passive long-term saving. Aim to become a long-term investor. This is not a daunting task if you are willing to start slowly and follow all the rest of the ten top tips.

iv Read about investing: Start to read the relevant information on money matters in your daily or weekend newspaper money sections. You do not need to spend hours on this reading. Nor should you worry unduly if there are terms or jargon you do not understand. Jot down any items you want clarified and either contact one of the companies who answer investors' queries over the telephone or wait until you have an interview with a salesman and ask him for some explanations.

It is better to understand a little than to misunderstand a lot

It is sensible to add one or two magazines to your reading to gain a broad coverage of the main areas you want to learn about. The *Investors Chronicle, Moneywise* and *Money Observer* are good choices. If you are counting your pennies, most public libraries keep the weekly copy of *Investors Chronicle* and also the daily broadsheet newspapers, including the *Financial Times*. In addition, books on investing can be helpful. They too can be borrowed rather than bought when you begin your reading programme to give you the opportunity to decide which, if any, you want to buy as reference books for future use.

v Learn about risk: This is one of the most important aspects of acquiring sound investment skills. There are many sensible ways to manage the risks, all directed at tipping the risk seesaw more in your favour; the more you know, the lower the risk. Throughout *The Money Maze* we have focused on many helpful ways to reduce risks of losing money. Careful preparation and attention to a proper investment plan are central to this. Being well informed applies on even the most basic levels such as knowing how to extricate yourself from a situation that has turned out to be unfavourable and greatly different to your optimistic plans.

vi Benefit from your mistakes: Small investors repeatedly make many mistakes which jeopardise their long-term financial interests. Always try to learn from your mistakes so you do not inadvertently repeat them. The most common mistakes can be avoided if you aim at a few main ideas:

a   Become a long-term investor and ignore short-term fluctuations.
b   Remember the 'money illusion' of cash deposits in 'safe' accounts.
c   Follow the markets to avoid buying at a peak.
d   Don't sell in a panic after the market has fallen steeply.
e   Ignore the latest investment fashions.

vii Become your own expert: In recent years there has been a sorry string of financial scandals; far too many for comfort. So it is vital you start to think about learning how to become your own financial adviser. This is the only sure way to be certain no one to whom you have entrusted your financial affairs will suddenly let you down. If you take control of your own finances as soon as possible, you will be far better able to cope with all the horrendous ramifications that might surface if you do find yourself caught up in a financial disaster, completely beyond your control.

Look after your capital with care, then it will look after you in retirement

As we saw, even in the last decade, this has happened far more frequently than anyone would have imagined possible. The numbers of victims can now be counted in their millions. Sadly, many passive savers are under the misguided impression that the authorities will bail them out of a financial mess that becomes a scandal. I believe it is hopelessly optimistic to rely on this. There are, however, five essential elements to address so you can become your own expert, as we discussed in chapter 4.

a   Take the simplest route.
b   Be a long-term investor.
c   Prepare an investment plan.
d   Follow the market action.
e   Diversify.

viii Start budgeting: Budgeting will play a mammoth role in helping you acquire money skills. First, it is vital for getting control over your spending, especially if that is currently out of control or if you are perpetually in debt. Second, and even more crucial for your long-term financial peace of mind, budgeting will help you to find a reasonable sum of money to save on a regular basis so you can begin to build up capital for your future. Budgeting is a wonderful tool for allowing the same amount of income to go further.

The objectives of routine budgeting are far larger than simply recording all the various items that you spend your income on every month. You must stay focused so you can discover exactly where your money is going. Set yourself maximum spending targets to keep a tight control over your expenses. Budgeting is a challenge in the same way that slimming often is. Cut out the 'between meal snacks' and your shape will quickly look trimmer. So it is with budgeting. If you simply learn how to cut out all the frivolous spending on bits and pieces that you often quickly discard, your finances will soon acquire a leaner, fitter look. Tackle the task with gusto, it is your passport to greater riches. Budgeting is one of the first tasks to establish in your investment planning.

Measuring risk
is an early
warning signal
to stay alert

ix Do a yearly wealth check: Do not be unduly depressed if when you have prepared your first wealth check, you discover it consists of a mass of debts and nothing else. When you know where the key weaknesses are in your current financial situation you are well on the way to correcting them. We discussed how to calculate your first wealth check in chapter 5. Keep a copy of this in a safe place. Then you can compare it with next year's result, to see if you have made any progress. Resolve to repeat the exercise on a yearly basis, so you can chart improvements in your financial situation. As they slowly emerge, year by year, this exercise alone will give your confidence a massive boost. Once you have outlined your first wealth check, you are ready to think about setting your financial goals.

x Set your money targets: These will include targets of varying lengths. Setting your money targets is yet another crucial step in preparing your own investment plan, so we will defer discussing them in detail until later in the chapter.

The last three top tips; starting to budget, doing your first yearly wealth check and setting your money targets all form part of your preliminary stages for designing your investment plan, to which we now turn.

The Investment Plan

Devise a proper investment plan so you can work with it to turn your plans into reality. By identifying your position on the investment staircase, incorporating the ten top tips and designing your financial pyramid, the essential core of your personalised investment plan springs into place. Clearly, as you mount the staircase, your financial needs will change, so you must pay attention to the group of key savings and investment needs most people should plan for.

Everyone of working age, from twenty to sixty-five should save and invest for retirement and future key events. People in work should also consider protecting their income in case illness prevents them from working. Unfortunately, many of the **permanent health** and **critical illness** policies which cover this eventuality have problematic small clauses or sickness limitations. These never seem to come to light until you make a claim and are feeling at your most vulnerable because you are ill and have lost the reliability of your regular income. Extra vigilance is therefore needed when buying these types of policy.

« Remember that time is money. »

Benjamin Franklin

People without family commitments, such as children or the twenty-plus and thirty-plus age groups, and those who are retired, should aim to save and invest for the future. The earlier you begin, the greater will be your gains. This goal is still relevant to pensioners, who may live to enjoy many decades of happy retirement.

Those in the thirty-plus age group with growing families still need to consider saving and investing for retirement and for major events. But in addition, they need protection for replacement income if they encounter a serious illness, protection for the mortgage plus any other debts, and life assurance to provide a replacement income for a widow and dependent children. If the breadwinner in the family dies prematurely, state provision for the surviving members of the family is totally inadequate as a replacement income to provide a reasonable standard of living.

Saving and investing for retirement becomes a top priority for the forty-plus and fifty-plus age groups. They will concentrate on building up a pensions fund and on stock market-related investments, mainly unit or investment trusts. More experienced investors or people with free time and the inclination to get involved, may want to consider building a portfolio of publicly quoted companies. This is an excellent way to increase your wealth over several years. Income and debt protection plus life assurance may still feature in your planning.

Preliminary Stages

To set up your investment plan, begin with a few preliminary stages of planning among which you should include starting to budget, doing your first wealth check, setting your money targets and deciding on your attitude to risk. We shall look at each of these in turn:

Start budgeting

First, prepare your current budget, to see where all the money now goes. Look carefully at the areas where you think you can reduce the outgoings to increase the size of your monthly cash surpluses. Then, rewrite the current budget as your target budget and monitor your progress weekly and monthly in your working budget to get a grip on the spending totals and find the money to save. If you are confused, re-read the budgeting section in chapter 5.

Do your first wealth check

When you have produced your first two budgets, the current and the target, you can do your first wealth check, to discover the full extent of your current assets (possessions) and debts. The wealth check should clearly reveal the degree, if it exists, of your present situation of overspending, especially if you have an overdraft or large and persistent credit card debts. You will see almost at a glance if you have any complementary accumulation of real financial assets. You can use your wealth check to assist you in clarifying your financial pyramid building blocks. Does your current wealth include the right range of assets which will match your existing or future requirements? With your wealth check in front of you, this question leads directly on to the next stage in your planning, namely setting out your money targets.

Set realistic targets

As a result of beginning to budget and calculating your wealth check, you may discover that your debt situation is far grimmer than you had imagined. Your top priority now is to escape from your debt crisis. All the rest of your planning must await that happy outcome. Refer back to the first half of chapter 8, to get to grips with your debt problem.

Your money targets will be designed to cover all your main savings priorities, which may have different time scales. Your short-term targets, for example, will span the next few months. They might include buying a new car or pay-

Every step on the route

ing for an annual holiday. Over the next two or three years, your medium-term targets might include saving for a deposit on your first

to success has to be

house, or the move to a larger house. For the longer term, there may be several saving needs: to help children through university, make weddings,

paid for, in time, effort

and build a pension fund for retirement. Do not be depressed at all the major future events where plenty of money will be needed. Just identi-

and hard cash

fying them all is the first step to sorting out the best way to save for them. Never forget that more than a million pounds may pass through your fingers during your working life. That should be more than enough to cover all your future plans, once you have focused on how to achieve them.

Always aim to set out your targets with realistic sums for the money that you are likely to need to achieve them, together with approximate dates for when you want that money to be available.

Here is an example to work with:

Date: March 1998

	goals	date needed	costs £
1	house deposit	1999	5,000
2	buy a second-hand car	1999	3,500
3	Kate going to university	2010	12,000
4	pension fund to age 60	2022	150,000

Don't worry unduly if your first targets appear to be more like stabs in the dark than realistic money goals. If you do a yearly wealth check you can revise these totals as you go along. Moreover, in the example above, if you wanted to take out a policy, perhaps an endowment to help Kate through university or a personal pension plan for your retirement, the salesman from the company you choose will be able to give you plenty of information about what size premiums you should aim to make to arrive at your preferred lump sum by the target date you have set.

Your attitude to risk

Before you establish your investment plan you must tackle the issue of your attitude to risk. If you are a naturally cautious person, until you have amassed enough expertise to feel comfortable with more highly volatile stock market-related equities, you should aim to choose investment schemes that match your psychological approach to risk. There will be plenty of time in the future, hopefully, to take a more risky approach to wealth creation, once you have gained more of the knowledge you need to feel comfortable with that approach.

At the outset, if you feel cautious, do not worry even if this means selecting more low-risk savings-related schemes for your earliest stages of pyramid building. You will be fighting yourself if you try to adopt a higher risk-oriented investment attitude that does not suit your personality. Later, when you feel more in command of the crucial principles, you can discard the cautious, savings dominated stance in favour of a more aggressive equities-related attitude. And this will apply, no matter how old you are. Once you have sufficient knowledge, making money is far easier than you could ever imagine. But it is extremely difficult to take successful investment decisions if they leave you feeling anxious or uncomfortable.

Financial Pyramid Planning

With your preliminaries sketched out, now is the time to begin planning for all the separate blocks in your financial pyramid. For most people, the first major investment step will be to address any weaknesses in their three essential foundation building blocks: buying a house, a pension and insurance-based savings. These are the big priority areas of wealth creation, the main corner stones for future financial security. Everyone should concentrate on these three areas right from the outset before focusing on the upper blocks on the pyramid. This is in every way the most appropriate starting point, as these three blocks focus mainly on the lower risk areas of savings.

This is where a little focused reading really pays off, especially when you are trying to decide between competing products for any one scheme you are planning to buy. And this will apply whether you are considering a mortgage, pension, insurance policy or unit trust. If you use an adviser, be sure that not only has he explained all the key points to you, but that you clearly understand them. Ask him to leave you all the important literature so that you can go through it on your own after the interview. By all means listen to his advice, but be determined to make your own financial decisions. It is your money you are spending.

Check the credentials of the company he is recommending or the company he represents, if he is a direct salesman. Make sure you fully understand all the crucial small print clauses and the total charges you will incur. Check the long-term performance of the product you are buying. You will want to find an insurance or pensions company or a fund management group who can demonstrate in writing a consistent performance stretching back over several years. This information should be provided either by the company or the representative you are using. Remember the high charges/low returns seesaw. High returns and low charges should apply to all the financial products you are likely to buy. If you can buy your pension with single premium payments, you may reduce the charges considerably.

Finally, take advantage of the so-called 'cooling off' period of ten days in which you may change your mind and cancel a policy contract. Do not be afraid to use this escape route if you have second thoughts about a plan, although this does not apply to unit trusts. However, all pension and insurance policies do contain a cooling-off period. It forms part of the essential paperwork.

Sift Through The Choices

When you begin to search for ways of building the top layers in your financial pyramid, one of your first problems will be to decide which particular investment schemes will be best suited to you. Several factors should be considered here.

First, which investment step are you on? If you are on the lower steps you will have a much longer period to build up your capital, so you can afford to take a more risky approach. But if you are on the higher steps a more cautious approach would be sensible. However, if you begin early enough in life, you can move from an aggressive growth investment approach to a more cautious income-oriented plan, as your funds build up over time.

Another major element that will affect your investment choices is whether your highest need is for capital growth or income. We saw in chapter 5 what a disaster it can be if you confuse these two. This again depends on which investment stair you are currently on. Obviously, people on the lower steps of the investment staircase will be keenest to build up their capital while those nearing retirement will be looking for sound income-oriented investments, to boost their current spending power, while hoping to maintain the purchasing value of their capital.

You can swing the odds

more heavily in your

favour by creating your

own made-to-measure

investment plan

We saw in chapter 2 that a very modest sum of money can grow substantially if it is left in real assets for a long period. This means that parents could put a small sum into an international growth fund for their young children and leave it to grow for fifteen or more years. Meanwhile, a young man in his late twenties could perhaps make a modest, one-off payment into a personal pension plan and leave it to grow over the next ten years or so, before he begins seriously to build up his pension. This one-off payment will help him to feel secure in the knowledge that over the period he had left his money in a pension plan, it would be building up a useful starting fund.

For novice investors who set out in their late forties or early fifties, as I did, if you are prepared to put in the necessary effort, you can follow a good progression in investments, linked to the rising level of your expertise. If you want to make higher returns, you can move steadily forward as you approach your early sixties, advancing from unit and investment trusts, then on to small fast-growing companies and on again to invest in the leading UK FTSE 100 blue chip companies. This route will enable you to increase your funds much faster than would otherwise be the case. Investing in small, fast-growing companies can be risky, as successfully managing their growth is one of the hardest things for them to achieve. They can be like the nursery rhyme about the girl with the curl:

« *When they are good, they are very, very good, but when they are bad, they are horrid.* »

If you decide to follow the fortunes of a collection of small growth companies, in which you have invested some money, you must be ready to watch them very closely for any signs of problems or a faltering in their growth. This can be time-consuming, but if you do not monitor them routinely, you may miss a sudden profits warning and lose a lot of your money. Unless you really want to become a millionaire, you can eventually plan to move on to the major blue chip companies, which do not need such continuous monitoring. Depending on which companies you choose, they may grow by 8 to 13 per cent a year. By the time you have progressed through all these stages and are ready to buy these major, quality blue chip shares, you can plan to hold them right through retirement. Then you will be the ultimate long-term investor, receiving regular, hopefully rising, dividends to supplement your income from a pension. Of course, you must still be willing to do a yearly review, so you know how these major companies are faring. In the review you will want to look and see if they are still performing as you had hoped. One advantage of major FTSE 100 shares is that news about these companies features regularly in the financial press to keep you updated.

In my opinion, this is an ideal scenario for pensioners who need reliable sources of income. You will not need to be so active with your investments, which leaves time to travel and enjoy your hobbies. This is what a happy retirement should provide for. You will also be able to enjoy the income benefits of your holdings while ultimately, you can bequeath your blue chip shares to other younger members of your family.

Just take one step after another on the route to investment success

One of my friends told me an inspirational story about his grandmother which I would like to share with you. I am filled with admiration for her foresight and hope that I might some day repeat what she achieved. Back in the early 1960s, she spent £3,000 on a block of shares in a British pharmaceutical company. These shares were still in the family in 1997, but were now in the hands of her grandchildren. Her initial investment had grown handsomely over the years, and was by then valued at well over £600,000, having risen a staggering 200-fold in thirty-four years. Of course, today, £3,000 seems such a modest sum to invest, but beware!

It's that devil 'money illusions' at work again. In 1963, £3,000 was the annual income of a young doctor, working single-handed in a practice in Islington. I know, as I was married to one who earned just that. So although £3,000 in 1997 terms, sounds quite insignificant as a lump sum investment, it was considerably more impressive in the early 1960s. If a young doctor in 1997 wanted to put the equivalent of one year's salary into one British company, he would have had to spend around £45,000.

The important point to grasp, however, is how fast the pharmaceutical company's shares have romped away, while doctors earnings over that thirty-four years grew by a far more modest 15-fold. These comparative figures all illustrate to perfection why long-term investments in solid British companies with great growth prospects win all the prizes for building beautiful nest eggs. My friend's grandmother certainly had a good idea. Choose the right investments and you and your family can live like a Lord on unearned income.

Pyramid Planning

To recap on the major stages of building your financial pyramid as you mount the investment staircase, the various stages of planning can be drawn up as a table with their low-, medium- and high-risk status clearly marked, as shown below.

Schemes to use in your Investment Plan

plan	no. of years	risk level	age groups
cash fund	indefinite	low	20s–60s +
national savings	1 or 5 +	low	10s–60s +
TESSAs	5–10	low	40s–60s +
endowments	5–25	low	30s–60s +

unit trusts (PEPs)			
1 trackers	5 +	medium	20s–60s +
2 international growth	7 +	medium	10s–60s +
3 emerging markets	7 +	high	10s–60s +
4 UK growth income	5 +	high	40s–60s +

company shares	3 +	high	40s–60s +

The Action Plan

Having outlined the stages for creating your own investment plan, we can now set about putting the plan into action.

Here, in the Action Plan section of this chapter, the investment plan is set out as a working guide for you to complete the various stages of your financial pyramid planning. The Action Plan will take you through a series of questions on which you will make the appropriate decisions, one by one. This will allow you to progress through the early stages in an orderly manner. With so much information available, the key objective is to focus on the pure essentials to keep the process of planning as simple as possible, so you can work your way successfully through the never-ending intricacies of the confusing money maze.

A first priority is to examine your situation in terms of your current debt position and the state of your tax affairs. People who have neglected their financial affairs for years will probably discover they are very poorly briefed on money matters. Having now reached the Action Plan, however, readers will hopefully feel ready and more willing to take a firmer control over their finances. Now is the time, therefore, to consider the important issues on dealing with outstanding debt and tax problems.

YOUR *personal* **Investment Plan**

The Plan in Action
1 Are you in debt?
Yes: – go to 2.
No: – go to 3.

2 Is your debt manageable?
Yes: – go to 3.
No: a) Work through the first half of chapter 8 again. Pay special attention to the table on page 198 on how to tackle a debt crisis. Then go to 3.
b) Seek professional advice. Contact the Citizen's Advice Bureau, or a debt counselling service. Then go to 3.

3 Are your tax affairs in order?
Yes: – go to 4.
No: a) Work through the second half of chapter 8 again. Then go to 4.
b) Seek professional advice. Contact your local Inland Revenue office for leaflets or more information.
c) Ask your friends for a recommendation or see list on page 237–8 to find an accountant to sort out your problems. Then go to 4.

4 Are your tax returns up to date?
Yes: – go to 5.
No: Reread the second half of chapter 8. Pay special attention to the table on page 206 on the tax calendar. Seek advice from the Inland Revenue or an accountant. Then go to 5.

5 Do you know your place on the investment staircase?
Yes: – go to 6.
No: Reread chapter 1, then go to 6.

6 Are you ready to start budgeting?
Yes: – go to 7.
No: Reread the section on budgeting in chapter 5. Then go to 7.

7 Is your main budgeting concern overspending?
Yes: Prepare your 3 budgets, current, target and working budgets using prepared grids on pages 227–9. Focus on reducing your spending on at least three 'black holes'. Then go to 8.
No: – go to 8.

8 Is your main budgeting concern not having any money to save?
Yes: Rework your current budget to create a target budget that includes a pay-yourself-first fund. Then go to 9.
No: – go to 9.

9 Is your main budgeting concern running up unexpected overdrafts?
Yes: Reread chapter 5, with special attention to the cash flow calculations, shown in the table on page 118. Keep a close watch on the cash flow section of your working budget. When you have managed that to your satisfaction, go to 10.
No: – go to 10.

10 Have you got emergency funds on deposit?
Yes: – go to 11.
No: Reread section on emergency funds in chapter 7. Rework your budget to find regular savings to build up your emergency fund. Then go to 11.

11 Is your emergency fund equivalent to 3 or 6 months annual salary?
Yes: – go to 12.
No: Rework your working budget to make provision for an emergency fund equivalent to 3 to 6 months of your annual salary. Then go to 12.

12 Can you prepare your first wealth check?
Yes: Prepare your wealth check and work out your assets and liabilities. Then go to 13.
No: Reread chapter 5, section on preparing your wealth check. Refer to table on page 120. Prepare your wealth check. Then go to 13.

13 Do you know what your money goals are?
Yes: Prepare your money goals and then go to 14.
No: Reread chapter 9, section on calculating your money targets using table on page 216, prepare your money goals and then go to 14.

14 Are you planning to buy a house?
Yes: Reread relevant sections in chapters 6 and 9 then go to 15.
No: – go to 15.

15 Have you got a pension?
Yes: – go to 16.
No: Reread section on pensions in chapter 6 and begin to prepare your pension plans. Then go to 16.

16 Will your current pension funding be large enough to give you a 70 per cent replacement income when you retire?
Yes: – go to 17.
No: Reread chapter 6 and revise your pension plans. Then go to 17.

17 Have you got policies specially designed for supplementary savings?
Yes: – go to 18.
No: Reread chapter 6 and make some supplementary savings plans. Then go to 18.

18 Have you got a mortgage or other debts?
Yes: – go to 19.
No: – go to 20.

19 Have you got life assurance to cover your debts, including your mortgage?
Yes: – go to 20.
No: Reread pages 150–2 in chapter 6 and make plans to obtain appropriate life assurance. Then go to 20.

20 Have you got life assurance to provide your widow and dependent children with a replacement income equal to 70 per cent of your current income?
Yes: – go to 21.
No: Reread chapter 6 and make plans to obtain the appropriate life assurance. Then go to 21.

21 Have you written a will?
Yes: – go to 22.
No: Reread chapter 6, then go to 23.

22 Is you will up-to-date?
Yes: – go to 23.
No: Rewrite your will so it is up-to-date. Then go to 23.

23 In connection with your will, do you have dependent children or financial complications?
Yes: Consult a solicitor, see page 238 for address of the Law Society. Then go to 24.
No: Buy a preprepared will form at a good stationery store. Prepare your will. Then go to 24.

24 Have you got any investments to top your financial pyramid – National Savings, tax-exempt plans or unit and investment trusts?
Yes: – go to 25.
No: Reread chapter 7 and make plans to buy toppings for your financial pyramid. Then go to 26.

25 Are you happy with your holdings of National Savings, tax-exempt schemes, unit or investment trusts?
Yes: – go to 26.
No: Reread chapter 7, adjust your holdings as necessary. Then go to 26.

26 Is it time to do a yearly wealth check, or fill in your current tax return?
Yes: Do your yearly wealth check and compare it to last year's wealth check to see if you are on target to meet your financial goals.
No: Make notes in your personal organiser so you remember to do a yearly wealth check and can meet the tax deadlines.

If you are approaching retirement, this could be the right time to begin considering the wide variety of annuity possibilities on offer. Reread the relevant section on annuity planning in chapter 6, if you are unsure how to proceed, and then work your way through the annuity maze, outlined on page 224 to decide which of the huge choice of annuities would best suit your situation. Having worked your way through the annuity maze I would still recommend that you use a specialist to arrange your annuity. Now, however, you will be more in command of the facts and will therefore be better able to understand the various options he suggests you should take.

Work Your Way Through The Annuity Maze

1 **Do you need all the income from your pension right away?**
   Yes: Use 75% of your fund to buy a pensions annuity now. Go to 2.
   No: Defer taking your annuity and consult a special advisor to consider using phased or drawdown schemes.

2 **Are you in good health or a non-smoker?**
   Yes: Buy a standard annuity. Go to 3.
   No: Buy an impaired life annuity. Go to 3.

3 **Do you want to protect part of your pension for your spouse?**
   Yes: Choose a joint life annuity. Go to 4.
   No: Choose a single life annuity. Go to 4.

4 **Do you want the maximum possible pension right away?**
   Yes: Avoid all the following options as they eat into the amount of your pension. Go to 8.
   No: Consider all the following options in turn. Go to 5.

5 **Do you want your pension guaranteed for a specific period?**
   Yes: Choose the guaranteed option of 5 or 10 years. Go to 6.
   No: Buy an annuity without a guarantee. Go to 6.

6 **Do you want your pension to rise in value over the years?**
   Yes: – Go to 7.
   No: – Go to 8.

7 **Do you want a fixed increase for your pension?**
   Yes: Choose either 3%, 5% or index-linked escalations. Go to 8.
   No: Consider with-profits or unit-linked annuities where increases depend on the growth achieved by the investment funds. Go to 8.

8 **Have you got a preference for how you want your pension to be paid?**
   Yes: Choose from monthly, quarterly, half-yearly or annually. Go to 9.
   No: You have to make a choice, as the pension has to be paid at set intervals as specified at the outset. Go to 9.

9 **Do you want to get the maximum amount of pension possible?**
   Yes: Use a specialist annuity bureau to find the best open market option for your age, sex and size of fund. You should also consider taking your pension monthly, quarterly, half-yearly or annually in arrears as this increases the amount paid out, although not by very much.
   No: Settle for immediate payments on the specified period of your choice using the company you built up your pension fund with. However, please note that this alternative will probably not give you the best result.

Stay On Track

With your full investment plan in place, now is the time to follow the guidelines and keep abreast of current financial affairs through your reading, by attending investment classes or seminars, by visiting money shows or conferences on specialist topics, or by joining an investment club. All these avenues allow you to meet like-minded investors for a lively exchange of ideas.

As you slowly put your plans into action, you can monitor how you are getting along. You should assess your progress on a regular basis, to ensure you are on track to achieve your financial goals. A yearly review of how you are getting on could coincide with your yearly wealth check. It might simplify matters if you organise to do this financial spring cleaning so it coincides with the tax year end. Then updating all your financial affairs can be focused on the month of March. Give yourself plenty of time to improve your financial situation, especially if, like me, you started out with huge debts and very few assets. There is no race to be won, although the sooner you have reached a state of financial security the sooner you can begin to enjoy the fruits of your efforts.

Failure teaches success

I like to keep all my notes and information in my personal organiser where they are all in one easily remembered place. Keeping a diary can also be very helpful. Computerised records on a palm-top computer is another method. If none of these alternatives appeals to you, try to devise your own method of recording your activities. Ideally, you want to have them all in one tidy place or filing system, so you can periodically review your progress. The main objective here is to analyse the results. You want to know when events turned out right, so you can hopefully repeat them. But more seriously, you must know what went wrong when things do not go according to plan. Then you can avoid this scenario in the future and learn as much as you can from your mistakes.

You have to become your own financial adviser to fully experience the pleasure that it brings

I think learning to become more financially aware is one of the most exciting hobbies you can cultivate. You can become your own financial expert whatever your age or circumstances. This is a hobby that will stand you in good stead right throughout your life. And you can pass this knowledge on to your children and grandchildren. And then, we haven't even mentioned how wonderful it is to see the success of your financial planning, when you have enough money not to worry unduly if you want to go out and spend some of it. The benefits of this pleasure far outweigh the modest amount of time and effort you will spend on becoming your own financial expert.

As you progress, you will achieve some of the most precious advantages life can offer today; financial freedom and the ability to make many choices on how you will spend your cash. You will secure the opportunity to fulfill your hopes and dreams.

« It is impossible to adequately describe the wonderful satisfaction of doing all this for yourself and becoming financially secure into the bargain. »

current budget

ITEM	Jan	Feb	March	April	May	June	*Totals*
income							
carried for'd							
salary							
bonus							
interest							
dividends							
gifts							
extras							
Totals							
expenses							
food							
mortgage/rent							
electricity/gas							
telephone							
water							
council tax							
insurance							
car expenses							
credit cards							
store cards							
travel							
TV licence							
clothes							
entertainment							
extras							
tax							
NI contributions							
savings							
Totals							
carry down							

The Money Maze

target budget

ITEM	Jan	Feb	March	April	May	June	Totals
income							
carried for'd							
salary							
bonus							
interest							
dividends							
gifts							
extras							
Totals							
expenses							
food							
mortgage/rent							
electricity/gas							
telephone							
water							
council tax							
insurance							
car expenses							
credit cards							
store cards							
travel							
TV licence							
clothes							
entertainment							
extras							
tax							
NI contributions							
savings							
Totals							
carry down							

YOUR *personal* **Investment Plan**

working budget

ITEM	Jan	Feb	March	April	May	June	*Totals*
income							
carried for'd							
salary							
bonus							
interest							
dividends							
gifts							
extras							
Totals							
expenses							
food							
mortgage/rent							
electricity/gas							
telephone							
water							
council tax							
insurance							
car expenses							
credit cards							
store cards							
travel							
TV licence							
clothes							
entertainment							
extras							
tax							
NI contributions							
savings							
Totals							
carry down							

glossary of TERMS

Active fund manager: one who aims to out-perform the market.

Actuary: expert in the theory of statistics especially of mortality, sickness, retirement and unemployment.

Additional voluntary contributions (AVCs): additional payments paid into company pension schemes by members.

Analysts: professionals who work for the big brokerage and merchant banking houses whose job it is to analyse and report on national economies, individual companies and various sectors of a stock market.

Annuity: a form of income, guaranteed and fixed for life, which is bought through insurance companies with an accumulated pension fund.

Annual bonus: a lump sum added to a policy every year it is in force, which cannot be taken away once it has been allocated.

Annual General Meeting: a yearly meeting when the directors of a company present the main items of business affecting it to the ordinary shareholders of the company.

Arithmetic growth: linear or add-on growth in a commodity.

Assets: physical and intangible goods (like goodwill) that a person or a company owns.

Auditor: an outside accountant employed to make routine checks on a business to ensure the company's accounts are being kept properly.

Balance sheet: the statement of the capital position of a company at any one time. It shows what it owns (assets) and what it owes (its liabilities).

Bear and **bull markets:** a bear market is one where prices are falling usually across the whole market for a prolonged period of weeks, months or even years. A bull market is one with a rising trend. Investors who think the market is about to fall are bearish while those who think the market will rise are bullish.

Bid: the price a fund manager is willing to pay to buy back your holdings in a unit trust.

Bills: a bill is a short-term fixed interest loan stock, often issued by governments or very large corporations. UK Treasury Bills have a life of three months.

Blue chip: a share in a very large, well established and highly regarded company. It is named after the highest value chip in poker.

Bond: a bond is a certificate of debt issued by companies and governments to raise cash. They usually pay interest and can be traded in a market. A bond is longer term than a bill. It is a fixed interest loan which guarantees to repay the capital at an agreed future date. UK Government bonds are known as gilts or gilt-edged securities because in the nineteenth century, when Britain was the centre of a thriving wealthy empire, they were considered 'as good as gold'. There are several time periods for UK gilts: short (under five years to maturity), mediums (between five and fifteen years) and longs (which mature after fifteen years).

Bonus: additional sums of money added at regular intervals, usually of one year, to a savings policy. Once added, the annual bonus cannot be taken away.

glossary of TERMS

Brokers: brokers are professionals who buy and sell on behalf of their clients.

Capital: an amount of money, a lump sum, that can be invested in assets or is available to invest.

Capital gains (or growth): the increase in the capital value of investments.

Capital Gains Tax: this is a complicated form of government taxation, payable on profits above a set level, from the sale of various assets, including stock market investments, particularly shares.

Capitalism: a form of economy where entrepreneurs put their own money or money they have raised into business in order to make profits. This money is called capital.

Cash flow: the amount of money which flows into and out of an account belonging to an individual or a company. The difference between the cash flowing in and out is the important number. If more money flows into the account than out of it, the account is cash positive. If more flows out, it is cash negative.

Collective funds: any scheme where investors pool their resources to spread their investment risks. Popular forms of collective funds include unit and investment trusts in Britain and mutual funds in America.

Compound growth: method of growth in which the interest is added back to the capital at each stage to enhance the total.

Convertible: a bond or share which has the option to convert into another bond or share at a fixed date or set of dates and under fixed terms.

Credit: credit is given by banks when they advance loans to their customers, and by businesses when they allow their customers to take goods and defer payment for them.

Creditors: companies or individuals to whom you owe money.

Critical illness policy: pays out a lump sum if the policy holder develops one or more of certain specified illnesses.

Default: to fail to pay a debt.

Defined benefits: see **Final Salary Pension** schemes.

Defined contribution scheme: or money purchase scheme, the contributions go into a pot whose growth depends upon the investment performance of the fund; at retirement the fund is used to purchase an annuity.

Deflation: the opposite of inflation; when general prices in the economy are falling.

Demerger: when a company splits off part of its operations as a separately quoted company.

Depreciation: the loss in value of an asset with time or through usage.

Discount: a discount occurs when investment trust shares are selling below the level of the total value of the shares held in its portfolio.

Dividend: this is the proportion of a company's profits or earnings which is paid out to its shareholders as a distribution. It is paid out twice yearly, as an interim and a final dividend.

Dividend yield: the ratio between the dividend and what was actually paid for the share.

Economic cycle: this is a round of economic events that proceed in an irregular succession.

Economists: professionals who study the behaviour of the economy.

Endowment policy: a life insurance and savings policy which pays a specified amount of money on an agreed date **(the maturity date)** or on the death of the person insured, whichever is the sooner.

Equity: commonly used to mean the **ordinary shares** of a company. They are freely traded shares in publicly quoted companies that do not carry a fixed rate of interest; instead they entitle their holders to a share in the growth of the company through an annual dividend payment. The equity holders are the company's owners.

Exchange Rate Mechanism of the European Monetary System: it ties European currencies together by confining them within set bands. If any currency starts to move outside the bands, the European central banks must take action to oppose the movement.

Final Salary Pension schemes: also called **defined benefits.** here the level of the benefits is fixed, regardless of the performance of the funds.

Fixed Expenses: expenses that are fixed or certain in amount for a long period.

Flotation: a flotation is a new issue of shares available to the public that occurs when a private company comes to the market and sells a percentage of its shares to whoever wants to buy them.

Front end load: when a major portion of the charges, including commission, is applied to an insurance, savings or pension policy at the outset and deducted during the initial years. These charges may be referred to as 'initial charges'.

FTSE 100 index: monitors the performance of the top 100 publicly quoted companies by market capitalisation (market value) on the UK stock market. It is weighted to take account of the largest and smallest sized companies within the hundred. It is updated throughout the day.

FTSE 250: this index works in a similar way. It monitors the performance of 250 medium-sized companies that together comprise this index.

FTSE 350: this index covers the performance of the FTSE 100 and FTSE 250 shares. All three indices are updated continuously throughout the working day.

FTSE SmallCap: this is an index that covers a range of the small companies traded on the UK stock market.

FTSE All-Share index: covers about 900 shares on the UK market. It is updated at the start of every working day.

Gazumping: a situation where a prospective house purchaser has been outbid by a second purchaser in spite of the original offer having been agreed.

GDP: Gross Domestic Product - the amount of goods and services produced by a country in one year.

Gearing: the relationship between the size of the borrower's initial debt and the lender's initial share of an asset on which a loan is outstanding. High gearing means high borrowing relative to a person's contribution to the value of the asset.

Geometric growth: growth on growth, where a commodity is growing by a percentage of its overall size.

Gilt-edged bonds: British government loans which carry a fixed interest.

Gold Standard: a system of valuing currencies against a fixed amount of gold. The British Gold Standard was first set up in 1717 by Sir Isaac Newton, the Keeper of the Mint.

Gross: interest or dividends for investors, means before deduction of income tax.

Guaranteed income bonds (Gibs): these bonds give a guaranteed income but do not give investors any capital growth.

Illiquid assets: assets or securities which are not easily transferable into cash.

Income: money you earn or receive from a regular and reliable source.

Income fund: a unit trust that concentrates on companies which pay out large dividends which can supplement an income.

Income plan: an insurance based product which provides income for elderly couples by utilising some of the equity tied up in their property.

Independent financial advisers: (IFA) an adviser committed to offering 'best advice' on a wide range of investments and financial products available in the marketplace.

Index: a selected list of publicly quoted shares which represent all others of that type in a stock market.

Index-linked: a security whose value and/or interest payments are linked to inflation, particularly index-linked gilts, pensions or National Savings products.

Individual Savings Account: (Isa) a new tax-exempt savings scheme due to be introduced by the Labour government in 1999.

Inflation: a percentage measure of the amount by which the prices of goods and services rise in the economy, over a period of time, usually one year.

Institutions: usually meaning financial institutions, the pensions and insurance companies in the UK. They handle huge sums of money on behalf of their clients, the policy holders.

Interest: a regular payment made usually twice yearly to savers who keep their money in deposit accounts with building societies or banks.

Interest only mortgage: the amount of the loan stays the same throughout the duration of the mortgage with monthly payments of interest due plus payments into a savings plan. The intention is that the savings plan will grow in size sufficiently to repay the entire mortgage at the end of the period.

Investing: putting money into real financial assets with the hope of increasing the size of the original **investment** through future growth at the same time as receiving a regular and rising income.

Investment trust: a company which is quoted on the stock exchange and exists to invest in the equity of other companies. It is used by large institutions and also small investors to gain a wide spread of investments.

Liabilities: an amount of money owed to other people.

Linear growth: regular incremental or arithmetic growth.

Liquid: a market for a financial commodity where there are many buyers and sellers so that it is easy to deal. Investors who hold cash are said to be **liquid,** as cash is the easiest commodity to use for buying any other asset.

Liquidator: a person appointed to wind up a company that has run into trading difficulties.

Low-start mortgage: designed to help the first-time buyer to meet the payments on the endowment policy plus the interest on the loan throughout the first five years of the mortgage.

M4: a measure of the cash in circulation plus that in bank and building society accounts.

Market capitalisation: a company's total value, that is, the number of its shares in issue multiplied by the share price at any one time.

Market maker: a person who offers to buy or sell securities on his own account, acting as a principal. This contrasts with a broker, who acts as an agent for the investor.

Money illusions: the failure to take account of inflation when assessing the purchasing power of money.

Money purchase pension scheme: the individual contributes to the pension plan with or without additional contributions from the employer. The size of the final fund depends upon the performance of the funds. These schemes are also called **defined contribution schemes.**

Money Supply: a measure of the amount of money in circulation in the economy used by governments and economists.

Mutual: a form of company structure where the members (usually borrowers, savers or policy holders) own all the assets of the company. It applies to building societies and some insurance companies, such as Scottish Widows and Equitable Life.

National Savings: low-risk savings schemes run by the UK government with attractive rates of interest where interest is paid gross.

Negative equity: a situation where the current value of your property is less than the amount owed on the mortgage.

Net worth: the value of your assets after deducting the full extent of all your debts (liabilities).

Nominal value: the numerical value of an item, ignoring the impact of inflation.

OEIC: open-ended investment company, an umbrella unit trust which can have any number of sub-funds within it, but with a single price for the whole fund.

Open Market Option: a scheme for an annuitant to purchase his annuity in the open market, not just from the company with which he built up his pension fund.

Ordinary shares: the commonest form of shares in a company; the holders own the company and receive dividends in proportion to its profitability.

Ordinary shareholders' funds: the money belonging to the ordinary shareholders in a publicly quoted company.

Paid up: a policy is made paid up when the policyholder decides to cease paying further premiums but leaves the accumulated fund in his policy to continue growing. This is a better option than surrendering the policy early because the policyholder cannot afford to continue paying the premiums. Surrender values may be low but if the paid up fund stays with the company to maturity, it will continue to grow and surrender penalties will be avoided.

PEP: Personal equity plan, a government sponsored scheme for investing up to £9,000 each year with all income and capital gains free of tax. The £9,000 is split into £6,000 for a general PEP, which can be invested in mainly UK-based unit or investment trusts or directly into shares, and £3,000 which must be invested in a single company PEP in which you can hold the shares of only one UK company at a time.

Profits: the amount of cash left in a business after deducting all the expenses from the revenues earned.

Premium: prices of the shares in an investment trust are selling at a level above their intrinsic value.

Pensions: a savings scheme whereby the contributions create a fund which from a specified date can buy an annuity to provide an income to the saver. Although contributions are generally tax exempt, tax will have to be paid on the eventual income derived from the fund.

Permanent health policy: pays out a regular income replacement if the policyholder is unable to work because of ill-health.

Publicly quoted companies: companies that are listed on a national stock market.

Purchase life annuity: can be purchased by anyone with disposable cash, not simply by those buying pensions annuities.

Purchasing power: the amount of goods and services you can buy with your money at any time.

Real assets: assets which hold or increase their value over time, in spite of inflation.

glossary of TERMS

Real financial assets: assets in financial investments that tend to hold or even increase their value over time, in spite of inflation.

Real growth: growth after deducting for inflation.

Real rate of return: the capital growth plus income earned on an asset after deducting for inflation.

Recession: a downturn in activity across the economy which lasts more than six months.

Recovery shares: these are the shares of companies that are expected to recover to a higher rating by the market. They include several types of company: those in cyclical sectors which will expand profitably as the economy recovers from a recession; good companies that have hit a problem or failed to meet investors' expectations; companies that are plagued by problems and may recover.

Repayment mortgage: the capital owing and the interest on it are paid off throughout the period of the loan. Therefore, at the end of the term, the entire debt will have been repaid.

Re-rated: when analysts and investors decide that a company has better prospects than was generally expected.

Reserves: money put aside out of the profits of a company to build up the internal resources the company holds for future use, including expansion.

Retail Prices Index: the official measure of inflation in the economy It is calculated by weighting the cost of goods and services to approximate to a typical family's spending patterns.

Risk: this word has various interpretations. Broadly, it is the amount of money which an investor stands to lose from any investment.

Saving: putting aside a sum of money for future use.

Second mortgage: a legal contract with the same or a different mortgage provider to obtain further cash on a property. Usually carries a higher rate of interest. Positive equity needs to be still locked up in the property to be able to obtain a second mortgage.

Securities: tradable financial products, such as shares or bonds.

State earnings-related pension scheme (Serps) a state pension in addition to the basic state pension, plus widows' benefits and invalidity benefits, based on earnings.

Stockbroker: see also **Broker;** stockbrokers are professionals who buy and sell shares on behalf of their clients. Private individuals and institutions are not allowed to deal in shares directly with the market makers, who are the people that set the prices. Stockbrokers act as middlemen between buyers and sellers.

Stock market: the market for equities, or 'shares', in public companies. In London called the Stock Exchange. A buyer is actually purchasing a share in the ownership of a company.

Tax collector: the official responsible for collecting income tax.

Tax inspector: the official responsible for assessing how much tax a tax-payer owes the Inland Revenue.

Terminal bonus: a final sum of money added to a policy on maturity as part of the total payout.

Term assurance: life assurance which covers a fixed term only.

TESSA: Tax exempt special savings account, a government sponsored scheme for investing up to a total of £9,000 over a period of five years with interest paid free of tax.

Total Return: the addition of the capital growth plus the dividend income received on an investment in real financial assets.

Tracker fund: a fund designed to follow some stock market index by investing in a range of shares which behave similarly to that index.

UK growth and income trusts: forms of unit trust which invest in companies quoted on the London Stock Exchange which will give investors exposure to either a high rate of growth or a high annual dividend payment.

Unearned income: income derived from assets and not by work.

Unit-linked annuities: an annuity that is linked to the Retail Prices Index, so that the pension payments rise in line with inflation every year.

Index: a selected list of publicly quoted shares which represent all others of that type.

Unit trusts: a form of investment where investors' money is pooled within a trust in order to purchase a large number of shares to spread the risk. This enables an investor to have exposure to a larger range of companies than individual resources alone might allow.

Unit-linked policy: an insurance or pension policy in which the benefits depend on the performance of units in a fund invested in shares, property or fixed interest investments. **Unsecured loan:** the lender does not require that you lodge other assets with him to protect the loan..

Variable expenses: expenses that vary from one month or one year to the next.

Volatility: a measure of the frequency with which share prices move up or down.

Voluntary Contributions: additional contributions to your pension plan.

Value-added tax (VAT): a form of indirect taxation borne by traders and consumers. It is levied on goods and services. If a business has more than a certain level of annual turnover it has to be registered for VAT with the Customs and Excise.

Variable rates of interest: the rates of interest vary, according to the general levels of interest applying in the economy.

Warrant: a long-term option to buy a company's share at a pre-determined price.

Wasting assets: assets whose value declines over time, and with use.

Will: a formal legal statement of a person's wishes as to the disposal of their assets after their death; literally a 'willing' of assets.

With-profits annuities: annuities which depend on the performance of an insurance company's investment funds.

With-profits policy: a life insurance or pension policy with additional amounts added at regular intervals to the sums insured. The additions take the form of bonuses, annual and terminal.

Whole of Life Assurance: life assurance that continues throughout your life, as long as you continue paying all the premiums due.

Yield: the annual rate of return on a share or a bond which the investor would earn from that security at the current market price.

suggested reading AND
USEFUL names and addresses

SUGGESTED READING

I have included a short list of books and leaflets which are a gentle introduction to the general topics of personal finance and investing. They cover a very wide range of views and different investment approaches.

Ballance, David, *Allied Dunbar Investment and Savings Handbook 1997–98*, Pitman, 1997

Drury, Tony, *Investment Clubs, the low-risk way to stockmarket profits*, Rushmere Wynne, 1995.

Help the Aged, *Managing a Lump Sum*, Help the Aged, Information Department, St.James's Walk, Clerkenwell Green, London EC1 0BE.

Lefevre, Edwin, *Reminiscences of a Stock Operator*, John Wiley, 1993.

Linton, David, *Profit From Your PC; How to use a personal computer to buy and sell shares*, Rushmere Wynne, 1995, and an updated version, *More Profit from your PC*, 1996.

Lynch, Peter, *One Up On Wall Street*, Simon and Schuster, 1989.

Philip, Simon, *Kelly's Financial Planning for the Individual* Gee Publishing, 1996.

Schwager, Jack D., *Market Wizards*, Harper & Row, 1990.

The Beardstown Ladies, *The Beardstown Ladies Common-Sense Investment Guide*, Hyperion, 1994.

Vintcent, Charles, *The Investor's Guide, Be Your Own Stockbroker, The Secrets of Managing Your Own Investments*, Pitman Publishing, 1995.

Which? Ways to Save and Invest, for details telephone 0800 252 100.

A useful book for the reference shelf is a beginner's investment guide as it will cover the main essentials. These books usually explain all the jargon in simple terms. They are an ideal reference for checking up on all the unfamiliar terms involved. Any one of the following four would be a good starting point. I have included my own book on investments for beginners because it deals extensively with how I learnt to handle the skills of investing for myself.

Chase, Lorraine and Adam Shaw, *Money and How to Make More of it*, Orion, 1998.

Cohen, Bernice, *The Armchair Investor*, Orion, 1997.

Gray, Bernard, *Investors Chronicle Beginners Guide to Investment*, Business Books Ltd, London 1991.

Slater, Jim, *Investment made Easy*, Orion, 1994.

USEFUL TELEPHONE NUMBERS AND ADDRESSES

National Debtline tel: 0645 500511.

Consumer Credit Counselling Service (CCCS), tel: 0800 138 1111. Nine offices around the country for face-to-face interviews.

National Association of Citizen's Advice Bureaux (Nacab). There are 17,000 bureaux around the country with general and specialist advisers.

Annuity Bureau, tel: 0171 620 4090.

Annuity Direct, tel: 0171 684 5000.

Association of Private Client Investment Managers and Stockbrokers, 112 Middlesex Street, London E1 7HY.

Council of Mortgage Lenders, BSA/CML Bookshop, 3 Saville Row, London W1X 1AF.

National Association of Estate Agents, for directory of members tel; 01926 410785.

Institute of Chartered Accountants in England and Wales, Moorgate Place, London EC2P 2BJ, tel: 0171 920 8100/8711.

Institute of Chartered Accountants in Scotland, 27 Queen Street, Edinburgh EH2 1LA, tel: 0131 225 5673.

Chartered Association of Certified Accountants (ACCA), 29 Lincoln's Inn Fields, London WC2A 3EE, tel: 0171 242 6855.

Institute of Financial Planning, Whitefriars Centre, Lewins Mead, Bristol BS1 2NT, tel: 0117 930 4434.

The Society of Financial Advisers, 20 Aldermanbury, London EC2V 7HY, tel: 0171 417 4419.

The Law Society of England and Wales, 113 Chancery Lane, London WC2 1PL, tel: 0171 242 1222.

The Law Society of Scotland, 26 Drumsheugh Gardens, Edinburgh EH3 7YR, tel: 0131 226 7411.

Solicitors for Independent Advice helpline, tel: 01372 721172.

Personal Investment Authority (PIA) helpline for pension mis-selling victims, tel: 0171 417 7001.

SIB Factsheet on the pensions review, tel: 0800 003 007.

BEST Investment provides a guide to PEP Best Buys, tel: 0990 112255.

NEWSLETTERS AND JOURNALS

Financial Times, Number One Southwark Bridge,London SE1 9HL.

Investment Trust Newsletter, The McHattie Group, Clifton Heights, Triangle West, Bristol BS8 1EJ.

Investors Chronicle, Greystoke Place, Fetter Lane, London EC4 1ND.

Moneywise, RD Publications Ltd, 10, Old Bailey, London EC4M 7NB.

Money Observer, Garrard House, 2/6 Homesdale Road, Bromley BR2 9WL or FREEPOST NB 2019, Bromley, BR2 9BR.

Company REFS, (Company Really Essential Financial Statistics), Hemmington Scott . Publishing Ltd, City Innovation Centre, 26031 Whiskin Street, London EC1R 0BP.

SYSTEMS

There are a number of software packages for budgeting, among the most useful are:

Microsoft Money and *Quicken.*

For Income tax and filling in your self-assessment tax forms on computer, *Which?* has produced

TaxCalc 1996–97 on CD ROM or disk, Which?, PO Box 89, Dept TP17, Hertford SG14 1TB

suggested reading **and USEFUL names and addresses**

Several software packages provide a variety of share price information, portfolio management or technical analysis. I have experience of using:

Market Eye, ICV Ltd, 23 College Hill, Cannon Street, London EC4R 2RA.

Synergy Software, Britannic House, 20 Dunstable Road, Luton LU1 1ED.

Updata Software, Updata House, Old York Road, London SW18 1TG.

WEB PAGES

AAA Investment Guide http://www.wisebuy.co.uk [facts on 93 different types of investments and savings]

Financial Times http://www.FT.com

Hemmington Scott (the publishers of REFS) http://www.hemscott.com

Electronic Share Information http://www.esi.co.uk

Mrs Cohen's Money on http://www.Channel 4.com

Updata http://www.updata.co.uk

Index

Index

Polly Peck 82
portfolios
    diversification 98–100
    pivotal ideas 167–78
positive attitudes 71–2
Premium bonds 163
premiums 164
    pensions 140–2
preparation, importance 72, 75–6
prices
    emerging markets 176
    houses 129–30
    investment trusts 164–5
    negative equity 190–3
    OEIC 166
    share fluctuations 19–20, 53–9
    tracker funds 169–70
    unit trusts 166
prison costs 67
products
    charges 139–42, 170, 179–80
    selection 88–9
public attitudes
    banking system 30
    shares 21–2, 49
publicly quoted companies 8, 13–16
    failures 18, 21
    geometric growth 43–4, 53–9
    global reach 18–19
purchase life annuities 147
purchasing power 126

Q
questionnaires 87, 90
questions, salesperson interviews 87–8

R
re-rated companies 174
reading 92–4, 211
    product selection 217
real assets 6–7, 105–6
    accumulation 4
    distinctions 8
    financial assets 5
        distinctions 7–9
        savings comparison 10–13
    houses 130

real rate of return, Equity Gilt Study (1918-97) 37, 51–2
real stock market assets 7–9
real value
    money illusions 49
    nominal value 47–8
recessions 43–4
    boom links 192–4
record-keeping 225
    taxation 203
recycled debts 196–8
reinvestment, dividends 38–9
rents 132–3
repayment mortgages 98, 131, 133–5
reserves, building societies 9
retail prices index (RPI) 51
    see also inflation
retirement 123–4
    income boosting 154–5
    National Savings 161, 163
    preparation 5
returns
    see also total returns
    Equity Gilt Study 37, 51–2
    realistic expectations 109
    risk links 35
rice grain legend 40–2
Riley, Barry 20
risks 211–12, 216
    confusions 95
    control 96–100
    diversification 91–2
    emerging markets 176–8
    equities 127
    fire analogy 49
    minimisation 108–9
    overview 72–6
    preparation 72, 75–6
    probability assessment 73
    reduction list 75
    return rate link 35
    seesaw 74–5
    stock markets 53
    tolerance levels 94–5
    tracker funds 169, 172
Roddick, Anita 141
Rogers, Jim 123